The Theology of a Protestant Catholic

Adrian Hastings

★

THE THEOLOGY OF A PROTESTANT CATHOLIC

SCM PRESS
London

TRINITY PRESS INTERNATIONAL
Philadelphia

First published 1990

SCM Press Ltd
26–30 Tottenham Road
London N1 4BZ

Trinity Press International
3725 Chestnut Street
Philadelphia, Pa. 19104

British Library Cataloguing in Publication Data
Hastings, Adrian
 The theology of a protestant Catholic.
 1. Catholic Church. Christian doctrine
 I. Title
 230.2
 ISBN 0–334–02441–2

Library of Congress Cataloging-in-Publication Data
Hastings, Adrian.
 The theology of a protestant Catholic/Adrian
 Hastings.
   p.   cm.
 Includes bibliographical references.
 ISBN 0–334–02441–2 : $19.95 (U.S.)
  1. Catholic Church—Doctrines.   I. Title.
 BX1751.2.H39 1990
 230′.2—dc20   90–31484

Typeset at The Spartan Press Ltd,
Lymington, Hants
and printed in Great Britain by
Richard Clay Ltd, Bungay, Suffolk

For all the members of the
Department of Theology and Religious Studies
in the
University of Leeds

Contents

Acknowledgments

Almost everything in this book has been written since I came to the University of Leeds in the summer of 1985. The exceptions are chapter 5 on Prophecy which first appeared in *The Burden of Prophecy*, ed. Neil McIlwraith (SCM Publications 1982) but has been largely rewritten for publication here; chapter 15, an end of session sermon for the Divinity Faculty preached in King's College Chapel, Aberdeen, March 1980 and published in the *Aberdeen Divinity Bulletin*, 22, Summer 1981; and 17, a memorial address of 1984 in Zimbabwe.

Chapter 2 was written for the Society for the Study of Theology conference at Exeter College, Oxford, April 1989; 3 was read to a Colson symposium on pluralism at Bristol in April 1987 and is included in the conference publication, *Religious Pluralism and Unbelief: Studies Critical and Comparative*, ed. Ian Hamnett (Routledge); 4 was written for a meeting of the Open Synod Group at High Leigh in January 1987 and appeared in *By What Authority?* ed. Robert Jeffrey (Mowbray, 1987); 6 was a paper for the *Societas Liturgica*, meeting at York in August 1989, and is published in *Studia Liturgica*; 7 was a York Cathedral lecture in May 1987 and subsequently appeared in *Anvil*, November 1987, and as a *Southwell and Oxford Paper on Contemporary Society* (June 1988); 8 was written as an address for Cuddesdon Theological College and later published as a *Southwell and Oxford Paper on Contemporary Society* (August 1987); 9 was written for a conference on contemporary South African theology held at St John's College, Cambridge, July 1989; 10 was first read to the Biblical Vacation School at St Anne's College, Oxford, July 1988, while 11 was a lecture for the centenary celebrations of Wakefield Cathedral in June of the same year. Chapter 12 was a lecture given at Sion College, London, in March 1987 and published in *New Blackfriars* the following September; 13 was a sermon preached at St Chad's, Headingley, in April 1986 and printed in *The Franciscan*, May 1988; 14 was the Ramsden University sermon preached at Great St Mary's, Cambridge, in May 1989, and 16 a sermon preached in Gloucester Cathedral in July 1988. 18 was the wedding address for my nephew Nicholas and Flavia, his mathematician bride, at St Dunstan's in the West, Fleet Street, February 1988. Chapter 19 was my inaugural lecture as Professor of Theology in the University of Leeds given in December 1986 and printed in *The University of Leeds Review* for 1987, while 20 was an address written for Yorkshire Television and later published in the Christmas edition of the *Tablet*, 1988.

★ 1 ★

Introduction

I would much wish to construct a far larger, more coherent, work of Christian theology than this but the writing of various histories, the editing of the *Journal of Religion in Africa* and the running of a busy and exciting university Department of Theology and Religious Studies ensure that I am unlikely to have time to do so for many years to come. *The Theology of a Protestant Catholic* is some sort of substitute. Any widely convincing doctrinal or theological coherence within Christianity, Catholic or Protestant, has come under increasingly severe strain in our time. Inescapably, yet awkwardly, more and more areas have been seen to require fundamental revision. Until relatively recently, despite the bitter and organizationally complete division between Catholics, Orthodox and Protestants of many sorts, they had continued to share a large common doctrinal core and pattern of apologetic – a body of ideas which long appeared deeply congruent with the culture and achievement of the West. The very scale of the real unity of belief between Christians makes their denominational separations look, in the light of today, curiously trivial. Nevertheless, that very core of consensus, both in its scriptural roots and later ecclesiastical branches, has come from the time of the Enlightenment onward under increasingly heavy challenge, not only from people who have ceased to believe, but also, almost equally, from theologians and other thinkers who have much wanted to go on identifying themselves as Christians yet have found more and more elements of Christian belief apparently untenable. The unanswered questions have multiplied. Today they seem almost out of control.

For a long while this whole intellectual process – philosophical, scientific, theological – appeared to affect the shape of the churches, their working theology, even their relationship to society, remarkably little. Theologians managed to be extremely 'liberal' in their more academic work while remaining remarkably 'conservative' in their ecclesiastical and social life, even in their preaching. But that could not continue forever.

As the various gaps between traditional doctrine, modern ecclesiastical life, contemporary theology and twentieth-century cultural consciousness grew bigger and bigger, desperate efforts have undoubtedly been made to bridge each chasm so as to establish, or re-establish, some sort of viable coherence between forms of belief, ecclesiastical realities and secular culture. These efforts have principally been of two kinds: a theological and scholarly one, focussing upon the interpretation of the scriptures and a range of philosophical and scientific issues concerning the nature of human existence and knowledge; a more institutional and spiritual one to rebuild the post-Reformation Christian world through the Ecumenical Movement. For a long time both types of effort were predominantly Protestant and Anglican, but over the last thirty years, since the announcement of Pope John's *Aggiornamento*, Catholics have been at least as vigorously involved in both. Yet from the standpoint of 1990 all these efforts seem largely to have broken down. At least any sense of theoretical coherence or of a shared goal – intellectual or institutional – conceivably attainable within the foreseeable future has disappeared. In a post-Barthian, post-Bultmannian, post-Rahnerian, post *Myth of God Incarnate*, age, Christian theology seems more shaken to pieces than reshaped even moderately coherently. Again, the Ecumenical Movement has largely lost both its earlier momentum and the sense of any plausible goal towards which it can convincingly move. The Roman Catholic Church, for its part, is now caught in the era of John Paul II in a huge exercise of 'Restoration' which is increasingly alienating its leaders both from those of other churches and from its own theologians. We are all in the dark.

Personally, I must confess to seeing around me almost infinite unanswered and seemingly unanswerable questions. Newman once wrote that a thousand difficulties do not make one doubt. I wish I could say the same. Christianity, more than any religion, has required of itself demanding rational evaluation of its beliefs and practices. It cannot do less today but, equally, despite its undoubted vitality in many areas of life and parts of the world, it at times seems hardly capable of responding any more to its own high requirements, let alone the jibes of outsiders. Near the heart of our dilemmas are questions concerning what authority, if any, the believer can appeal to reliably, questions concerning the basic shape of the church and its ministry, questions concerning the relationship between Christianity and other religions. What, above all, can we say of Jesus, even of God?

Is Christianity just one of the 'world religions', a very vague group of entities indeed, with no claim to superiority over any other even in terms of its own theology? May women be ordained to the ministry when, before the present century, they never were? Should they be? What authority has the church, the words of scripture or, indeed, anything else? Of course, these are only a selection of the more urgent issues before us. Trying to respond to question after question I have found it increasingly impossible to adhere very closely to Roman Catholic doctrine as I was taught and accepted it when young, and still less the particular form of it now insisted upon by Pope John Paul. Yet I remain convinced that there are elements relating to what Newman called 'Development' within the Catholic tradition which are more serviceable to the needs of a viable Christian doctrine than either conservative or liberal Protestantism. It may even be that the rather too biblicist mood of most Catholic theology in the Vatican II era has actually been unhelpful to a resolving of the deeper issues of theological coherence in post-biblical time facing us. Being a Catholic has less to do with dancing to the tune currently called from Rome than with a committed sharing in the faith, hope and struggles of the central communion of the Christian world. I remain then – in so far as I remain anything very specific – a Catholic theologian, yet – most certainly – a Protestant Catholic: protesting not only against the rigidities of late mediaeval Catholicism perpetuated in Ultramontanism (rigidities whose intellectual justification is incredibly weak but whose organizational defense intensely tenacious) but against far deeper rigidities within the whole central Christian tradition. The essays in this book wrestle with the inescapability of pluralism in all its forms, while continuing to uphold that singular cornerstone of Christian belief: the mysterious universality and finality of meaning of Jesus the Christ.

It is true that I have here focussed that meaning much more upon humanity than upon divinity, upon the implications of incarnated-ness than upon that which is incarnate: a christology of Adam, New Adam but still Adam, humanity, past present and to come, male and female, black and white. Humanity is infinitely diverse, Jesus is historically singular. Much of the strain of theology and an acceptable shaping of the church is to be found therein: a christological reconciliation of the perceived particularity of the incarnate divine with the vast pluralism, religious, cultural, histor-ical, of humankind.

In practice the church, and particularly its Roman Catholic form, has consistently failed the challenge, opting instead for models of uniformity drawn from one age or another of church history – patristic, mediaeval, Victorian – each, as a model of universal catholicity, intrinsically fallacious. The best hope for the church today would seem to me to lie in accepting gratefully and unambigu-ously both the Lordship of Christ and a truly anarchic diversity of ecclesial forms representing the diversity of human understanding, culture and experience, linked together institutionally by no more and no less than sacrament: the sharing in communion of the body of the Lord. If one can say 'Amen' to the eucharistic canon, it is enough. Intercommunion, from which only the scandalously evil should be excluded, seems to me the key to a true ecclesiology, anathema as this is to both the sectarian and the ultramontane. Of course all sorts of ministries, local, regional and universal are needed to serve the communion and to fulfil its responsibilities, but their acceptance and ordering is consequent, not preconditional, to the loving sharing of the sacrament which constitutes the church.

This volume is only a collection of essays, lectures and sermons, anything but definitive in form or content, even in the mind of their author. If we cannot answer all the questions now, or perhaps any of them completely, it is still necessary and helpful to go in the present as far as one can. All theology is provisional, whether its authors recognize this or not, and every moment needs its own theology, even a moment so agnostic (but also so credulous) as our own. In this year of the centenary of John Henry Newman's death, I would wish to be able to share some measure of his doctrinal confidence. Throughout his life he recognized that Christian doctrine was disintegrating around him under the impact of a 'liberalism' which he did not at all like but in fact, to a larger extent than he realized, actually shared. He saw the process largely as inevitable but remained one of the last really great minds able to share in the ancient consensus. The chapter devoted to him in this book is not – as some modern Newman contributions tend to be – a slightly triumphalistic salute to the great precursor of a modern Vatican II type of renewed Catholicism. He was far too anguished and ambiguous a figure for that. Yet perhaps if I had written it ten years ago, it would indeed have been intended as such. Now it is more wistful, less assured, yet still intended to suggest some underlying continuity of purpose despite the vast intellectual change effected by the twentieth century.

Christian faith, theology, hope, are precarious things and never more precarious than now. I cannot write with more assurance than I feel but the very struggle upon the edge of the abyss of unmeaning to assert patterns of coherent truthfulness, despite the thousand difficulties and many resultant doubts, may itself contribute a little to the assurance and enlightenment of others. I can do no more and, perhaps, a Professor of Theology may also do no less.

★ 2 ★

Community, Consensus and Truth

Setting the Scene

What is truth? It is reality perceived and appropriated as accurately as humans may. All human society is intrinsically dependent for health and integrity upon its objective pursuit and acceptance. Its validity depends upon a recognition of objectivity outside ourselves yet it is no less the case that in perceiving the truth and, still more, in collectively appropriating it within society, we do in fact fashion it profoundly. The truth is not detachable from its appropriation. The struggle for truth – a struggle which is absolutely central to all worthwhile human living – is, nevertheless, a struggle for the objective, for the surmounting of each new ridge of recognized appropriation. At every level, personal and communal, human living is deformed by commitment to non-truth, or even by a strategy of being economical with the truth – common as such strategies are and frequently advantageous in terms of short–term profit. Personal and social life flourishes only upon the basis of a commitment to what is honestly seeable and sharable as true.

If humankind is committed to truth, Christians have a double share of this commitment (as indeed they should have in regard to each and every human value) to truth of every sort but, especially, to the truth in their belief that in Jesus they do, in some unique way, attain with certainty to a central integrating ray of reality, concerning its inner and ultimate meaning, hidden to a more or less complete degree from the unbeliever. Almost every concept central to the Christian hermeneutic – revelation, belief, doctrine, kerygma, catechesis, theology, tradition – makes no sense if not seen as, in one way or another, vehicular to a divine word of truth, not obtainable by mere observation or science, offered historically, but with absolute reliability, by God to humankind in a process centred upon the figure of Jesus of Nazareth, himself pre-eminently God's word.

In classical theology the person of Christ is identified with the Word, but we cannot know a person, human or divine, except through personality, and we cannot know a personality except through words and deeds. Again, words and deeds themselves do not usually possess much instant or self-evident authentic meaning, apart from context, reference, tone, response; the linking up of this saying or doing with other sayings and doings. Everything has to be teased out. A sentence or action normally possesses a rather limited nuclear meaning, at least that is only the start of a fuller meaning. The full meaning of what we say and do draws upon a complex collectivity and continuity of experienced existence, its context in time and eternity. If the actor in question is – whatever that may mean – the 'word of God' uniquely present in this single life and time and yet present on account of all lives and all times, then it does not seem fanciful, it might rather seem absolutely necessary, to conclude that the whole of human history may somehow be required to tease out the fullness of that meaning, to provide an adequate context of interpretation.

Believing that Jesus is the Christ, the Lord, the Saviour, the Son of Man, the Son of God, the Word of God, the Second Adam, does not imply understanding very much about what these strange titles mean. And you will not get there simply exegetically by solving the riddle of the most likely accepted sense of the 'Son of Man' title at that time. The very multiplicity of titles suggests from the start both inadequacy and provisionality. They do not contain a definitive definition but constitute a riddle to start one off upon a pilgrimage in pursuit of meaning. They and the whole tense network of clues derived from cross, resurrection, stable, beatitudes, parables, the sheer experience of others knowing and passing on their encounter with this unmarried, homeless, paradoxically-minded, pacifist way-side teacher, all constitute the opening phase for an inherently enigmatic and open-ended on-going tradition of a truth which has never been static and possessed. It will, on the contrary, for ever be constituted and reconstituted not only by varied integrations in the minds and formulas of later believers of the many original symbols, but also by their thought-through, theological, interpretation in relation to anything else and all else in human life: the total context. The truth of the new Adam can only be understood by Adam in terms of Adam's understanding of Adam. Thus, until we know the end – whether, for instance, human life is to be ended by a series of nuclear explosions set off by Adam – we cannot by definition and existential limitation interpret holistically the meaning of the new Adam. Which means that every interpretation in time of Christ is of necessity a provisional and revisable interpretation, offered in response to a still partial body of evidence, yet no less contemporaneously important and even decisive for that. As humanity grows in the understanding of itself it can and must grow in its understanding of God-made-man. Christian truth is in some way unchanging because it is always rooted and centred in the single historical figure of Jesus, but it is no less true that Christian truth is also always and necessarily changing. It would not be true if it didn't. CT1990 cannot be the same as CT1970, CT1600 or CT33. It is not a mathematical or merely factual truth but a cultural and moral one.

The one thing Christianity is not is a religion of a book or of a law. Islam is both, Christianity neither. Of course, books remain important. The life of Jesus and everything else that matters, from apartheid in South Africa to the ecology crisis, have continually to be interpreted 'secundum scripturas', in the light of the scriptures. But the Jesus word is not encapsulated within scripture. Very wisely he himself wrote nothing except in the dust, so far as is recorded. There is no finality in what he imparts. On the contrary, he insists that his followers cannot understand everything now: the Spirit will teach them later, but not at one time. Pentecost is a beginning of the process, not an end, otherwise there would have been no need for Peter's vision or those anguished discussions at Jerusalem and Antioch. The relevant truth of Christ, New Adam, is to be teased out for the Adamite community across innumerable generations. The teasing out would begin before any of the specifically Christian scriptures were composed; it would continue when some or all of them were written but still widely not known – for it would be many generations before the community as a whole was conscious of the precise extent and authority of this new collection of sacred scripture. And when it was, the ever onward march of teasing out would still not end. Indeed the collection, while providing benchmarks and ever so many evidences of this and that, basically made the process that much more complex. It certainly did not provide ready-made answers to many of the questions which then and later the community was asking itself.

This does not mean that there was not a deep confidence that answers could somehow be authoritatively found within the church. It was, of course, quickly recognized that untruths too could be taught within the church, that indeed a struggle between truth and untruth was taking place almost as much within the church as outside it (probably, indeed, there was quickly far too polarized a conception of that whole process, though the experience may often have been less polarized than the conception) but there was an underlying conviction that the community could go on being absolutely sure of Christian truth though now more and more separated in time from both Jesus and the apostles.

Confidence in the truth was grounded – especially against the claim of gnostics and others to additional sources of insight, revelation and vision – in the historic continuity of the community kept faithful to the true memory of Jesus by eucharist, apostolic succession and scriptures, in the power of the Spirit and within a communion of local churches. Augustine could argue against the Donatists that the non-African Catholic consensus was with him and against them. The criterion of consensus for truth was hardly formulated in patristic ecclesiology (until its rather late and ahistorical over-statement by Vincent of Lerins) but it was implicit in almost all that was done. The Council of Jerusalem in Acts 15 provided the model: we start with 'no small dissension and debate' which is followed by an assembly in which representatives of different churches and standpoints are 'gathered together', speak freely and in due course come to formulate a consensus of 'the whole church' as to how to proceed. The developing ecclesial praxis of a far-flung communion of churches implies within it a consensus in the faith from which heretics have departed in mind and must, in consequence, be excluded. But this consensus in the faith was not one of adherence to a static formula. As H. E. W. Turner concluded in *The Pattern of Christian Truth*, 'Orthodoxy in the second century must be differently interpreted from orthodoxy in the fourth or fifth', thus there was an on-going 'development of orthodoxy'.[1] The

[1]H. E. W. Turner, *The Pattern of Christian Truth*, Mowbray 1954, pp. 16, 483, 497.

Councils – greater and less – were the mechanism of consensus which the church developed especially from the fourth century to ensure the maintenance of truth within a process of on-going orthodoxy. In theory at least, the bishops collegially represented their churches and the faith of their churches: if bishops gather from the whole *catholica* their common voice seems to guarantee through apostolic tradition and contemporary consensus the true faith. In practice the lasting authority of such a gathering could depend upon many things. The bishops present might have been too deeply intimidated by imperial power for their voice to be altogether credible; some might repudiate what happened and appeal to others who were not there; they were, anyway, never all, or even nearly all, the bishops alive at that time. Did the whole church truly accept the council's pronouncements? Was it truly 'received'? The authority of the gathering, solemn as it might be in its dogmatic formulation, was finally controlled by the authority of a larger and slower consensus, the abiding judgment of the church as a whole. The church had come to use councils pretty pragmatically without first defining constitutionally what their authority really was. Later on such definitions might yet prove more misleading than undefined practice because the real authority of consensus can hardly be formulated with precision in terms of when, where and how.

It was, maybe, in part the very difficulty of using and interpreting either an 'ecumenical council', or a recognizable consensus, whether of theologians, or of the whole community, whether of the past as well as the present, which drove the West towards the simpler expedient of papal authority and infallibility and the East towards a position which more or less implied that the central doctrinal march forward had come to a full stop, producing a somewhat static and historically backward-looking ecclesiology. In each case development was to be controlled by locatable 'organs'. Newman had a very strong intellectual sense of the inevitability and inherent rightness of onward movement. He became convinced from the historical evidence that you could not appeal satisfactorily to a consensus and so he came to make a powerful case for claiming, in *The Idea of Development*, that the whole logic of Christian faith and church history requires the continued existence of a 'living voice' and that – if there is still a living voice in Christendom – then the only plausible place to locate it is Rome. He never cared for an ultramontane papacy but he had come to believe profoundly in the historic necessity of an authoritative papacy and precisely because he did not find that an appeal to consensus worked as a matter of fact when one considered ecclesiastical history. He did not, of course, wholly reject the importance of consensus-finding. On the contrary. Hence his cautiously worded, but no less distressing to ultramontanes, article on 'Consulting the Faithful'.

A Personal Pilgrimage

Theologically this is more or less where my own thinking began. My *One and Apostolic*[2] was published in 1963 and included a chapter entitled 'The Development of Orthodoxy'. The book was in substance my Roman doctoral thesis defended in October 1958 and written well before Pius XII died. I left immediately afterwards for Uganda and remained in Africa without a break for over six years. In 1958 the thesis had been rejected for publication, largely because there seemed at the time too little interest in 'progressive' Catholic ecclesiology – at least in Britain – but five years later in the changed Johannine atmosphere John Todd wrote to suggest it might now be publishable with some revision. I had, however, been engaged for all that time in pastoral work and secondary school teaching and was rather out of touch with the developing conciliar theology. Hence, while 'advanced' for Pius XII's reign, and profoundly conciliar in its central thesis that the church is best conceived as 'communion', the book may appear in some ways a bit conservative in terms of the second session of the Council which was when it actually appeared. The thesis had not, in fact, included either 'the Development of Orthodoxy' or the next chapter entitled 'Authority and Unity', which were both added while in Uganda I prepared the book for publication. However, they were both – so far as I remember – substantially written in the 1950s for inclusion in the thesis and then omitted from its final text. They represent, then, so far as I am concerned, the 50s rather than the 60s.

Central to my argument in 'The Development of Orthodoxy' was the evidence culled from Turner's *Pattern of Christian Truth* which I used to reinforce the Newman position as against Richard Hanson's

[2]*One and Apostolic*, Darton, Longman & Todd 1963.

claim that the idea of 'the living mind of the church' represented a 'theological will-o-the-wisp' possessing a 'bizarre fecundity paralleled only in Hinduism'. He thought it absurd to suggest that 'the "living mind" of 1954 is not the "living mind" of 2004, which will in its turn be superseded by the "living mind" of 2054 and so on, until the Last Judgement'.[3] I replied (inspired to some extent by three articles by Henry St John in *Blackfriars* for the last three months of 1955, 'The Authority of Doctrinal Development') by enquiring whether this was so different from asserting, with Turner, that 'Orthodoxy in the second century must be differently interpreted from orthodoxy in the fourth or fifth'. What is 'orthodoxy' but the 'living mind', and why should a process recognized as inevitable and indeed desirable in the first half of the first millennium be seen as an absurdity in the second half of the second millennium? However, while stressing the continuity between the two concepts in developmental terms, I did more or less dismiss the significance of the discontinuity in terms of the consensuality of the process itself, holding at the time a rather high view of early papal history.[4] Like other Catholics at the time,[5] I did, of course, accept the teaching of Vatican I on Papal Infallibility as also the Papal definition of the Assumption as absolutely certain and definite.

At the time I thought 'The Development of Orthodoxy' a conclusive case and I still think its inner logic a strong one. Certainly I already recognized – a great deal more, probably, than most of my fellow Catholics – that there had been serious errors in papal teaching of a secondary kind, (the instance of the Johannine Comma and the Pontifical Biblical Commission first convinced me of that in 1948, as an Oxford undergraduate) but I regarded them as sufficiently marginal not seriously to imperil the plausibility of the main thesis. Over the years I have come to be convinced that this is not so. The number of points and the seriousness of many of them on which I find it impossible to accept the truthfulness or pastoral opportuneness of the Roman 'Living Voice' have become just too many and too considerable to leave the central thesis untouched. Just

[3] *Theology*, 1954, p. 383.
[4] See my article on 'The Papacy and Rome's Civil Greatness', *Downside Review*, 1957, pp. 359–82.
[5] Karl Rahner, for instance, see his essay 'The Development of Dogma' published in German in 1954 and in English in *Theological Investigations*, vol. I, Darton, Longman & Todd 1961, pp. 39–77.

as Newman's earlier ecclesiology broke down in his own mind on grounds of historical evidence, so in my mind the reliability of a Roman magisterium as expressed by Vatican I (or even the precise wording of Vatican II) broke down on similar grounds. For years I got along with an ecclesiology which was respectful of history by distinguishing sharply between infallible and non-infallible teaching and reducing the former to a minimum, but in doing do it really rendered infallibility otiose. Yet to question infallibility *per se* would of course have imperilled one's very existence in the post Vatican I church.

Magnificent as papal history has been in many ways, studded with outstanding figures (as well as some rather nasty and some very feeble ones) and strengthened by much prudential wisdom and occasional brilliance, I have come to see that if the papacy has often served the wider church highly responsibly it has also led the church astray and kept it astray over many things of profound importance to an extent that renders any ultramontane or Vatican I orientated view of the papacy simply absurd. Does this historicist rejection of a really very ahistorical conception of ecclesiastical authority wholly rule out a 'living voice' doctrine of the relationship between church and truth?

I do not think that is necessarily so. It does rule out the only Catholic view of the matter I had to hand in the 1950s – an essentially Vatican I doctrine of papal authority dominated by the 'infallibility' syndrome, an authority working on its own quite uncollegially, exercising a unique 'petrine ministry'. The fact that I was personally prepared even then to stress the possibility of mistaken non-infallible papal teaching (e.g. over *Apostolicae Curae* – see a controversy in which I was involved over this in the *Downside Review*, 1957–8) did not mean that I had any alternative model for the positive reformulation of reliable teaching. I had in point of fact thought far too little about the conciliar option. Papal and conciliar conceptions had in the past quite failed to coalesce in any form that did not either displace the papacy to a degree that I could not at all contemplate at that time, or alternatively, leave councils as no more than papal lap-dogs. Doubtless attempts were made by some less ultramontane theologians to stress that the Pope was still in the habit of 'consulting' before he spoke and even that, subsequent to definition, a time to test it on grounds of 'reception' was required before one could be quite sure. Many of us have, of course, been grateful to Newman for emphasizing these things. In the ecclesiastical context of my youth, they did not get one very far. However, from such hints and survivals of a more consensual past, Vatican II revived the theory of collegiality and relocated Roman authority within a basically consensual model of a sort that history makes pretty clear was the dominant theoretical one in the early centuries. By doing this, and despite the anxious hedging-in of collegiality by the *nota praevia*, the Council did inspirationally at least open a Pandora's Box which has dominated Catholic theology ever since. In the understanding of collegiality, what is important is less a sort of technical test as to whether in given circumstances collegiality has or has not been exercised according to canonical criteria, but much more the underlying moral one required for any authentic process of authoritative decision making. Truth seeking through consensus is an exercise in listening, praying, sharing, dialogue, cool rational discussion, openness, forbearance, mental tolerance, in a way that mono decision-making cannot be structured to be, being fundamentally oracular. So when it came to *Humanae Vitae* in 1968 one was armed with something of a new ecclesiology which, while it did not reject the possibility of authoritativeness exercised through the living voice, did require that in a matter of high theoretical or practical moral importance that authoritativeness should be seen to be genuinely collegial and consensual.

In the days immediately after the publication of the encylical, I was invited by Simon King of Burns and Oates to contribute a chapter on 'The Papacy and the Church' to a symposium entitled *On Human Life* published later that same year (this chapter was reprinted in 1978 as chapter 3 of *In Filial Disobedience*[6]). Some fairly lengthy quotations from it may be justified here as it was the 'scandal' of *Humanae Vitae* which more than anything else hammered into my own mind the absolute necessity of a theology of consensus:

> It is the whole Church which is the pillar and witness to revealed truth. . . . It is not easy to judge of this *consensus*. When the passing of time and development in society and thought present to men new problems, new questions as to what is and what is not acceptable to the mind of Christ, there is no easy way through for

[6] *In Filial Disobedience*, Mayhew-McCrimmon 1978.

the Church of God. There is no oracle to which men can turn; only by honest living and prayer and discussion and an openness to the Holy Spirit, can the Church (hierarchy and laity combined) come little by little to an understanding of what is and what is not implied in the once delivered message of salvation . . . The mind of the Church becomes clear through the process whereby the *sensus fidelium* (the mind of the faithful) within the many local churches grows little by little into a *consensus ecclesiarum* (the common witness of the churches). This, formulated and expressed by the chief pastors of those churches, becomes a *consensus episcoporum*, the witness of the bishops of the one Catholic Church in and with their head, the bishop of Rome.

Attempts to short-cut this process, to ignore the reality of the Church as a communion of churches, to treat it as if it was but a single Church ('The Church of Rome' as non-Catholics mistakenly call us), to regard the Pope as an oracle who can, apart from human processes and the in-built constitution of the Church, pontificate with certainty upon any subject, is to misunderstand what the Church of God is, to make of the Pope what he is not, and to lead the faithful grievously astray. The condemnation of Pope Honorius by an ecumenical council and its ratification by Pope Agatho is surely in itself sufficient evidence of the fact that the Pope can err. And we have in fact a whole tradition of erring papal teaching . . . (78–9)

By refusing to allow the problem to be discussed by the Ecumenical Council or by the synod of bishops, by rejecting the advice of a large majority in his own commission together with a Resolution of the World Congress of Catholic Laity, he has placed himself in the position of an oracle. This was bad ecclesiology. It cannot be regarded as surprising if, when a Pope, with however sincere intentions, so totally ignores the ecclesial 'signs of the times' placed before him, and acts in a manner which accords neither with the conduct of a normal prudent man nor with the known constitution of the Church as an ecumenical council has just delineated it, God permits him to make a bad mistake, just as he has – without any possibility of doubt – permitted many Popes to make such mistakes in the past. (83)

The problem with a theology of consensus remains how to pin-point any particular expression of that consensus. In regard to questions that are not an issue for anyone at present one may well be able to acknowledge consensus of a rather passive kind, but this is of its nature of little use and the thoughtful person may well question whether it would survive if the matter in question did become one of contemporary relevance. But the formulation of a consensus in regard to the relevant (and therefore, also, almost surely of the at least potentially controversial and divisive) does require some sort of organ and focal point. It is appropriate and reasonable that councils or a collegially-functioning papacy should act as focus, precipitant and final formulator of the consensus. That is functionally accept-able, but how sure can we be in the particular case that it has functioned quite right? In relationship to truth, functionality is not enough. A theology of consensus is not just a check upon papacy and council to ensure adequate prior consultation and appropriate mechanisms for the formulation of doctrine to ensure its harmon-ious reception. Rightly understood it must take us into larger and far more difficult areas, questions which I personally had still hardly faced up to in 1968.

By 1981 I had come a good deal further and my next quote is from a paper I read to the Scottish Church Theology Society 22 January 1981 (or rather its subsequent published summary):

If there is a reliable *regula fidei* or 'living voice' it must be located somewhere; there really is no other plausible candidate than Rome, and yet the evidence of history is too clear that the voice of Rome has gravely let down truthful christian witness time and again. This does not mean that I conclude that the whole sense of christian orthodoxy as it has always existed in the church is a mistaken one, but that it certainly cannot be tied securely to some particular structure, but only to the continued presence of the Living God in the Church, in and above all the structures, using a Council here, a Pope there, a creed, a martyr, a prophet, a theologian. Moreover, God tolerates more error in any and every part of the church than the purist has ever wanted to admit for his own part of it. So effectively the true 'traditio' is always mixed up with a mass of false, inaccurate and misleading ideas. God tolerates error in the Church and provides no immediate mechanism for picking out the errors with certainty. There is just no rule of thumb for distinguishing a prophetic reformer raised up by God from a pig-headed heretic . . . We should all be restrained by a far greater sense than we have had of the value of human and christian freedom, the frailty of the historic magisterium, and of the power of God's truth of itself to prevail just because it is the truth: *Magna est veritas et praevalebit.*

Perhaps at that point I was going almost too far in the direction of an unstructured and unstructurable 'Living Voice', dependent only upon confidence in God, and it is noticeable that in that paper I had nothing to say about consensus. Is it possible to salvage rather more in consensus terms?

Consensus and its Limitations

My presupposition in 1968 was that the presence of the Holy Spirit of God has been guaranteed to the church and that there are formulable and recognizable conditions in which his presence can be so counted upon as to guarantee the truth of ecclesiastical teaching. Those conditions would have included that it is the teaching of the Church Catholic rather than of a mere part of the church, that a large measure of collegiality has been exercised and that adequate time has been given to open and rational discussion as also to prayer. Presumably the more all this is done, the more we would all be agreed that the consensus thereby reached merits acceptance. It was because there was genuinely so much of all this in the work of the second Vatican Council – so much learning, discussion and responsible listening to a wide range of convictions, not only within the national diversity of the Roman Communion but also in the voices and traditions of the observers from other churches – that many of us found the major teachings of the Council so reliable, even though the Council explicitly withdrew from any claim to be teaching infallibly.

However, looking back upon Christian history, when can we really be sure that anything like this actually happened? Hardly at the first Vatican Council. Nor, to be honest, at most of the early Councils either. Nicaea, Ephesus and Chalcedon may be defended in terms of what they proclaimed but not so easily in terms of their expressing a contemporary consensus. Each provoked major and disastrous schism, while their membership was far from fully representative of the church at the time and their proceedings were often arbitrary and even violent. No Council has ever had an adequately balanced representation from the whole contemporary church. Luther appealed from the authority of the Pope to the authority of a general council but later decided that councils could err too. It seems in practice hard to disagree. We may well say and believe that a truly ecumenical council will not do so, but have we ever had a truly ecumenical council? The modern Roman theology of the infallibility of both Pope and council hinges upon the ecumenicity of Vatican I. But in terms of modern Catholic ecclesiology it is increasingly difficult to deny that, at least, the great Orthodox communion, Greek and Russian, is – and was in 1870 – part of the visible church. In which case Vatican I was surely not ecumenical and – if it had become so – its minority would have become the majority. As it may still seem parlous in Roman Catholic eyes to question the full ecumenicity (and, therefore, conceivable ability to teach infallibly) of Vatican I, it is worth at least referring to the excellent study of the Jesuit Luis Bermejo, *Towards Christian Reunion*, with its lengthy chapter discussing 'the relative value of Vatican I' (pp. 134–88) and to the obvious fact that other councils in the past have been deemed ecumenical for a while and then disallowed. There is certainly no fully reliable judgment – even in Roman Catholic tradition – upon which historic councils have been ecumenical and why. It is the historicity of the undergirding of the whole concept of infallibility, both conciliar and papal, which is in question. The absolute reliability of Christian witness and interpretation of the gospel provided by a fully ecumenical consensus might seem, then, to be rather something the church has continually, and appropriately, sought for in history but never quite unambiguously found. In this, as in other notes of its being, it is more in pursuit of its nature than in possession of it.

Again, the very concept of a 'living voice' speaking with authority to today within an ever-advancing process of time and culture, of the understanding of the world and of humanity, must really imply that however authoritative some piece of ecclesiastical teaching was in the past, within a given culture, that teaching is not necessarily in quite that form appropriate in after ages. Doctrinal development is

controlled less by an inward process of deductive explication carried
on by the church and its theologians and far more by response to
huge alterations in human consciousness. Of course, there are
greater continuities in culture than many a spokesman of contemporary modernity may like to admit, nevertheless it can also be very
difficult even to understand what significant meaning is to be
attached – then or now – to the formulas of past ages. Moreover,
where in the past there was most consensus, it may often be
concluded that the consensus derived very little from the inspiration
and conscientious interpretation of revelation, and far more from a
given of culture unquestioned at the time but – in many cases –
almost wholly discarded subsequently. In such cases consensus may
almost come to be an indication of untruth and in practice the rare
dissident voice (*Athanasius contra mundum* or whatever) may be much
more the carrier of Christian truth than the apparent consensus of
the 98%. In practice neither an institutionalized consensus nor the
reality of an uninstitutionalized but populist community consensus
guarantees truth either absolutely or even that little measure of truth
which might really be within the grasp of this time and these people.
All may pray and proclaim the gospel emphatically enough, but all
may be wrong. In historical terms it is hard to deny that. We may
want to conclude that in such cases the praying was hypocritical or
shallow, that there was little thought and much unkindness and that
such things explain why the consensus went so wrong. The point is
that while we must needs pursue true consensus, we can never be
sure that we have reached it and should often feel adequately sure
that we have not. It remains something to be sought, rather than
something possessed and easily pointed to. False consensus, now as
in the past, can be a deceptive thing, naturally attractive, but
dangerously destructive of much else when imposed upon the
questioning. In practice churches nearly always function in part in
terms of a false consensus, and faced with it only the prophet, lonely,
awkward, reviled, liable to be stoned and certainly in a small minority
may be able to carry on a truly living proclamation of truth – and
perhaps he too is proclaiming less the truth than simply the right of
truth *not* to be identified with something far too small and
ephemeral. It is the paradox of the dialectic of truth that it is both
pursued through consensus and blocked by consensus. A theology of
the vindication of truth in community must include the lone voice of

the prophet quite as necessarily as the voice of Sanhedrin, *Collegium* or Council.

No community can exist without a core of consensus, its shared understanding of that truth which is relevant to its life and functioning. But that truth may be constructed entirely by the community, its own justificatory myth, and will in time be fashioned and refashioned by that community. Community, consensus and truth stand together indeed, but the truth in question may well not precede the consensus but be its consequence, though it does in time come to assume a sort of independent existence. If a community divides into two, whether through agreement or schism, each part inevitably functions out of a new consensus which will include an interpretation of the separation. Of course the two interpretations may conflict, while sharing a number of basic facts – just as Catholic and Protestant communities in Northern Ireland see the 'truth' of Ulster's history very differently while agreeing over, for instance, the date of the Battle of the Boyne. If we are dealing with football clubs or, for that matter, African tribal cosmologies, we are not much worried by this model of the relationship of truth to consensus. In regard to the Christian church it is different. We presuppose an external *Res*, that which objectively is as it is and is known by us through God's word and the progressive unfolding of its meaning within the community of the church guided by the Spirit. The consensus here is taken as evidence that we have got it right. If there is a schism in the church and, as a result, two opposing consensuses emerge in two opposing communities, we infer that one of them is wrong. With the football clubs or the tribes dividing, we do not really do so: we simply see the two new consensuses as constituting the necessary cohesion for the two new and distinct communities: they have made their truth – each is socially appropriate, and one may not be truer than the other. We may not reduce the church's consensus to that level but we should not exclude at least partial analysis in such terms.

Look at things now from another viewpoint. The Christian tradition had understood itself very consciously and consistently in terms of a consensus model, symbolized by councils, by the retention of ancient creeds and other formulas, even by the image of Rome as 'see of unity'. It has not, to anything like the same extent, developed a dialectical model of self-interpretation in terms of the creative fruitfulness of disagreement and even conflict. We have tended to view doctrinal conflict as between orthodoxy and heresy, between truth and falsehood, in which heresy is defeated and truth triumphs, rather than in terms of a dialectical process through which a new form of the truth, appropriate to the circumstances of some new age or culture, emerges and can only emerge across conflict and debate. In fact Christian history, intellectual, pastoral and spiritual, is incomprehensible except in terms of the positive fruitfulness of profound disaccord.

Such processes tend to begin with attack upon what has become in point of fact a false consensus adhered to by an ecclesiastical authority with which it has become closely identified. To mount such an attack a 'prophet' may well be needed. Catholic tradition has tended to hold that the line of true prophets came to an end with the apostolic age. Henceforth their work would be carried on by the episcopate. But the consensus-challenging role of the prophet is just what a bishop is normally not equipped to do. His job description is quite a different one, though of course some bishops may be prophets too. While a prophet may initially be almost alone in denouncing the existing consensus for failure to be truly truth-bearing for now, it may well also be the case – and often is – that he is saying that what the authorities have claimed to be consensus is really not so at all. The poor and the voiceless are thinking something quite different. The fact that bishops the world over declare such and such to be the church's common mind does not necessarily mean it is so: they may be speaking in reality, not as representatives of the common mind of the church as a whole, but only of the clerical body and its running dogs, or again of the upper class, or the middle class (if lord bishops themselves have moved down that far), or just of males. When a 'prophet' challenges this sort of phoney consensus, he may be burnt, or he may survive but produce a schism and the setting up of two rival consensuses, one of which will eventually canonize him within its new foundation charter, or, perhaps, perhaps, he may be able to survive within the community despite everything and thus create a new dialectical relationship out of which a genuinely altered and improved consensus will in due course appear. And even if he does not personally survive, his ideas – or some of them – may do so. Of course, while Christian doctrinal history is far more dialectical and more consensual than is usually admitted, the dialectic is still finally subservient to the consensual. However much the consensus does in fact change, the community cannot survive without a consensus of some sort. If fixed by integralists the consensus is likely to prove in the long run a threat to the vitality of the community by its rigidity, if fixed by pluralists the threat may come rather from the absence of sufficient identity, but some form of consensus there must be. The question is, perhaps, how best to ensure that the maintenance of a sufficient consensus to ensure identity does not at the same time stifle the opposite process of on-going pluralistic dialectic. The only tenable answer to that question would seem to lie in one's ability to respond 'Amen' to the eucharistic prayer. The consensus upon which the church's communion and identity depend is finally, and only, liturgical.

The snares lurking within a consensus model may now be summarized as follows: first, the relationship between community and consensus is such that the latter may signify no more than what is socially appropriate as communal mind for this group of people now: it does assure 'truth' but of an essentially subjective kind; second, 100% ecclesial consensus at any given time is far more likely to reflect the least questioned aspects of culture rather than a mature unison in the understanding of the gospel; third, the achievement of consensus has often been obtained only through a subsequently played-down silencing or exclusion of those who do not share it (involving denial of the dialectical nature of advancement in truth) and this has been a recurrent phenomenon in ecclesiastical history; fourth, apparent consensus is in reality often only a consensus of the vocal and the power-holding minority, largely determined by class and group interests, whether that minority be the hierarchy only, or all the clergy, or whites, or Latins, or males, or the upper classes. Again and again, where consensus is proclaimed or appealed to, it proves, on strict analysis, to be inherently defective upon one or more of these grounds.

All this must appear pessimistic enough. It is hard not to be so when confronted with the never-ending follies of ecclesiastical history. We certainly carry what treasure we may have in earthen vessels. Nevertheless, the pursuit goes on in the belief that God exists beyond humankind, that we not only engineer the truth but also discover it, that a heavenly vision must be shared. It is dangerous to over-value the achievement or rediscovery of consensus at any given moment of time as definitive. Nevertheless, what matters most in the long run remains what is shared 'in my name', and seen to be shared, and somehow that sharing of conviction is not only with contemporaries but also with past and future too. Every time we really find consensus it should delight us, like oil running down the beard of Aaron or dew on Mount Hermon, a foretaste of the kingdom, that 'quaedam inchoatio beatitudinis' which is what the church's life is really meant to be. Oh, would that we were there!

In the meantime we must seek consensus, while not forgetting to seek other things too, and we should cherish all suitable organs for achieving consensus – synods and councils, pastoral congresses, the joint letters of theologians, even the Petrine see of unity itself. All may serve. But if Peter was not only rock but Satan, what lesser tool of truth and unity will not also be double-edged? Let us close with a happening. I doubt whether the Catholic Church – and even the Christian community far more widely – ever experienced a much greater measure of genuine consensus than in the years 1962–67. It was open but not unstructured, it listened, it prayed, it argued and it learnt. All sorts of cobwebs, which a few years earlier would have been seen as elements of some undying consensus, were swept from out the corners in the house-cleansing of that great aggiornamento. Perhaps it could not have gone on, a necessarily temporary expression of the state Victor Turner has labelled *communitas*. At least it did not, and we are – in a way – all the more polarized twenty years later in consequence. But it did exert its own authority. There was an authenticity in the conciliar experience of consensus which is not easily to be set aside. The prophets and thinkers – the Congars, the Rahners, the Beas – were woven into its rich tapestry. They were needed first to be firm in their singularity but in the long run what mattered most was the consensual witness they were enabled to serve, not only within the theological community but in the ecclesial community as a whole. That is already history, a *memoria*, but for us who remain and still seek the truth and within that community which we call church, it is also rather more.

★ 3 ★

Pluralism: Theology and Religious Studies

Pluralism is, I believe, a matter of absolutely primary importance for theologians, philosophers, students of religion, human beings, because human and religious experience is irremediably pluralist. But pluralism has come to have so many forms and meanings which require to be distinguished rather carefully if their consideration is not to become hopelessly confused. My intention in this chapter is to consider one quite limited, almost methodological, aspect of the subject by focussing on two rather closely linked developments within the recent intellectual history of the Christian West: one, the transformation of university departments of 'theology' into departments of 'religious studies' (either by change of name or effectively); the other, the proposed transformation of Christian theology itself, with its hitherto irreducible core of particularism, into a pluralist 'world theology' which gives no centrality or primacy to any specific religious tradition of revelation or salvation. The latter programme is particularly connected with names like John Hick and Wilfred Cantwell Smith. These two developments have gone very closely together, the one often appearing as the justification of the other. They might well be claimed to represent collectively the most characteristic contribution of the late 1960s and 70s to the theological area of study.

I will begin with what might be called, a little simplistically, an attempt to delineate the *Sitz im Leben* of John Hick's *God and the Universe of Faiths*.[1] The establishment of a *Sitz im Leben*, as should be

[1]John Hick, *God and the Universe of Faiths*, Macmillan 1973; see also his later *God has Many Names*, Macmillan 1980, *The Problems of Religious Pluralism*, Macmillan

obvious (but often isn't), in no way demonstrates the truth or falsity of an idea, but understanding is undoubtedly helped by the contextualization of its genesis. The book was published in 1973 and represents the most influential example in this country of the re-writing of Christian theology to accommodate the apparent require-ments of a religiously pluralistic world. It is closely paralleled by the work of Wilfred Cantwell Smith[2] in America, among others. To understand this exercise, and the apparent need for it, it seems to me helpful to consider the cultural world which had finally broken up a few years previously. It was not, strange as it may seem in retrospect, a pluralist world. It is true that from the seventeenth century at least, the west was laying the intellectual and religious foundations for pluralism. It is true also that for two hundred years the British Empire had straddled cultures and faiths with, on the whole, remarkable tolerance and aplomb: India could not have been ruled otherwise. But it was only, and very deliberately, tolerance up to a point. Indian culture and religion, it was officially agreed, were good enough for Indians, but they were not something open to an Englishman – however affectionate a Kipling or a Forster, at least, might be towards them. The underlying tragedy of *A Passage to India* lies precisely therein. Indian culture and society could be a tourist attraction, but it would be very dangerous for all concerned if they became more than that.

The Victorian model coupled a world-wide empire and com-merce with the most emphatic commitment, explicit or implicit, to the mental, moral and religious primacy of Western man, conceived in a unitary and rather missionary way. Despite the growth of a multiplicity of denominations, a pluralism of public experience was not significantly reflected in a pluralism of world view but rather in an unquestioning consciousness of superiority, guaranteed by printing press and gun, railroad and telegraph. Perhaps there was no other way in which Europe's political domination could have been appropriately justified or motivated. If a diversity of culture and

---

1985, and 'Religious Pluralism', pp. 145–64 of *The World's Religious Traditions*, essays in honour of Wilfred Cantwell Smith, ed. Frank Whaling, T. & T. Clark 1984.

[2]Wilfred Cantwell Smith, *The Meaning and End of Religion*, 1963, reprinted SPCK 1978; *Towards a World Theology*, Macmillan 1981.

religion was all the same admitted, it was then not on a fully pluralistic basis but on a strictly two tier model: ours and theirs, and never the twain shall meet.

Our was not as such necessarily Christian – or at least it did not remain so. Take that much-used nineteenth-century phrase 'civilization and Christianity'. For some people the one took primacy, for some the other. The missionary, expatiating upon the power and wealth of Queen Victoria's empire to a bemused petty African potentate might wave the Bible before him and declare impressively, 'Here is the explanation of Britain's greatness', but the late Victorian mind was increasingly regarding the Christianity element in the package as expendable, and for some colonial officials it was just a nuisance. One remained no less firmly convinced of the inherent superiority of Westernness.

Certainly the typical missionary, mini-theologian, or person in the pew rather easily equated the most particularist claims of Christianity, of Christ, of Bible, the *'solus'* of Reformation theology, with the inner principle of the West's primacy, the conclusive reason why Britain was *super omnes*. England's providential role, declared Frederick Temple, at the time a young man, but later to be Archbishop of Canterbury, was 'the sublimest position ever occupied by any nation hitherto, that of the authoritative propagator of the Gospel over the world'.[3] The theological and religious particularism always inherent in the Christian gospel took on or coalesced with, in the context of the nineteenth-century, this world-embracing Western cultural particularism of political, even racial, domination – a domination which would not exterminate other breeds and faiths, but regulate them, study them conscientiously, hopefully perhaps in due course convert them. *Christus vincit* melted into 'Britannia rules the waves' and the more confident one was in the inherent superiority of Victoria's Britain, the more affected one might be both with a high sense of protectionist duty towards lesser breeds and by the call of the Student Christian Movement's new watch-word 'The evangelization of the world in this generation'.[4]

Of course I am simplifying, even perhaps caricaturing a little, the

[3]*Memoirs of Archbishop Temple*, ed. E. G. Sandford, 1906, p. 54.
[4]T. Tatlow, *The Story of the Student Christian Movement*, 1933; H. Hans Hoekendijk, 'Evangelization of the world in this generation', *International Review of Mission*, January 1970, pp. 23–31.

world view of our ancestors – the world view in which at least some of us were still brought up. But not too greatly. In the first half of the twentieth century it was expressed less crudely and less confidently, yet it survived and, indeed, a large working empire continued to require it as a sort of civil religion. The final collapse of this civil religion came only after the Second World War and even then not too quickly. But the conditions which both needed and stimulated it were rapidly disappearing. The economic and political decline of Britain in particular was obvious. By the mid 1960s the Empire had virtually disappeared. The United Nations had generated a new ethos of egalitarian international relations. Japan, China, Indonesia, India, Pakistan were major powers. Christianity had lost such world-wide political significance as it possessed prior to the 1939–45 war. Even within Europe the ding-dong struggle between religion and secular humanism which had continued within the Western tradition for many generations seemed to have reached a new phase in the ever more apparent triumph of the latter.

The 1960s were the decade in which the customary ideology of the West became manifestly unnecessary and hence patently absurd. It happened coincidentally, but perhaps not wholly coincidentally, with other, less easily to be anticipated, cultural revolutions: a general deriding of structure and tradition, a discovery of permissiveness, community and experience: culture-free, gender-free, race-free.[5] The quintessential qualities of the sixties seemed all that the Victorian spirit was not. This transformation, partially but by no means wholly ephemeral, was made a great deal more complex for Britain by an extra but not unrelated development – the arrival of hundreds of thousands of Carribbean and Asian immigrants, the latter bringing their own non-Christian religions. Britain itself was becoming religiously a highly pluralist society in which Muslim, Sikh, Hindu and Buddhist communities were important, just at the time when its Christian commitment was, at least in numerical terms, declining more rapidly than in any previous decade of the century, and just too as the old model of a two-tiered humanity was disappearing as absurd.

Western man had lived hitherto – even, paradoxically, if he lived in

[5]For an assessment of this see Part VI of Adrian Hastings, *A History of English Christianity 1920–1985*, Collins 1986.

India or Malaysia – in an essentially unpluralistic society and that society was motivated by an unpluralistic Western religion, whether Christian or liberal humanist, the two accommodatingly interwoven. All that was now over. In the sixties our Western world became stridently pluralist. The model was no longer Eton but California. Strangely enough, just as the traditionally unitary and missionary West turned in aspiration pluralist and undogmatic, much of the rest of the world began to move with almost equal suddenness and even cruelty towards unitary, anti-pluralist models. The late 1960s can be seen as a crucial moment for both developments. So much so that Western society's rather hastily embraced pluralist ideals, intended especially to accommodate the religions of Asia, could become for others new grounds for suspicion rather than any obvious bridge. It is within an almost world-wide anti-pluralist surge that the modern Western concern for pluralism must be assessed.

In the late 60s, however, that was not evident and the newly perceived cultural pluralism of the West could well be seen as standing in need of a civil religion grounded in an appropriate theology. No faith should be established, yet each should be accorded appropriate respect and drawn into the functions that society asks of civil religion. There was an implicit need of an intellectual framework for the new religious order, even if that order could not fully be brought into being all at once. The inter-relationship of religions could, of course, be looked at in purely secular sociological or historical terms, even in Marxist ones, but to a religious sympathizer such terms would be reductionist and demeaning. Civil religion and the theology behind it must not be that. Parallel approaches to a number of different religious traditions must inevitably generate institutions which are in principle religiously pluralist – that is to say, orientated sympathetically to religion in general but to no specific religious tradition in particular. For such approaches and institutions to be genuinely attractive to believers themselves, it could then be argued that they ought to be justified not in merely secular terms but in those of an over-arching theology, an umbrella religious outlook, a 'global or human theology' as Hick called it,[6] in terms of which all these various religions could intercommunicate and, in good Durkheimian manner, contribute

[6]*God and the Universe of Faiths*, pp. 105 and 106.

religiously to the onward march and moral health of the contemporary city. That, I take it, forms a large part of the agenda behind Hick's *God and the Universe of Faiths*. Of course he did not, and doubtless does not, see it quite like that. It would indeed be socially reductionist to see it merely like that. The point is that a consciously pluralist theology looked appropriate to the contemporary context, especially the context of Birmingham. Hick in all honesty stressed that the whole subject of the relation between Christianity and other religions was one he had 'largely ignored until coming to live . . . in the multi-cultural, multi-coloured, and multi-faith city of Birmingham and being drawn into some of the practical problems of religious pluralism' (xiv). Precisely. As a result of this experience he found it personally no longer possible to maintain a Christ-centred or 'one's own-religion-centred' theology. Instead he made what he called his 'Copernican revolution' to a God-centred or, later, a 'reality-centred' theology. He tells us that 'for at least twenty-five years' he had believed that 'those who do not respond to God through Christ are not saved but, presumably, damned or lost' (121). 'I believed by implication that the majority of human beings are eternally lost . . . this was the position in which I was for a number of years concerning the relation of Christianity to other religions . . . but as soon as one does meet and come to know people of other faiths a paradox of gigantic proportions becomes disturbingly obvious' (122, cf. 100) – the paradox that these people are far too good to be 'lost'. Hick, of course, went on to re-examine traditional Christian theology, criticize it and develop his own 'human' or 'global' theology. But I don't think I am altogether mistaken in judging that for him the theological re-analysis was secondary and that it indeed looks rather weak in strictly theological terms. The 'Copernican Revolution', while claimed as a splendid clean fresh start, is too evidently committed to its conclusions in advance, yet too confused as to what those conclusions really are. The overwhelming impression I am left with is that for Hick the revolution was an experiential rather than a strictly theological one. He had previously lived in a Christian world and taken for granted a fairly simple Protestant Christ-centred view of salvation, doubtless more devotional than theological in essence and hardly thought out at all. Entering into a professorial role in a genuinely pluralistic world, he felt quickly compelled to discard this over-simple and dubiously Christian evangelical view of salvation and damnation and create instead what he thought of as a new 'global' theology. As he himself stresses, theology derives from a particular cultural situation. So it is not unfair to point out how very closely his own does so.

This was, similarly, the situation within which new university departments of Religious Studies suddenly flourished. The university department of Theology, supported in the past as an honoured part of a national university, itself maintained by public funds, was an appropriate – almost necessary – part of a religiously single world. It existed primarily to develop a coherent on-going rationale for society's dominant faith or ideology – in the case of Western Europe, some form of Christianity – and hence to service a major public profession, the church's ministry. Theology was needed to relate church to society, and it was needed by both sides. From the 1960s, however, such a department was increasingly anomalous. By theology I mean what it has traditionally meant, a discipline which is not merely concerned comparatively or historically with sacred scriptures and religious doctrines, including an understanding of humanity, but which does so from a position of faith. I remain unable to see how without faith one can have theology – a history of theology, yes, but theology itself, no. A department of Christian theology implies in principle staff and students working together from and within a common faith, though doubtless a vigorous department could reasonably carry, and indeed benefit from, the questioning challenges of the odd deviant. It seems to me perfectly proper in principle to have such a department. In an Islamic country a national university can appropriately maintain a department of Islamic theology; in a Christian country a department of Christian theology. Indeed the absence of such a department was socially dangerous, the existence of a vigorous academic theology being the best defense against the dominance of irrational and intolerant fundamentalisms.

In reality, however, the one nation-one religion model has long been an anachronism almost everywhere, and the pursuit of it as an ideal in the pluralist reality of society may be a highly dangerous one. In a pluralist society a department of pure theology can only exist appropriately at a more private level, yet withdrawal from the public arena of a genuine university is likely, all in all, to be disadvantageous for theology – though it may still be the right, even the only, option in some circumstances. There can be little doubt that from the 1960s the department of Christian theology became less and less appropriate as a university institution in Britain. Our society as such no longer retains that degree of coherent Christian faith to require and justify university departments of specifically Christian theology, at least on the scale that they had existed hitherto. Nevertheless religion and churches (that is to say, communities of faith) remain an important reality of life, personally, nationally, internationally. It requires study, sympathetic yet scientific, critical yet constructive. Room is still needed for the construction of theologies – the rational critique of human life, material existence, political, religious and social structures on the basis of the faith of significant minority communities. Such a critique is needed by society as much as ever, but it can only be done on the basis of a faith of some sort. As there is no more a majority faith in society, it must be done on the basis of one or more minority faiths. Certainly Christianity in Britain today has the right (in terms of social significance) as well as the capacity to mount a critical theology. Such a theology has no right to a university monopoly, but it has a right to be present there – and as something more than the mere systematizing of an individual's belief. Indeed society itself would be dangerously the loser if influential religions within it were denied the opportunity to theologize effectively at university level and thus encouraged to fall back upon fundamentalism and quietism. The Department of Religious Studies in which all this should now be done is as understandable a development of post-6os Britain as is the theology of Hick, yet while the one seems to me an absolutely true and necessary development, the other appears a superficially attractive but over-hasty misdevelopment.

Departments of Theology, even where they retain the name, seem to be effectively transforming themselves into departments of religious studies. Most elements of a modern course of theology are in point of fact tackled with absolutely no necessary sense of religious commitment. Indeed the specifically theological element within a theology course in most English universities is now quite a small one – probably too small. This should not, however, mean that it is unimportant, nor that theology cannot exist, even flourish, within a department of religious studies, whether so-called or not. It can. But it does so on the basis of the work of individuals and groups, bringing their personal or community faith commitment creatively to enlighten one or another area of study. In much the same way it is not appropriate to have a department of Marxism, but many a Marxist works creatively within departments of history, sociology, philosophy or, indeed, religious studies. We may note here that if religious studies is in its way very much wider than theology, theology also remains in its way very much wider than religious studies. Religious studies is, inevitably, the study of religion – all religion, including the relationship between religion and anything else. But theology is not, as such, necessarily about religion at all. It is about existence in its totality seen in the light of a faith. In the same way an appropriate department of religious studies in Britain today will be in principle pluralist, open to and, hopefully, containing Christians, Muslims, Jews, Marxists, agnostics. They are united, not in faith – as they should be in a department of theology – but in a serious concern with the phenomena and significance of religion in a wide sense and in recognized skill in studying and interpreting such phenomena from a variety of standpoints. What exactly do we mean by pluralism from the viewpoint of religious studies? First, a recognition that the diversity of religions is a substantial, not a marginal, element within our subject, and that for an understanding of religion, it is crucial to consider the evidence of different traditions (including, especially, those outside ones own). Secondly, by pluralism in our discipline, we must mean the principle that one religion is not to be systematically interpreted in terms of another, and that the department has no over-arching principle of interpretation other than that of liberal scholarship. This does not mean that the comparison of religions is excluded, nor even the criticism of one in terms of the theology of another religion or any other appropriate terms, only that the department is not committed as such to any single religious or critical viewpoint. I cannot see any other way the subject can or should survive within universities in a society such as ours, however much it may be the case that in any one department all or most of the staff are in point of fact representative of a relatively small spectrum of belief. It seems sensible that in different departments the spectrum should be different.

It was natural enough, in the late 60s and 70s, that, as the department of theology turned effectively into a pluralist department of religious studies, and as its concerns with religious traditions other than the Christian grew considerably, there should have been a feeling, an expectation, that theology itself had to respond pretty drastically. In some way, indeed, it had to. The absence of serious consideration in nearly all post-mediaeval theology – to go no further back – of other religions and their significance vis-à-vis God, man and Christ is obvious enough. The question really was, in what way should it do so?

Hick presents his 'Copernican Revolution' as the only appropriate intellectual development for a Christian theologian in the pluralist city. Is it? It would be dangerous to imagine that just because a particular intellectual development appears on the surface appropriate to a particular context, it is therefore the correct development, or that there may not be other perhaps less obvious but better grounded approaches. That Hick's was truly in its way extremely appropriate in terms of cultural and social context, I have already tried to show. Was it, however, theologically appropriate? It is, quite obviously, necessary for Christian thinking to change in response to cultural change. Yet it is equally true that Christian thinking can be inappropriately hijacked by the spirit of the age into sudden developments alien to its own proper self. A Copernican Revolution in theology can certainly not be finally justified in terms other than theological. This, of course, Hick fully recognizes and his arguments relate to the confused state – as he sees it – of the earlier theology of the relationship of Christianity to other religions (the number of 'epicycles' it had, he argues, been forced to develop) in order to justify change.

The companion volume to *God and the Universe of Faiths* should undoubtedly be seen as the symposium *The Myth of God Incarnate*, edited by John Hick in 1977 after three years of preparation.[7] The aim of the book was to argue that the incarnation, usually regarded as the centre-piece of specifically Christian belief and theology, the key component of Christianity's distinctiveness, was no more than a myth or a shibboleth and one which today, 'the new age of world ecumenism' (168, Hick's phrase), could very well be dispensed with. This, the Preface indicated, would have 'increasingly important practical implications for our relationship to the peoples of the other great religions' (ix). No longer, Professor Wiles observed in the opening chapter, would Christians be able to believe in 'the superiority of one religion over another in advance of an informed

[7]John Hick (ed.), *The Myth of God Incarnate*, SCM Press and Westminster Press 1977.

knowledge of both faiths. Such a change can only be regarded as a gain' (9). Jesus would no longer be claimed as in some way 'the way for all peoples and all cultures', but as one of a number of powerful spiritual figures in human history who have taught the world about God. 'We should never forget' Hick confidently declared, 'that if the Christian gospel had moved east into India instead of west into the Roman empire, Jesus' religious significance would probably have been expressed by hailing him within Hindu culture as a divine Avatar and within the Mahayana Buddhism which was then developing in India as a Bodhisattva' (176). One wonders how he knows.

'A divine Avatar' or 'a Bodhisattva'. One among many: a guru within a pluralistic world. That was the intended message of the book and one suggested succinctly in the Epilogue by Dennis Nineham. Professor Nineham summed up the matter, clear-sightedly enough, not in terms of the incarnation but of the uniqueness of Christ. That too, under any form of words would have to go. Now it is obvious enough that an explicit incarnation-type theology is only one of the ways in which the New Testament writers endeavour to expound the mystery of Christ and various writers in *The Myth* correctly stressed this pluralism in New Testament theology as, of course, within subsequent Christian theology. Does the vocabulary of the incarnation doctrine, either in its Johannine or its Chalcedonian form, speak to us today? Does it contain christology *tout court*? Or is it just one way to talk about Christ among other ways? May we not use other ways? Of course, we may. But beneath such questions there is slipped in an essentially different one: do we need assert in any verbal form at all that Jesus is 'necessarily in principle unique' (202)? The Hickian function of the book is to deny it (though not all its contributors might have gone along with that denial). Now the book's appeal is intrinsically to Christian theological scholarship – an examination, principally, of the coherence of the Christian tradition's internal thinking in regard to Christ. Yet what it actually had to admit – as sound New Testament scholarship must admit – is that while the terms and images chosen for the formulation of Christ's religious uniqueness vary, the affirmation of that uniqueness can be found with basically equal weight in every New Testament writing as in all subsequent Christian credal affirmation. That embarrassing claim to religious uniqueness on behalf of one man, Jesus of Nazareth, and a consequent ultimate universality of significance, have remained the central characteristic of the Christian tradition, formulate them as you will. Deny the uniqueness and defend Christianity as the appropriate folk-religion for the European West, and you are, I would hold, denying Christianity intrinsically, however many bits and pieces of Christian wreckage you may still find serviceable. Maintain that uniqueness and universality, in whatever linguistic form, and you maintain the continuity and vitality of the Christian claim, however many bits and pieces you may discard as unserviceable.

That seems to me the heart of the matter. Christian theology can only function as such in accordance with Christianity's own central internal logic as a way of faith and of life. That logic is certainly not provable: the sound scholar can tackle the evidences with much good will and not find it adequately convincing, because the claims of that logic seem so improbable. But that is not theology, which remains and has to remain a discipline issuing out of a faith. It is philosophy, one form of common sense, religious studies, what have you. A theology operates according to its own awkward logic, a logic which functions rationally in judging probabilities, seeking coherence in systems, examining seemingly contrary statements, but all within the context of some great basic presupposition. All Christian theology, from the earliest Christian communities prior to the writing of the New Testament – in so far as we can know them – has operated on the basis of this great supposition, the qualitative uniqueness of Christ. No evidence of a pluralism, internal and subordinate to that unanimity, can possibly justify, in theological terms, an abandonment of that presupposition in favour of a quite different religious or secular world view. The attempt of Hick and of *The Myth of God Incarnate* to justify a rejection of that presupposition in favour of an ultimate religious pluralism within human history should be in principle a theological non-starter. It must also, existentially, be destructive of Christianity as a coherent religious reality. It is a strange stipulation that, in order to enter the age of pluralism appropriately, you must first cease in principle to be what you have been for two thousand years. It is not one which makes theological sense (or sociological sense in relation to Christianity's on-going community identity) and, equally, it should not be one required by the integrity of religious studies or a genuinely ecumenical approach to the situation of pluralism. That integrity requires, I would suggest, on the contrary, acceptance of the logically non-compatible claims of different religions, rather than the attempt to relate them all systematically within an imagined 'world theology', which would be recognized by the believers of no tradition. I am arguing, then, for an explicit dualism: recognition of the quite different requirements of 'religious studies' and 'theology'. For the former the remark of Maurice Wiles is eminently correct: here we must, of course, not assert 'the superiority of one religion over another'. A department of Religious Studies could function on no other basis. But such a department operates in terms of a pragmatic secular liberal commitment to mutual respect in the pursuit of learning, not in terms of an implicit or explicit theology of its own. This may seem to privatize theology, but there can be no alternative other than the setting up of a bogus 'global theology' as a sort of civil religion for the department: bogus because it relates to no recognizable community of faith.

Essentially different are issues such as an adequate theological evaluation in Christian terms of the relationship of other religions, ideologies and moral commitments to the uniqueness of Christ, or again the limits of credal and denominational pluralism within the large historic tradition of Christian belief. The trouble with the Hickian and *Myth of God Incarnate* approach was that it mixed them all up. Such questions can not, of course, be other than immensely important and their conclusions may well be significantly corrective for the thought and practice of the Christian community. Thus it should in fact be painfully evident that the very simple model of salvation through explicit faith in Christ alone, taken for granted by the younger Hick, was really not the central traditional Christian one at all – though doubtless it had been taken for granted over many generations by countless Christians, Protestant and Catholic. It is too evidently false to the full data of the tradition – including especially the explicit and breath-taking insight of Romans 5 that the grace of Christ has abounded more widely than the sin of Adam. Basic to the tradition was a tension between the every-frontier-breaking-down universality of salvation and the particularity of its symbolic personal initiator and centre-piece. The abandonment of neither is acceptable. Again, basic to the tradition, was the relationship between old covenant and new, whereby the adherents of both were included within a single history of salvation 'ab Abel', whether or not they knew anything of Jesus of Nazareth. Any appropriate advance in the Christian theology of salvation or of the relationship of religions might best start at this point. The fact of that *both* should, from the start, have ruled out a narrow 'Christians only are saved' doctrine. It should not be too hard to evolve a theology of other religions and other scriptures too drawn from the paradigm of Israel, much as most theologians have failed to do so. Earlier covenants are at least an under-analysed and under-used category in theological thought. But such a development would remain an evolution, not a Copernican Revolution and not an epicycle either. This would not be a pluralist theology but it would be a Christian theology open to the full pluralism of human experience and able to build upon a wide rather than a narrow model of divine revelation and the way of salvation.

Different again, of course, is the question as to whether, philosophically, belief in Christ remains a very plausible belief; or whether Christianity is not now a dissolving reality without a future, because without a sufficiently coherent set of beliefs with which a thoughtful twentieth-century person is able to identify. That, perhaps, was the true unwritten agenda for several of the *Myth of God* writers. A theologian can well come, theologically, to such a conclusion: he may come to decide that it is impossible to construct any more a credible and coherent system upon the basic Christian presupposition, and thus come finally to cease to be a Christian theologian, because no longer a Christian. If Christian theology is based upon a false premise it should in due course wither, like many other dead ideologies and religious systems of the past. A theology, while grounded in faith, has still of its nature to establish an adequate and intellectually coherent and convincing system linking together a range of ideas relating to the basic aspects of contemporary human existence in the light of a central faith principle. This Christian theology has always tried to do and often effectively. If it can do so no more, it must crumble. But that is not a matter of pluralism, just one of the intellectual and spiritual senescence of a religious tradition.

It is manifest that an environment of radical pluralism must put an immensely much greater strain upon the theologian, just as it does upon the ordinary believer, than an environment of shared belief. In the latter a scholar can easily tend to harmonize his conclusions with public faith without quite realizing he is doing so, in a way that simply ceases to happen when there is no longer a public faith of that sort. Such is the condition of modern Britain and such is, accordingly, the condition of a modern department and the discipline of religious studies, within which the academic theologian has now very largely to work. It can certainly be a strain to be loyal to the exigencies at once of religious studies and of a theology. Each of course has a variety of possible approaches to pluralism. A department of religious studies will, then, have to carry along with it an internal pluralism, including a plurality of attitudes towards pluralism itself. Indeed the tension of that plurality may be experienced within a single person. But such strains can be carried; indeed they have to be. In fact there is really no field of modern life and study in which a genuine loyalty at once to liberal and pluralist structures and to ones particular convictions, not shared with all ones colleagues, may not tax ones resources. It is really an unavoidable predicament. People who reject Christianity should not imagine that if they have principles and integrity they can escape it, though clearly some world views may seem more awkward in their scholarly consequences than others.

Today's is certainly a much harsher environment in which to assert the Christian claim to an absolute religious particularity than was the privileged bondage of the European past. Maybe it will prove too harsh and the battle will, quite quickly, be abandoned. But it should not, I think, be abandoned at the first moment that the new terms of service are read out, as the theologian recognizes around him a pluralist world instead of Christendom. He should have been more on his guard, ready for the moment when the Christian claim would cease to be bolstered up by the claims of mediaeval or Victorian Christendom. After all, they did not start together. Christianity's non-pluralist commitment to the absolute particularity of Christ in relation to the ultimate meaning and purpose of humanity, God's will for the world, originated within a religiously pluralist world and among its poor, and triumphed in that world. Faced with a multitude of cults it was unyielding in relationship to them. The absolutist claims of Christianity were, one might suggest, masked rather than manifested in their true import by their subsequent connection with absolutist claims of Western culture and political power. Now that the latter have so largely collapsed, as has the connection between the two (though not, of course, in much current American ideological warfare which unites a highly fundamentalistic Protestant Christianity extremely closely with American world power and 'civilization', very much on a British Victorian model), it may well be an appropriate time precisely to speak forth the true scandal of Christian particularity in such a way that it can at least be heard for what it always claimed to be – the scandal of God's foolishness, not of British cleverness; of the weakness of the cross, not of the power of the maxim gun.

If the clever and the powerful of today's world have not time for such a message, seeking instead a more socially mellifluous new civil religion (inclusive or exclusive of God, 'reality-centredness', the tomb of the unknown soldier, Lenin's birthday, or whatever), it may be that the poor of the third and fourth world will think differently. Maybe they will be right to do so, finding in it indeed 'the way, the truth and the life', or maybe they will simply be missing out on the most reliable intellectual advances of the twentieth-century in pursuance once more of an opium appropriate to their state of misery. In philosophical, historical, religious studies terms, we cannot quite say which is the case. And a pluralistic department of religious studies must be open to all the possibilities. But a theologian, operating loyally within such a department and the pluralistic world it reflects, will still – if he is able to stick to his last, at once believer and scientist – maintain that the Christian faith has always had at its heart a paradoxical assertion of the improbable, never contemptuous of reason, scholarship or other revelation, yet able again and again to outflank the broader ways of human wisdom and religion with the narrow particularity of a cross, a tomb, a tortured body, a resurrected hope, unique, yet everyman's experience. Such an assertion is in some way fulfillment of every aspiration of the most pluralistic of worlds, yet it remains no less committed to a singularly single salvific symbol, one no less improbable in the first century than in the twentieth, but which for both may still – just conceivably – contain the power and the wisdom of God.

★ 4 ★

The Authority of the Church, Universal and Local

In regard to the life of the church the authority of the church is, in a practical sense, final. It comes at the end of things, not their beginning. Every other authority – reason, the Bible, God – has to be mediated within it, through it, so that if the church is the most rightly judgable of all things, so has the church too to judge all things. To it has been given a mission of witness and service and authority to fulfil it, an authority from which there is no form of constitutional appeal. For one's own life one may appeal to conscience and go ones way, but for the church's life the church's authority is inevitably final – which does not mean that it may not be fallacious. There is no way in which the church as a recognizable and public body, a fellowship of women and men joined by sacrament, belief and common purpose, can evade the requirements of its own authority. However much it may proclaim and be conscious of its subordination to God and to revelation, it is still, within its on-going life, the church itself which resolves the relationship of revelation to Bible, the frontiers between Bible, reason and experience, how God has spoken and how God's word has this here and now implication and not another. It may appeal to the power of the Spirit, it may pray, it may cast lots, it may discuss, it may vote, it may consult the faithful or limit its debates to the bishops, it may leave all to the Pope or nothing to the Pope, but in none of these ways can it avoid the simple truth and basic responsibility of its own authority without thereby ceasing to be the church.

All this is the more obvious when we are concerned with such issues as those of ministry, the who and how of ordination, the authority of synods. These are, most eminently, church matters: they have no standing at all, no sense, apart from the church and precisely because they are essentially – and in no derogatory way – so churchy, the authority which the church possesses must be exercisable in regard to them most appropriately.

Nevertheless this is not, of course, the primary area of concern for church authority. Far from it. The church is a missionary, preaching, witnessing body. What power it has it must exercise, first of all, in witnessing to the Father of Our Lord Jesus Christ, the death and risen life of Jesus, the power of the Spirit, the meaning of reconciliation, the life of justice and holiness to which in Christ mankind is called. All this comes first by sheer ecclesial necessity. It did and it does. But the exercise of that witnessing, the internal guidance of the communion of the faithful, the structure and handing-on of the ministry across the generations, into new lands and an ever-widening circle of the faithful – numerical, geograph-ical, linguistic – required a secondary exercise of church authority, in matters then which were not so much given to the church as generated within the church's history, matters over which the church should appropriately exercise a conscious control which it does not have in the primary area. It is not accidental that in the course of Christian history and theology, the doctrine and theology of the sacraments, of the ministry, of the very nature of the church and its authority are rehearsed, take some sort of formal shape and are (occasionally) even 'declared' far later and far more accidentally, pragmatically and indecisively than the doctrine and theology of God, Christ, redemption, grace. They are tools rather than ends; servants not saviours; socially and culturally conditioned and reconditioned in a way that – it is true – our grandparents seldom appreciated but which we, fortified by the historical and anthropo-logical perspectives of the modern mind, can not ignore. The conditioning is not an invention of our time, only in some sort a discovery.

The church, then, is and always has been struggling to update, to shape and reshape its consciousness and structured ministry so to be able here and now to fulfil, with as little unworthiness and ineptitude as may be (yet it will still be with much, being composed of unworthy servants) its single calling in new, changing and varied circum-stances. The struggle to do all this is not new. It has been there since, precisely, apostolic times. And because of the intrinsic nature of this whole area of church life and ministry, the pragmatic development of actually living and ministering has somehow to predate the authorization of the church, especially of the world-wide church. So it always was. The church did not begin with a doctrine of ministry. It began with a very simple praxis of ministry which grew and grew and as it grew its branches had to be blessed and pruned – perhaps very occasionally one needed actually to be lopped off. But it was and is of the very nature of Catholic ecclesiology and ministry that the development preceded the formal and ecumenical authorization. Even the canon of the New Testament, so decisive subsequently for the life, teaching and self-understanding of the church came in its authoritative and ecumenical form – and could only come – long after the development within local churches whereby separately written books were linked together and set apart to share a kind of divine and inspired authority already recognized in the books of the Old Testament.

A muddled process in a muddled church. So it was and so it still will be, if we are going to adhere to a model of a living rather than mummified catholicity, the model of a pilgrim church, whose rules are never quite laid down in advance. Nobody seriously studying the history of Christianity from the second to the fifth century could, I think, doubt the basic truth of that model. Different local churches in communion with one another but with no agreed procedures for settling problems in advance or universally had to feel their way forward when faced with issues which, in the circumstances of the day, required a solution with an urgency which the same issue had not previously seemed to have. In due course the Emperor Constantine pressed upon the church the practice of an ecumenical council – a boon, if also a curse in the scale of secular political influence it witnessed to. But it came after two hundred and fifty years of coping otherwise – through local councils or the pastoral decision-making of individual bishops, the seemingly haphazard moving forward of the Christian conscious-ness. And Nicaea did not end all that. The ecumenical council has remained a way of responding to already well advanced develop-ments and disputes rather than a way of plotting out a theoretical line of advance in hitherto unexplored territory and the role of the Papacy at its most beneficial has been mostly of the same sort – what the Second Vatican Council in its Decree on Eastern Catholic churches spoke of as that of 'supreme judge of inter-church relations' (art 4).

I am assuming, of course, in speaking to Anglicans that the Church of England (or the Anglican Communion) is genuinely a part of the *Ecclesia Catholica* about which I am talking. But I cannot speak trying to be an Anglican theologian when I am not – trying to think what an Anglican theologian could most reasonably say on this theme and in this predicament, if he or she also happened perhaps to share some of the ideas I myself have. No, that would not do. I can only speak as myself, a Catholic theologian baptized and ordained within the Roman communion and – I trust – still within that communion, even if my own disagreements with its canonical insistances have placed me in an anomalous position within it. Now Pope Paul called the Church of England 'a sister Church' and while that was not an infallible statement, it is at least consistent with many others and may be said to represent the praxis of Rome today, even if there is in Rome itself hardly a coherent theology to make full sense of it. Vatican II went some way towards providing one, but not a full way. Since then documents like the Malta Statement and those of ARCIC all stand, upon the Roman side, with at best ambiguous authority. We are out of one ecclesiology but hardly into another. Here again praxis goes ahead of theory. The church is a communion of faith, sacrament, fellowship, but this communion – Vatican II does tell us – can be partial as well as complete. I take it that in point of fact the true fullness of communion is here and now unrealizable for anyone. There are degrees of holiness, catholicity, unity, also degrees of communion. The partiality of possession of all its other marks is precisely the mark of the church as historic, a church on the way to being itself. Of course, not all diminutions of fullness are equally grave. Of course, the Church of England in particular – as this is what we are concerned with here – is, we must certainly recognize, not all that it should be. Of course, it was a grave lack of appropriate communion that at the Second Vatican Council there were no Anglican voting members (nor Greek Orthodox either). But that indicates a lack upon both sides and, of course, if it is not hard to point out other Anglican defects, one can hardly deny some Roman ones as well. The point is that, in all sorts of different ways, the church here and anywhere is *semper reformanda*. Every local church fails to be fully and recognizably what a local church ought to be and yet – so long as its members cling on to Christian faith and baptism, eucharist and creed and penitence for sin, and an unfailing hope in God who is God – it is not and cannot be basically unchurched. A sister church, in partial communion, is still a local church. The key fact about the pilgrim church is that it is not kingdom, it is not perfect, it is not arrived, it is in history, it is in a very real way creating itself as it moves along in the darkness of faith, a company of sinners striving, pretty pathetically most of the time, to be saints as well. The truest ecclesiology will be one very largely of imperfection, fallibility, partial communion.

That, I believe, represents a fair rough picture of Catholic ecclesiology, refertilized by the better insights of Vatican II. And the Church of England may see itself in such a context. In this great 'Ecclesia Catholica' it has to recognize and carry its responsibilities as just part of the whole, a local church, an 'ecclesia particularis' in the Council's frequently used phrase. It is a local church suffering for historical reasons certain disabilities (such as non-representation among the voting members of Vatican II) but also enjoying, even thereby, certain considerable advantages. Above all, it should have now a great freedom, relatively unbound by the restrictions of Roman canon law and control upon the one hand, royal and parliamentary bondage upon the other. This exceptional freedom could make of it not so much a bridge church, more a pilot church. But basically it might do well to behave – theologically but not canonically – as if it had been at Vatican II. It is a local church, and should not pretend to be the universal church. The universal church exists as a communion of local churches and the local church is subject to the universal church. Hierarchically and sacramentally the wider communion remains a bit upset at present – though not so much as it used to be – but the Church of England can only behave responsibly as if it were there. Clearly General Synod cannot claim the degree of authority that a universal council can claim: *Securus judicat orbis terrarum*. That should certainly not be forgotten. But, of course, even Vatican II with its 2000 plus bishops was not fully *orbis terrarum*. It did matter that Constantinople and Canterbury were not there. Alas: We cannot in present circumstances engineer *orbis terrarum*. If we denied that Constantinople and Canterbury and Moscow had anything to do with the church except as a matter of history or individual faith and good will we could declare – as we did on the old Roman ecclesiology – that Vatican II and such like were totally ecumenical. Full stop. But we can't. The very words and deeds of the Popes, as much as the sheer witness of religious and Christian reality, make that today too difficult. Once we are forced to recognize that the great Eastern schism really could not have excluded either Latins or Greeks from the visible apostolic church, we have to cope with the provisionality of not having a contemporary *orbis terrarum* effectively to appeal to. Yet it remains in principle and in practice more in Vatican II than in Lambeth, yet not wholly in one when it does not include the other.

The church is a communion of churches and sub-churches – from the house church to the province which links together a group of dioceses. All have their proper ministry and authority. All must see themselves, respectfully, humbly, but creatively and adventurously too, within the wider apostolic *communio ecclesiarum*: to be heirs of the apostles does not simply nor primarily mean to be a repository of apostolic teachings, harking cautiously back to a *depositio fidei*, but to have the sort of adventurous apostolicity which took Peter and Paul out from the established confines of the church of the circumcision to the challenges and new rule makings of the church of the Gentiles. Remember that the Council of Jerusalem – our scriptural paradigm for ecclesiastical problem solving – came together and provided a ruling after, not before, the crucial initiatives had been taken locally elsewhere. There were plenty of uncircumcised Christian believers, some among whom had already even been appointed as elders with prayer and fasting (Acts 14.23) before the Council ruled 'It has seemed good to the Holy Spirit and to us to lay upon you no greater burden' (Acts 15.28). Apostolicity really lies in adhering imaginatively to that total model: the courage to take local initiatives, which are sure to be roundly condemned by others as untraditional and unapostolic, as well as the ability to accept in due course the decision of the whole church when it has been properly reached.

Of course, a local church could not absolutely know that it was not mistaken when it decided that the uncircumcised might be baptized and made elders, or that after persecution *traditores* might be reconciled, or that – despite Paul's teaching in I Timothy – an unmarried childless celibate might be chosen as bishop, or that infants might be baptized, or confirmation separated by years from baptism, or whatever: all more or less revolutionary decisions taken first in fear and trembling by one or another local church, somewhere, sometime, long before the universal church had 'declared' that it was right.

The local church is not infallible. It may be wrong. It may even be in danger of becoming schismatic if it presses ahead with some missionary or pastoral innovation while the wider church too strongly disapproves. But, equally, if it does nothing, if it procrastinates indefinitely, when the need is there, it may still more surely come under judgment and dry up like the fig tree, correct but nevertheless fruitless. The point is that new pastoral decisions have got to be taken again and again in the course of history and they cannot initially be taken from the centre or by a general council. Without such decisions the church is bound to dry up, tied to an anachronistic shape. The guidance of the Spirit is to be seen more in the courage to move than in the prudence which resists innovation. Again and again in history circumstances somehow re-enact that first moving out process from Jew to Gentile. Adhering unchangeably to a previous pattern of ministry until the universal church decides otherwise is not to follow the apostolic model and is a recipe for ensuring that the universal church never decides anything. Apostolic fidelity requires, on the contrary, the courage of local churches to jump the gun while doing so utterly unschismatically, determined to maintain all that it can of catholic unity (but not uniformity), aware that there are bound to be painful confrontations – just as there were at Antioch – but clear above all that mission and pastoral need come first and can not be resolved simply in terms of fidelity to past practice – even in apparently major matters. Catholicism is a living, developing organism of understanding and ecclesial structure or it is nothing. Any sort of fundamentalism which could settle the shape of the church or the formulas of her faith once and for all in terms of how things were in the fifth-century or the second or at the death of the last apostle or whenever, has absolutely to be rejected, and precisely out of fidelity to the growing historical catholicity which has always characterized Christian history, the intrinsic developmentalism of the New Testament itself which presents itself not as closed law but as a model to take with us into the unknown future.

When one considers the relationship of local church authority to universal church authority, it is impossible to say that some matters can be put into the one box only, some into the other. Many of the greatest doctrinal issues were considered in local councils; quite little pastoral matters could be legislated about in ecumenical councils. Of course, not all that is done is done wisely or rightly. But what we cannot do is to exclude certain types of decision and initiative because, for instance, they are too important to be taken locally. On the contrary, the most important decisions must come locally first. What is required in the councils of the local church is to approach such matters with a sense of high doctrinal and pastoral responsibility – not only for oneself, but for the whole *Catholica*.

Are there no limits we can theoretically pose to the power of the church, universal or local, to reshape its own constitution and ministry? It is hard to think of many with assurance. There has, undoubtedly, been a strong tendency to want to push back almost all the contents of this secondary category of concern into the primary category, to fundamentalize it, one might say, and of course we can't divide the two completely – the eucharist and baptism in particular are essentially bridging elements coming from the one into the other. So too may be a differentiated ministry, as well as a still more especial 'Petrine' thread of authority, or – again – the mediatory power to express the forgiveness of sin even apart from baptism. We have to be careful how we tamper with such as these. And yet, of course, the whole central history of the sacraments and the ministry has been that of one long tampering with such central inheritances. The shape of the Mass, developing over the centuries, and differently with different liturgies, is proof that we can and even have to tamper with them. We could only begin to justify some of the main lines of the mediaeval Papacy or, again, religious orders with an immensely flexible and developmental kind of ministerial theology. And if we should say – as Roman theology has often tended to say – that some rather precise things we cannot touch: that we cannot, for instance, in any way touch the matter of the eucharist, it has for validity to be wheaten bread, then we would be forced to conclude that the St Thomas Christians in south India, celebrating their eucharist for many hundreds of years wheatless, but using some sort of rice cake instead, never really celebrated Mass, renewing the sacrament of the Lord's Supper. They were geographically incapable of so doing. How absurd. How could we think God so foolish! In the later Middle Ages, a number of Popes undoubtedly gave permission for various abbots, who were not bishops, to ordain priests – thus anticipating John Wesley. Again the Council of Florence quite formally declared the 'matter' of the sacrament of ordination to be the 'handing over of the instruments' ('traditio instrumentorum'), a practice which never existed at all before the Middle Ages. All such cases argue emphatically against any sort of sacramental fundamentalism.

A brief consideration of two other issues may help us further in understanding the way the church has developed, its authority has been exercised and recurring doubts about sacramental validity overcome.

The first is that of confession and absolution. The church's continual sense of being a community in which sin is forgiven by the power of God has taken a variety of sacramental forms – some more public, some more confidential. The church at any particular time may prescribe the forms but it is not bound by the forms of other ages. Certainly in the Middle Ages people often confessed their sins to the laity; the last Catholic bishop of Iceland indeed did so to his wife when on his way in 1550 to lay down his life for the faith at the hands of Danish Protestants. That event does not seem outside the frontiers of acceptable Catholic tradition.

The other issue is that of baptism by women, much controverted in the Church of England in the sixteenth and seventeenth centuries. The bishops were anxious to defend the validity of baptism by midwives; some more extreme Protestants denied that it could be done. It may be that the underlying attitudes and arguments used then and now are not so very different. The traditional Christian insistence that women can baptize, coupled with the reluctance of some Christians to allow it to happen, has a good deal to say to the question whether, when pastorally opportune, a woman can be ordained.

The moral I would draw from these and other examples is that the church has the power to construct and reconstruct its ministry, its sacramental forms and hierarchy, and has in fact done so (more or less wisely and imaginatively) according to the culture and pastoral needs of the age – even though it has not for the most part been self-consciously aware of that power. Hugh of St Victor thought there were thirty sacraments. I am not entirely sure that we were wise to agree instead with King Henry VIII (and, of course, many better theologians before him) and declare that there are only seven, and I am not entirely sure that in the future the church will not profitably reconstruct some of those other twenty-three.

It may be helpful, finally, to point to the way in which the World Council of Churches and its Central Secretariat has developed since the 1940s. Theology did not come first here, at least consciously. What came first was a spiritual aspiration and the response to an international pastoral need, which had at first almost ostentatiously to disavow ecclesiological significance. And yet of course that significance has been enormous in re-establishing, outside the world of the Roman Communion, the sense of the *Ecclesia* as requiring the embodiment of a universal ministry and centre of unity. One might indeed say, paradoxically, that behind modern Geneva is none other than a petrine theology of a 'see of unity': unable to tolerate its present realization in Rome because of the latter's exaggerated pretensions and practical intolerance, it has been necessary to realize it *pro tem* elsewhere. A very ancient theology may then be implicit in this modern praxis, yet almost unconsciously. And that is what one finds again and again. When some seemingly revolutionary development has taken place, one can recognize within it in altered dress the imperious requirements of the 'faith once delivered to the saints'. So too in some apparently traditional adherence to the precise pattern of the past one may at times only too clearly detect a form of faith now crucially at variance with the central message of the gospel.

If a local church – laity, bishops, priests – faced with a need for a radical pastoral initiative, think and reason about it, pray, seek the guidance of God's spirit and then act in such a way as to adapt the structure of the church and its ministry to express better in today's world Christ's abiding truth, then ecclesiologically it cannot be faulted. Ecclesiologically, it is not wrong because it has not been done before. Ecclesiologically, it is not wrong because the *orbis terrarum* has not yet pronounced upon it. Ecclesiologically it would be wrong, after such a process, to be afraid to act for no other reason than that the universal church remains partly uncertain, partly opposed. The rightness of the particular decision must be hammered out pastorally, christologically, soteriologically, anthropologically, but not ecclesiologically. Ecclesiologically, the world church in its full authority can only say to the innovators who have thought it out in those other dimensions, and prayed and gone ahead, 'Brethren, since we have heard that some persons from among us have troubled you with words, unsettling your minds, although we gave them no instructions, it has seemed good to us in assembly to send to you with Barnabas and Paul, Judas and Silas . . .' to confirm not just the legality but the immense pastoral and missionary desirability of some seemingly controversial novelty. That, I believe, is what the *Catholica* will in due course say yet again but, of course, 'some persons from among us' may well say quite a lot of other things first.

★ 5 ★

Prophecy

The crucial role of the prophets of Israel from Elijah to Jeremiah and the way in which Jesus was both hailed as a prophet and behaved as a prophet may make one ask why Christian theology has so played down the possibility of post-New Testament prophecy and whether really for Christian theology prophecy is something only of the past and not also for now.

Prophecy is a function of moral interpretation which may operate, and may be needed, within any society. It is a societal role – vocal yet marginal but almost, if not entirely, uninstitutionalized. It is the voice of the 'fool', the child looking at the emperor's clothes, requiring imagination and the courage of an uncomplicated truthfulness, but also a symbolism associated with the poet's mind rather than the scientist's. Like every role operative within the biblical and Christian tradition, it exists also and, in a sense, primarily outside that tradition. There is a continuity of experience between 'secular', religious and biblical prophecy and any attempted analysis of such experience needs to call on the whole range of phenomena. No highly institutionalized and hierarchical society wants to listen to a prophet – the very institutionalization of the court fool was a way of reducing prophecy to insignificance – but no highly academic society has much time for a prophet either. Yet prophecy – while no substitute for government or science – remains peculiarly necessary, if largely ignored, within any society's pursuit of wisdom.

Prophecy in the biblical-Christian tradition is not equivalent to the revelation of things unseen, nor is it teaching about such revelation, though it does in its judgment presuppose revelation, that is to say it presupposes the reality of a God of justice and love. But it is a word to the world about the world now, about the immediate or coming human situation, about what is wrong with society. It is not in the Bible given as human opinion, but as God's judgment upon humanity, upon the predicament of Israel or Nineveh. The prophet is, in the deepest sense, a religiously minded person, concerned with nothing more than the doing of the divine will, almost fanatically so. But, while a constant religious tendency is to ecclesiasticize and ritualize, to sacralize human behaviour, turning human concern away from the seen to the unseen (sometimes rightly so), the prophet breaks in on ecclesiasticism, ritualism and mysticism to locate the finally most valid religious behaviour – that is to say the behaviour which most adequately expresses the worship of God – in justice, compassion, generosity, the loving service of one person for others, in truthfulness. And he locates this true religiosity in just those aspects of justice and compassion which matter most here and now, but which contemporary society and the contemporary church may be most prone to sin against.

The prophet, then, stands, by the sheer necessity of his role as the outspoken bearer of awkward truth, on the knife edge between the religious and the secular, between sacralization and secularization. The professional temptation of the religious is to establish a complex 'special' world of religious rites, rules and institutions, as apart as possible from the normal secular round of human affairs: a church apart, a religious world of meaning apart, in which the duty of the religious person is mostly located. In a religiously respectful world, it is hoped, that 'special' religious network will be the most central, privileged area. That is sacralization. The secularizer breaks in on it to declare religious rites unimportant and boring: what matters to people is not the specifically religious, but the pragmatic world of kinship, sex, commerce, politics, human relations in all their forms. Now what the prophet declares is a judgment upon both sacralizer and secularizer. What matters to God, he says, is not 'The temple of the Lord, the temple of the Lord, the temple of the Lord' (Jer. 7.4), not religious ritual, not 'Lord, Lord' (Matt. 7.21), but secular relations, all that seems most non-religious but is in fact the very stuff of the City of God as much as the City of man. It is in the market place and the prison that the two cities are divided, sheep from goats, and by no 'religious' criteria at all, but by that of the service of one's fellows. You fed me when I was hungry, gave me drink when I was thirsty, visited me in prison. Or you did not. But when, Lord? – When you did or did not do it to the least of my brethren.

The prophet relocates the heart of religious meaning within the secular world from which the professionally religious person, the religious institutionalizer, had subtly withdrawn it. But in doing so, he does of course overturn the whole theory of secularization. For nothing is now secular. Nothing is irrelevant to the worship of God. There is no area of life from which we can keep religion out: neither politics, nor sex, nor slavery, nor buying or selling. The 'religious' person and the secularizer are really in alliance. They want the lines well drawn and tended: religion here, secular life there. Sundays for God. Weekdays for modern man. Keep religion out of politics. Keep all the dirty linen of the 'modern world' out of the church. Of course, the clearer such lines are drawn, the more irrelevant do Sunday and church become until the Sunday is secularized too and the church closed.

No, says the prophet, it won't do, for religion is the worship of God, and God happens to care far more for what is characteristic of the weekday than what is characteristic of Sunday. For the prophet true religion is far more about morals than about ritual, but by morals one means the great divide in human life between bullying, cruelty, organized oppression, the cults of affluence and power upon the one hand, and generosity, self-sacrifice, the care of the weak, the fellowship of the poor, sheer love, upon the other. The hard core of human immorality derives from the hierarchy of earthly power, political and commercial, and its ruthless urge to exploit the weak and to enrich the strong. Now exploitation and cruelty are inherently untruthful – they can hardly admit to being as they are and survive. So injustice is continually cloaked in a veil of untruth. It is the specific function of the prophet to expose the tawdriness of that veil, setting it against the way in God's world things really are.

Why in a Christian society can't all this be said and done by the church itself and its regular ministry? That, indeed, is the assumption of standard Catholic ecclesiology. If this was the role of Christ, then it is the role committed to the church, and it is for the Pope, the patriarchs, the moderators, to carry it on. And don't they do so? To a very important extent they do. The sheer reading of the scriptures, the celebration of the eucharist are prophetic and very dangerous exercises, proclaiming human freedom, equality, fraternity, and so calling into question every inhuman structuring of society. You cannot expurgate Catholic Christianity of its prophetic threat. But you can, of course, try – and many an establishment ecclesiastic has done his best to do so: to make of organized Christianity a sanctioning of blatant injustice in society (to be put right only in the next world), instead of a challenging in the light of the life, death and teaching of Christ of the sinfulness of contemporary humanity, particularly powerful humanity.

Of course, church leaders have been true prophets on many occasions; nevertheless, as we can see very well from even a little look at church history, it has too seldom happened. If it does not happen, it is chiefly for three reasons. One is that, especially in a Christian country (that is to say, a country with a majority of at least nominal Christians among its citizens), the church itself very easily becomes part of the wealthy establishment of power. Bishops become barons and then members of the House of Lords. The vicar is next in the village hierarchy to the squire. The more church leaders are incorporated within the secular structure of power, the less able they are to challenge it. They come instead, not merely to be silent about the sins of society, but even to share in them. So, in the eighteenth century, the Society for the Propagation of the Gospel owned a West Indian estate worked by slaves, just as other wealthy people did. Missionary Society as it was, it could not agree that its slaves should be preached to or baptized, lest their labour be impaired thereby, to its great economic loss. A Pope, who was also ruler of the Papal States of central Italy, was largely controlled in his attitude to government everywhere by the need to maintain his own position, repress revolution, keep the right allies. These may seem extreme cases, but they are not really very extreme in terms of Western Christian history from the fourth to the nineteenth century and they symbolize a position from which church leadership seldom wholly escapes: it is chained by prudence if not by actual participation in the crimes of the strong. A preoccupation with the diplomacy of institutional survival of a privileged sort leads it to practise complicity with governments which offer to protect that privilege and so secure a very large measure of church silence.

The second reason is that of the marked tendency of the professionally religious to retreat from the secular to the sacred, to declare the insignificance of – and their own relative lack of interest in – what goes on outside the 'soul' or church doors, so long as religious rites and institutions are not affected, and so long as they are not prevented from preaching about the next world to their faithful. Purely doctrinal teaching, and strongly other-worldly teaching – stressing the virtues of patience, obedience, poverty, disregard for the things of this world – can be so imparted as to be downright anti-prophetic. Such teaching somehow dodges all the real issues and crimes of contemporary society. Hence it seldom leads to the persecution of the preacher. This in fact brings us into the third reason: a recurring tendency within the church's moral teaching to invert true Christian morality: to play down the duty of serving the needy, to play up sexual sins, especially the sexual sins of those who have been deprived of power (of women rather than of men, therefore); to play down the duty of speaking uncomfortable truths, to play up the virtue of all forms of obedience, ecclesiastical and civil. Such teaching appears highly spiritual, it is a morality of the sacred rather than of the secular, and it won't upset the powerful. It obviously fits in well with an other-worldly spirituality of religious withdrawal. No society can operate without a morality, without collective standards of approved and condemned behaviour; but moralities vary greatly and for centuries ecclesiastical morality has had a markedly different character from that which the gospels ascribe to Jesus.

Collectively these tendencies produce a church whose leadership very seldom takes on its shoulders the truly prophetic burden of its founder. On the contrary, the church and its leadership come to reflect only too well, in a sacral mode, the very disorders of society against which it should be protesting.

In such circumstances, if Christ's message is to be proclaimed in all its cutting power, with all the danger that that implies for its proclaimer, it is only too clear that this will not be done by church authority as a whole. Here as elsewhere the mistake has been the monopolization of roles by the hierarchy. In practice the institutional and sacerdotal roles cannot easily be combined with the prophetic role. They were not in Jesus. The prophet in point of fact will need to address the institutional church, to witness indeed against the church, at least as much as against society. The world can indeed be expected to be the world, but the church should certainly not be a pious replica of the world; hence the true prophet will frequently need to be more scoffing about the church than about the world – about the Sadducees and Pharisees than about Pilate and Herod. It is sometimes comfortably suggested by church people that the true prophet will not be church-minded and should leave the church alone while addressing the world. Is that not the implication of being an anti-sacralist? Yet that is just what the true prophet cannot do: the reason he cannot do it is *not* because he is concerned with religion and 'sacred' things rather than with 'secular' issues of justice and mercy, but just because his task is to whip the church for being concerned with 'sacred' things, in a false or secondary sense but not in the deepest and primary sense in which the sacred is precisely justice and mercy. His role may be less to point out the sins of the world than to point out the sin of the church in falsely analysing the sins of the world. He has to lay bare a pious but essentially ungodly pseudo-morality and offer instead a true one. Of course, if he does this, he is threatening the leaders both of the church and of the world and the complicity that runs between them. For he will be saying that the rich get richer and the poor get poorer, that the weak are denied justice and even land and food, that the powerful are strengthened in their oppression by the smiling opportunism of ecclesiastical tame cats purring beside their hearth rugs, by the black mantilla which the President's wife deferentially wears as she is given a very special papal audience, by the shares in the state bank which the church would hate to lose, by the dry Martini which Caiaphas sips on Pilate's verandah. 'Woe to you, scribes and Pharisees, hypocrites! For you build the tombs of the prophets . . . You witness against yourselves. You are the sons of those who murdered the prophets' (Matt. 23.29–31). There may indeed be little for it but to kill the troublesome prophet. Later on, at a safe distance in time, we can, of course, give due honour, put up the memorial tablet, establish the commemorative lecture. But first of all he must be removed. Thus in El Salvador, Archbishop Romero was proving altogether too dangerous to the establishment. And as he raised up the chalice of Christ's blood at Mass in March 1980, he was shot and killed, and his place as archbishop-prophet in a nation at war between oppressors and oppressed was left unfillable.

Not all prophets, of course, are murdered. Though Archbishop Helder Camara is still alive, his house was riddled on occasion with machine-gun fire – more, perhaps, a salutary warning than an attempted assassination. Who else have been prophets in our time? C. F. Andrews was a prophet against imperialism in the British India of the 1920s, Dick Sheppard was a prophet of peace in the 1930s, Dietrich Bonhoeffer was a prophet who would not submit to nationalism even when his country was at war in the 1940s, Trevor Huddleston has been a prophet against racialism for longer than most of us can remember. Solzhenitsyn was for decades a prophet against the oppression of ordinary decent Russians by the Soviet system. Today prophets and 'schools' or 'sons' of prophets (II Kings 2.5) abound in Latin America, and such disciples may often be murdered too, for disciples are no better than their masters. Thus, six months after the martyrdom of Romero, three American nuns and a fellow worker were murdered in El Salvador on 2 December 1980: Sisters Maura Clark, Ita Ford, Dorothy Kazel and Miss Jean Donovan. Ordinary names for four women gunned to death for their fidelity to the example of Oscar Romero.

But it is not perhaps the most useful exercise to search around the church identifying individually true prophets, especially as it is of the nature of the prophetic role that it can be a passing one. The true prophet has no claim to be one for life, no right to object to a divine declaration of redundancy, no permanent charism of infallibility! He can be called for a purpose and then dropped by God, and he has no ground for complaint. But the poor man having had his taste of the pulpit, or the microphone, may not so easily recognize this and go on pontificating about many things on which he is quite incapable of prophesying. He is, after all, human too. And the prophet may well be odd or struggling with asthma and a pretty mixed-up personality, as was Dick Sheppard; a man of fits and starts. The prophet does not work from nine to five, at least not as a prophet.

The point is that a prophet can come from anywhere and be of any type. We have just named several archbishops as prophets – hardworking, reliable priests, people in fact combining two apparently very different roles. Don't they give the lie then to the view that the official church cannot prophesy? Yes and no. The official church can prophesy, and Archbishops Romero and Camara have clearly done so – both to their own countries and to the world. Even a Pope may be a prophet. After all, God can act in the most improbable of places, and if institutionally the Papacy is the least likely place to find a prophet, spiritually it is the most desirable. Pope John XXIII challenged the church and the world and, precisely, the church's relationship to the world in a way that was both extraordinarily unexpected and quite distinctively prophetic. He was hardly by temperament a prophet, and yet his word came to his contemporaries with an amazing personal authority – really much beyond the authority even a Pope can claim. His own church may never have quite forgiven him for doing so. Ideally, what John XXIII and Oscar Romero have done (two temperamentally quite conservative people, yet caught by a prophetic fire), every Pope and archbishop and moderator can do. But, of course, most don't.

There is in the clarity of message, the personal courage, the loneliness of stance, of such as these a quality that is not easily shared institutionally by many. As a matter of fact, they stand not quite alone but apart from the great mass of the Catholic episcopate, and their message does challenge the church's leadership itself in its self-understanding, its deep connections with oppressive secular power. It may be, ideally, that the whole Catholic Church should stand shoulder to shoulder with an Archbishop Romero, but it is quite certain that it did not and is not at all likely to do so, and even that the dominant power in the church both in Rome and in Latin America has rather little sympathy with such as these. A Cardinal Baggio, an Archbishop Lopez Trujillo, sees the priorities for the church and the maintenance of its established position within the power structures of this world in very different and more ecclesiastically prudent, more Sadducean, terms. If Archbishop Romero was a prophet, he was speaking to and judging, not only the government and society of El Salvador and South America, but almost primarily the church herself and the way in which for generations she has provided a sacred veneer of respectability for such societies while gaining a comfortable share of the privileges therein.

Maybe there are times when only an archbishop can really deliver that message effectively. And so while the prophet can be anyone, a prophet who is to be heard by a hierarchical church is likely enough to be a priest, even a bishop. Yet a prophet to a hierarchical church may also be wholly unhierarchical – as was Catherine of Siena. God raises up a voice within the church to speak to the church, in order that the church may speak with evangelical directness to contemporary humanity. The true prophet is characterized, then, by a lot of things: his or her message has a note of unambiguous fidelity to the sheer awkwardness and absoluteness of truth and its claims and yet is also unambiguously contemporary. It does not require complex interpretation because it is not obscurely, technically or diplomatically phrased as so many ecclesiastical and academic statements are. Yet its contemporaneity does not involve any basic dependence on contemporary ideology. On the contrary, its specific power may depend on speaking to the age without identifying with the age's own view of itself or with any contemporary power system – and all contemporary ideologies belong to one or other power system. The prophet is committed, vulnerable, at risk. Prophecy is not philosophy. It is not sociological or theological analysis. It is not intellectually the most sophisticated of communication techniques. It just points with painful clarity and intensity to what are, in the light of the divine and the ultimate, today's moral priorities and to how they are neglected.

The theologian of liberation or 'political theology', even the very proponent of the importance of the charismatic, may conceivably be a prophet, but is not necessarily so. One can write whole books, useful books, on liberating praxis, on justice, on charisms, but never in truth be part of any such praxis. Or, again, one can be genuinely part of it yet not prophetically: the sympathetic analyst of prophecy is not thereby a prophet. A theologian of liberation and a prophet of liberation are different things, and may well even express themselves in quite a different sort of language. Both are needed. Modern political theology has favoured the socialist mode and that is one that very largely omits the personal role, while the prophet – and it is weakness as well as strength – is irredeemably personal. It is the very priority of particularity in the role that makes its formulation so difficult. You cannot draw up laws to define the role of Lech Walesa or Francis of Assisi, or William Shakespeare. Prophets are no substitute for theologians, nor for bishops, but a church without prophets, just as a world without creative writers and artists, is like salt without savour.

If William Shakespeare had died as a child we would all, and for ever, have been without *Hamlet*, *King Lear*, *A Midsummer Night's Dream*, and would have been immeasurably the poorer. A theology of the prophet as of the poet revalues the significance of the individual against the primacy of institution or theoretical system and for human and religious life that is part of its value.

It is very clear that all the qualities of the prophet are found most powerfully if most enigmatically in Jesus of Nazareth – least ritualistic, most truly religious, most humane of humankind: teacher of the Beatitudes and the parables, defender of sabbath-breaker and adulteress, the outcast of Calvary. A Christian prophet's vocation is not formally a matter of *imitatio Christi* but it can be some comfort against outrageous fortune to remember that a disciple is not better than his master and that whatever else Jesus was, he was certainly a prophet.

A question may here be asked: how far is there room for prophecy within a 'liberal' society or a 'liberal' church? The more oppressive and authoritarian a society, the more it is tailored to the judgment of the prophet: Nazi Germany at war, the Gulags of Soviet Russia, South African racialism, the 'National Security State' in parts of Latin America – the role of prophecy in all these atrocious situations is clear enough. But the liberal society, even if it includes great injustices, somehow muffles prophecy – by an over-coverage of all issues, grave and trivial, largely to the financial profit of the media; by the blurring of edges inevitable in such a society; and then just by being nice to prophets and asking them to speak at society luncheons and student conferences. Few true prophets can survive that sort of treatment for long. There is also, it is to be admitted, very often a complexity within the socio-moral problems of, say, modern Western societies which almost defies prophetic treatment. The prophet can so often trip up his genuine message by succumbing to the simplistic. The same, of course, is true of the more 'liberal' church. A really reactionary church is good ground for effective prophecy, but you have to be a very cool but powerful prophet indeed to get under the skin of a progressive church, smug in its progressiveness. Yet it can be done. George Bell and Barbara Ward would both seem good examples of effective twentieth-century prophecy. And as modern Western society becomes less liberal, it becomes again more obviously in need of a prophetic witness.

The better the church is functioning, the more prophetic it is as a whole. The more that is so, the more its leaders are speaking to the world really with the voice of Christ, the less need there may be for the individual, uninstitutional prophet to goad it on. The prophet must live what he preaches: somehow he is himself a living of the message, for it is no detached academic subject he offers, but a burning word which is burning himself up too. If the church and its leadership are really burning up with the message of the cross which brings life, of the freeing of the poor, of the judgment of God upon the heartless and the legalistic, and if this is manifest in the church's own life, then they are truly prophetic. *Deo gratias.* The individual prophet is here unneeded. But if the church and its leadership, while with conscious sincerity preaching the Christian message, in fact confine their ministry of justice to the pronouncement of banal and opaque generalizations, while showing an unyielding preoccupation with institutional and sexual regulations, with the maintenance of an essentially secular power structure, with the enforcement of law rather than the proclamation of the gospel, then they are in no way being prophetic. *Miserere nobis.* The individual prophet is here most necessary.

The church is led, it would seem, in three ways, more or less corresponding to von Hügel's three dimensions of religion: the institutional, the intellectual and the mystical. The first way is that of the historic institution, the apostolic succession of ministers, of Popes and bishops, of handed down creeds and liturgies and ministries. Dull and bureaucratic as this may often seem, it is a necessary part of the Christian economy, linking us in every generation with the objectivities of a visible and historic fellowship. Abandon that entirely and you fall subject either to the dominance of the academic or to a still more dangerous world of indefinable spirit, charisms which seem the more compelling the more extraordinary they are. But it is not the whole way in which God leads either the individual or society. The second way is that of a theology open to the whole range of scientific achievement. The thoughtful, rational interpretation by theologians in monasteries, schools, universities or wherever, without the authority of office but with that of learning and reason, has always been an equally important way in which God has guided the church. The third way, the charismatic or prophetic, presupposes the continuities of the other two. Grace leads both individual and society in ways which cannot be foretold. God responds anew to each new person and each new age of the church, not with novel revelations, but with new inspiration. It simply must be so, if there is any relationship at all between a living church and a living God. The spirit breathes anew in every age, choosing what messenger she will, to challenge the age, to demonstrate in quite

unexpected ways the relevance of the old gospel to new circumstances, new signs, new social disorders. This inspiriting is not
indeed only related to the specifically prophetic, though it may here
seem most recognizable. There is a universality within and without
the church of the Spirit's action. But within the communal
leadership of the church these three ways need all to be recognized.
The total guidance of God is not to be found in one or the other
alone, but in each even when joined in conflict. Neither one nor
another can be ignored, though on occasion one or another may have
to be defied – but defied still within one single, often agonized but
still abiding communion of the Body of Christ.

A danger in a theology of the prophetic could be to put all one's
eggs in a single basket, to deride the institutional and the rational
while taking one specific and particularly enigmatic form of social
leadership (the charismatic) at its own self-evaluation as some sort of
infallible short-cut to the divine. It may then turn out to be no more
than a particularly irrational road back to fundamentalism for those
disillusioned with bureaucracy. Over-confidence in the charismatic
can well be as misplaced and as dangerous as confidence in the
validating role of martyrdom or of a day-to-day infallible papacy.
The attractions of the prophet and the martyr can be particularly
great for Christians because the biblical and Christian tradition has
indeed owed so much of what is best in it to both and must remain
centred in Jesus who was at once prophet and martyr. Yet historic
Catholicism has in fact been singularly anti-prophetic, so a re-
evaluation of prophecy within a Catholic context is less a defence of
the received tradition than a critique drawing upon both biblical
roots and a major dimension of universal social experience to correct
a built-in one-sidedness derived from a dangerous subsuming of the
charismatic into the bureaucratic. Prophetic leadership as a social
phenomenon is no more infallible than any other and can at times be
quite disastrously misguided, especially when either institutionalized within a formal charismatic (or 'divining') role or triumphalized.
A Rasputin or a Khomeini may well exceed in the harm they do
almost any other kind of religious leader.

Prophets would be a very poor substitute for bishops or theologians: a healthy church, as a healthy society, needs the inter-action of
all three while recognizing that the prophetic, to be true to itself, is
the least predictable of them. And they do, of course, overlap. The

authority of an Ambrose, Basil or Augustine was that of a combination of bishop and theologian. Again, if bishops can be either theologians or prophets, so can theologians and scientists be prophets. Perhaps all in all the truest prophet of the modern Catholic Church has been Fr Yves Congar, utterly a theologian and scholar, but something more too: more willing to risk, more courageous, more determined to be heard outside academe, more urgent. In the Middle Ages, the prophet may have been diminished to a clown but of course a good prophet is no fool, he has done his sums, read his books, yet the final form of his public witness, moulded by a sense of personal calling, has somehow digested all that into a less conjectural mode. He is not a populist, indeed his immediate role is likely to be anti-populist, but he has to speak and act from the margin with something of the populist's certainty.

In conclusion, let us think again of the relationship of prophecy to the 'sacred' and the 'religious'. The Christian is faced with two temptations – one is to be sacralized, the other to be secularized. If one's heart, one's concerns, one's understanding of religion become preoccupied with religious things – ceremonies and church buildings and doctrinal orthodoxies and religious orders and papal visits then one has succumbed to the first temptation. If one's heart and one's concerns become preoccupied with the problems of the contemporary world in such a way that one is simply seeing and judging according to some ideology of the contemporary world – capitalism, liberalism, hedonism, Marxism or what you will – then one has succumbed to the second temptation. The power of true prophecy, which is here at the very eye of Christian living, is to be concerned above all with the things of this world, in a fiercely 'unworldly' way. To manage this, we do indeed require the 'sacred': scripture, eucharist, prayer. Here is a fount of vision. Celebrating the 'memorial' of the man who freely chose to die and is forever alive, finding the very heart of meaning in something so seemingly absurd to the modern world as a ritual meal, repeating week after week, 'This is the cup of my blood shed for you and for all', and finding it not a bore but unbelievably pregnant in power, we can be immersed in the secular without being secularized. The eucharist is not dissipated by such a context; it transforms it. And it makes its participants different. It asserts a pattern of meaning throughout the rest of life, a programme of revolutionary priorities for human relations, which sets one both intellectually and socially at odds with the secular continuum. To belong and not to belong. To be wholly part of the world and yet to be intensely, painfully marginal, because the faith within one refuses to acquiesce in the rightness of standards of collective and individual selfishness, class war, tribalism, nationalism, racialism, or just a bored satisfaction with affluence.

The value of the 'religious life' in the old-fashioned sense (the life vows of chastity, poverty and obedience, or some equivalent) may find its principal Christian justification in freeing people for prophecy. The vows make them into marginalized people, delivered from many of the ordinary day-to-day obligations of life, and so able to throw themselves, as Christ – that most marginal of celibates – threw himself, into the challenging of the world for the sake of truth, justice and mercy. Alas, time and again, 'religious life' has not freed people at all, but delivered them mind and body through a grievously over-institutionalized concept of religious obedience into the legalistic bonds of sacralized existence. Without deep piety – a sense of God and the need for grace and prayer – we cannot be prophets. Yet deep piety, Catholic or Protestant or Orthodox, is better than any other trap for removing us from the task of prophecy into the pseudo-religious world of a detached sacrality: a world all the worse for the ease with which it enters into alliance uncritically with the most reactionary *status quo*. Nothing should make someone a better prophet than monastic spirituality; in practice and generally speaking – at least until recently – nothing has removed people more effectively from the role of prophecy than monastic spirituality. Trevor Huddleston, many a Latin American Jesuit, Sisters Maura Clark, Ita Ford and Dorothy Kazel, and indeed lots of other religious in recent years have shown that this is no longer true – that religious life is rediscovering its prophetic justification. Nothing much more important may have happened within the church since the Council.

Paul of Tarsus, Catherine of Siena, Martin Luther, Simone Weil, Barbara Ward, Oscar Romero: whom are we to choose as Christian prophets par excellence? Everyone will make his or her own choice.

There is no defined 'apostolic succession' of prophets. No guarantee that an Elijah will always be followed by an Elisha. And there is no need to agree as to who was, who was not, a true prophet. Jesus Christ was, that is sure. And he suffered for it. His call for disciples is, above all, for men and women to take on the task of prophecy, its fierce intellectual honesty, its bearing of the burdens of the weak, its condition of marginality, its promise of unpopularity, its refusal to take refuge in the temple but its equal refusal to see the world through the spectacles of the world's own justifying ideologies. Such is the call. Who will hear it?

★ 6 ★

Liturgy and Cultural Pluralism

The Second Vatican Council devoted chapter two of the first part of its Constitution of the Church in the Modern World, *Gaudium et Spes*, to 'The Proper Development of Culture'. It may not, all together, have proved a terribly good chapter, but it does perhaps at least deserve the degree of approbation Dr Johnson made of a woman preaching. It is like a dog walking on its hind legs: the wonder is not that it is not done well, but that it is done at all! (31 July 1763). For a General Council to attempt to wrestle with the problems of defining and describing culture was undoubtedly something extra-ordinarily novel: it was indeed one of the most telling expressions of the Council's own culture – an already slightly strange-looking, and not altogether convincing, mix of sixties optimism and social inclusiveness upon the one hand, an underlying if relatively softly edged Roman traditionalism upon the other. But in this chapter – as in most of *Gaudium et Spes* – it is the former mood that dominates. The Council is wrestling with the relationship of unity to diversity. It speaks of a 'plurality of cultures' and stresses that each human community has 'its proper patrimony', 'a specific historical environ-ment' (53). Nevertheless, 'a more universal form of human culture is developing' (54), something which may, in the singular, be termed 'the culture of today' (57) but which may well, the Council fears, 'jeopardize the uniqueness of each people' (56) and threaten the preservation of 'the particular features of the different cultures' (54).

The Council sees all this as a modern problem. Nowhere does it confess that the church itself has, in the ecclesiological or liturgical realm, systematically jeopardized the preservation of particularities. Yet it does recognize that cultural diversity should be embodied in liturgical as in catechetical and theological diversity. The church, it claims, 'can enter into communion with various cultural modes'. 'The discourse of different cultures' can be used to give the message of Christ 'better expression in liturgical celebrations and in the life of the diversified community of the faithful' (58). The church, through the fulfilment of her mission, 'stimulates and advances' human culture and even her liturgy may thus 'lead men toward interior liberty' (58). These are large claims when judged historically against centuries of liturgical centralization, Romanization and Westernization – a process imposed not only upon the churches of Western Europe and all newly evangelized peoples whether in Asia, the Americas, the Pacific, or Africa but also upon the existing rites around the eastern Mediterranean and South India. The history of Roman Catholic liturgy in the post-Tridentine period is anything but characterized by the pursuit of liberty and cultural pluralism.

But the mood of the Council was clearly different, if rather uncritically different. It neither adverted to the vast gap between its bland aspirations and the past and present historical reality it represented, nor did it spell out the future implications of these somewhat cryptic sentences of *Gaudium et Spes*. They were, however, more or less repeated in various other places. The Decree on Eastern Catholic Churches did, of course, confirm that all Eastern rite members should be convinced that 'they can and should always preserve their lawful liturgical rites' (6): differing liturgies do not harm the unity of the church but rather make it more manifest (2). The Decree on Missionary Activity declared that 'from the very start' a new Christian congregation will be 'endowed with the riches of its own nation's culture' (15). Students for the priesthood should be 'versed in the culture of their people', while the laity must express their church life 'in the social and cultural framework of their homeland . . . acquainted with its culture' (21) so that 'Christian life can be accommodated to the genius and the dispositions of each culture' (22).

It was only – and naturally enough – in the Constitution on the Liturgy (articles 37–40) that a few brief norms were actually spelt out 'for adapting the liturgy to the genius and traditions of peoples'. These norms are somewhat revealing for the establishment of the mind of the Council in this matter – positive enough towards some diminution of uniformity, but extremely limited in any acceptance of the implications of such a diminution. It declares, first of all, that 'the Church has no wish to impose a rigid uniformity'. On the contrary, she 'respects and fosters the spiritual adornments and gifts of the various races and peoples . . . sometimes in fact she admits such things into the liturgy itself' (37). The very next clause, however, insists that 'legitimate variations and adaptations to different groups, regions and peoples' should only be allowed 'provided the substantial unity of the Roman rite is maintained' (38). In the final article 40, nevertheless, it is declared excitingly but dangerously vaguely that 'in some places and circumstances, however, an even more radical adaptation of the liturgy is needed' and goes on to speak of 'elements from the traditions and genius of individual peoples' which 'might appropriately be admitted into divine worship'. It has never been explained, then or since, where those 'some places' might be. Such things should be prudently considered by the local ecclesiastical authority and then submitted to Rome.

The Vatican Council almost entirely lacked experts and any strong consistent pressure group among the bishops representing a genuinely non-Western European viewpoint. Perhaps among major conciliar voices only the Patriarch Maximos really spoke for the rest of the world. It was not enough. There was, in consequence, absolutely no attempt to spell out the implications for the liturgy of the non-Western world, missionized very much *modo Latino* in the post-Tridentine period, of article 40 of *Sacrosanctum Concilium* or article 58 of *Gaudium et Spes*. There is, above all, no hint of the sheer pointlessness in southern hemisphere terms of insisting upon the near universal maintenance of 'the substantial unity of the Roman rite'. No more widely applicable lesson is garnered from the oriental experience. In consequence the maintenance of the rites of the oriental churches is portrayed in a rather backward-looking way with an insistence upon 'return to their ancestral ways' rather than as a forward-looking model for the universal church as a whole. There is a note here more of the preservation of a historic house or a nature reserve than of a genuine Catholic and Roman discovery of a model of ecumenicity in which unity no longer requires uniformity. While the cultural pluralism of the world was hailed by *Gaudium et Spes* as integral to the human experience together with the intrinsic bond between culture and liturgy, the Council baulked at the obvious conclusion that the imposition upon other cultures of the Roman rite was a denial of that bond and a piece of sub-catholicism.

The problem with all this is that it not only gave rise within the liturgical field to two quite differing models for the development of worship in the major churches of the third world, but it also provided almost no serious guidance to help with the immense difficulties involved in attempting a more radical inculturation of the sort which the Council did appear, at least in article 40, to be calling for. Yet in fact a programme of inculturation in depth centred upon the liturgy has been at least as central to the churches of the southern hemisphere in the post-conciliar period as has been a theology of liberation. If the latter may well appear the most characteristic expression of the renewal of Latin American Catholicism in this period, inculturation has been equally central to Catholic renewal in Asia and Africa. Yet, in so far as they have attempted to move beyond the modification of quite minor details and the importation into the liturgy of rather fringe motifs drawn from local culture, in so far then as they have attempted to move effectively beyond the horizon of article 38 of the Liturgy Constitution with its insistence upon the maintenance of 'the substantial unity of the Roman rite' to that of article 40 proposing 'an even more radical adaptation of the liturgy', they have in practice found themselves decisively blocked by Roman authority.

It is not my task here to discuss this situation in ecclesiological terms. Nor have I to examine the liturgies proposed, such as the Indian anaphora composed by the staff and students in the theological faculty in Jurseong or the Filipino Misa ng Bayan in Tagalog and English. What does seem clear is that there is absolutely no possibility of responding to the Council's principled commitment to the need and catholic authenticity of a liturgical pluralism corresponding to the world's contemporary cultural pluralism, and somehow comparable to the liturgical diversity which developed in the church of the first centuries, if a judgment upon the acceptability of every rite has to be made, and instantly made, not by people within the culture concerned but by a central authority whose officials are both entirely foreign to that culture and permeated by the ecclesiastical culture of Rome itself.

The basic model for cultural diversification of the liturgy should remain the way worship actually did develop in the early church. The Council's very insistence upon the protection of the Eastern rites must necessarily validate the early pluralist development of the liturgy out of which both those rites and the Roman rite emerged. Every rite, including the Roman, is the fruit of a specific historical inculturation. Each has its own culture or, rather, bears the marks of successive inter-related cultures. And this is true of all major manifestations of group or popular culture. It is not the creation of a single moment or mind. Rome had not the same culture in the sixteenth century as in the seventh or the fourth. A workable liturgy needs emphatically to be participatable now, it requires then a living relationship with contemporary culture and consciousness, but its relationship to the culture of the present is rather a different one – or should be – from, say, a pop song: its function as a vehicle of meaning, a *memoriale* of all that mattered most in the past, and a gateway to the transcendent, really requires that its relationship to contemporary culture be not too close a fit. It has not only to engage but also to bond together in communion – across both time and space. As the central ecclesial bearer of 'tradition', it needs to incorporate within it something of the Christian culture of past times. It has also, most certainly, to remain master of every new culture it engages with in that it has a meaning to pass on far more significant than the meanings it receives. In the south, as in the north, in the east as in the west, in the present as in the past, there can be an inculturation, a symbiosis, a transformation by the values of the receiving culture which is in fact destructive of the fullness and uniqueness of Christian meaning. All this means that good liturgy, while not ceasing to be particularist in a cultural way, must not be so narrowly. There is, appropriately, a living family relationship between all liturgies, a common self-understanding of what it is finally all about, the ability to share in a universal communion of liturgies. Christianity has in fact what one might call a liturgical culture, which is not or should not be a separate and total culture, but, while being inter-culturally recognizable, has yet to be integrated within very different cultures – different in space and time, different in both secular and religious terms. Christian liturgy, able to recognize itself as such, should somehow be at home and integrated with each yet not wholly integrated with any. It needs too to retain in each a dimension of strangeness. The challenge of its unique significance can only be warped or dissipated by the total domestication of a too successful inculturation.

Every culture has qualities and limitations which may be more or less recognizable to the sympathetic outsider, but she or he too is never cultureless. The paradox of culture is that we can never be culture-free in any instant of our consciousness or in any dimension of our judgment and yet still do find it possible, and indeed humanly obligatory, to commune in an ultimately universalist way across cultures both timewise and spacewise. Of all cultural artefacts, liturgy should be most open to that communion. But that cannot authentically be so, if we declare our own culture-point, or our own liturgy, to have an absolutist value. And that is emphatically as true of the Roman liturgy as of any other. A long history of successful imperialism, ecclesiastical and liturgical, does not constitute a culture-free vantage point from which particularist cultures can be safely assessed. But that is not easily acceptable to those who still feel themselves heir to the message, 'Tu regere imperio populos, Romane, memento'.

Every branch of European culture has, since at least the early Middle Ages, been impregnated with biblical and Christian meanings – symbols, terminology, a fund of stories, moral and social values and practices. Christianity and Western cultures share so many elements in a common story that it is hard to tell them apart and impossible to disentangle them. It is, of course, the non-personal dimensions of popular culture that are both most pervasive and least open to assessment. Bible and Mass may well be seen as providing the innermost core of the European cultural tradition, as David Jones has, among modern writers, most evocatively affirmed. This remains the case for Europeans who have personally and explicitly rejected Christianity – their cultural atmosphere remains Christian though this is undoubtedly becoming rapidly less true in regard to the contemporary, as distinct from the historical, face of European culture, and for Christians as well as for non-Christians. Yet in the historical too there is infinite variety. To turn, for a moment, to the English classical literary experience: the culture of Milton, Donne, Herbert, and Blake was religious and Christian at its depth in a way that the contemporary culture of Shakespeare, Jonson, Vanbrugh, and Gibbon was not. Nor is the Christian content and impact upon one form of European culture necessarily even compatible with that elsewhere: Scotland and Naples may both have been decisively shaped in their traditional culture by the Christian religion but in profoundly contrasting ways.

The very celebration of Christmas could be central to the one, almost outlawed in the other. In England the Mass was probably most integrated with public culture in the fifteenth century, but the integration was far from being a completely healthy one: on the contrary, the Mass had been so domesticated and malinterpreted within the current preoccupation with death and purgatory to produce a vast multiplication of chantry chapels, 'private masses' repeated by the hundred for the souls of the rich and a quite unbalanced liturgy. Liturgical inculturation is not invariably a gain. Yet Western Christians tended – at least until recently and not only in Rome – to regard their own form of liturgical-cultural mix as being the definitively correct one, while in reality amidst a ceaseless flux no form was definitive and most were deeply flawed.

The range of early liturgies as the range of early theologies derived from the experience of local churches wrestling with the worship of God and the expression of the Christian mysteries within specific cultural and linguistic contexts, while fully conscious of a wider communion of faith which – from the very start – crossed very considerable boundaries, geographical, linguistic, cultural. Such wrestling between pluralism and unity was not a modern discovery, it was a necessary experience of the *Catholica* in every age, in so far as it was true to itself. The increasing dominance of a single liturgical form was simply the expression in the West of an over-ecclesiasticization of the Roman imperial heritage which turned in mediaeval times into a centralizing monarchy unable to bear the true strains of catholicism. Ecclesiastical and liturgical pluralism are required precisely because of the world's inherent cultural pluralism. In this, in essence, Catholic Christianity is quite unlike Islam. It has no primary culture or language. The trouble is that, faced with the long battle with Islam, Roman Christianity in fact adopted an almost Islamic approach to world ascendancy, a Christian culture self-judged in principle monolithic came to be identified with the culture of Western Europe. Nineteenth-century Western secular imperialism came later to overlay the earlier Roman ecclesiastical imperialism to create the situation with which we have to cope in this under-end of the twentieth century. While in article 40, the Council for an instant appeared to grasp the nature of this predicament, in article 38 it quite failed to do so. In the last twenty-five years, third world liturgists have increasingly sought the liberation of article 40, Rome has increasingly fallen back upon article 38.

It is a sterile confrontation. While it cannot be resolved by any process of centralized liturgical supervision, it will not be well resolved either by a simplistic abandonment of existing liturgy. Good liturgy is not created at a stroke. Liturgies have in the past grown organically out of one another, and it is this that they should be allowed to do now.

Christianity remains in point of fact the most historically changeable of religions, able again and again to adapt itself to new races, cultures, languages and philosophies, to drop large parts of its apparently traditional baggage and absorb seemingly discordant novelty. But in absorbing it must necessarily transform or endeavour to transform so that new and old may function in some sort of organic harmony and eventual fusion. It is really not conceivable, nor appropriate, to drop all post-biblical luggage at any given point of time: 'Tradition' always retains rights and the formation in new circumstances of any new Christian-related culture will, like the formation of new theology and new liturgy, draw on all sorts of post-biblical Christian elements from Augustine to Bonhoeffer. Yet Augustine, for instance, so central to past Western Christian culture, is surely becoming a great deal more marginal even to it. If within the West we have never needed to sit so loosely to our cultural Christian luggage as now, how much more so Christians elsewhere.

There is nothing of beauty and the pursuit of meaning and truth in any human culture, however historically remote from Christianity, which cannot in principle somehow be drawn into one or another living Christian synthesis. But this should not principally be seen as the detaching of some single cultural element or symbolic form, judged suitable, and its isolated 'baptism' into a pre-existing Christian ritual or context (though, of course, a musical instrument is more easily 'baptized' than a christological myth or even a different pattern of colour symbolism). Symbols, myths, forms of expression and life of every kind make and retain their sense only within larger systems of meaning. It is with the latter that one has mostly to wrestle. It needs to be as parts of a living network of cultural, ecological, and economic meaning that individual elements enter into a Christian and liturgical context. When that former network is too tight a one, powerfully controlled by a world of meaning and institutional structures still vigorously alive, it may well be genuinely almost impossible to transplant major elements of it into a Christian context: the strains of seeming contrary references may be far too great for those involved. But if a network is more open-ended, if it can be seen as in itself correlative rather than contrary, precursor rather than alternative, or if perhaps it is in fact waning as a viable world of meaning in its own right, then a massive relocation of symbol may well be possible and in a way which means synthesis rather than syncretism. Only people to whom both networks somehow belong and for whom both have some real meaning can conceivably carry out such work, perilous as it still must be: the integration of two open-ended religious and cultural traditions within a new unity, a unity in which the primatial Christian vision and sense of human destiny takes a new historical and particularized shape through a culture which has itself been hitherto more than a culture, so that the new culture and its new inculturated worship is genuinely and recognizably in continuity with both a hitherto non-Christian religious culture and the central historical thrust of the Christian (and even largely Western) 'tradition'.

The eclectic adoption of motifs from other religions carried out hurriedly and over-optimistically in the early post-conciliar era may not have been a liturgically healthy way forward. Culture is a coherent whole. It cannot be religion-free, unless it be religion-less. The culture of a Christian community in a Hindu society should certainly include much in common with that of its Hindu neighbours and yet the culture of the two cannot be the same. A hurried adoption by intellectuals of symbolic forms deeply meaningful to other religions may well produce not a significant new liturgical synthesis but a jumble of deeply jarring rites, baffling to the unlearned worshipper. Or so it may at first seem, yet the power of absorption by living worship of new forms is very great and what seems discordant at first may be the breath of life later on. Third world Christians, for generations disciplined to worship according to rubrics laid down in the West, may not immediately recognize freedom when offered it: the freedom to be more themselves. While it is almost impossible to imagine an authentic modern Christian liturgy of a sort which does not draw deeply upon the long history of the Christian church and its cultural baggage derived from scripture and tradition, that history must always remain an open one in which the experience of new cultural contexts both reinterprets and adds to what has been handed down. And that history from now on and for quite a long time to come will be predominantly a southern hemisphere one. However shaped, its liturgy will remain both *memoriale* of things past and the sacramentalization of things present in expectation of things to come.

It is impossible to put formal limits to the process of authentic inculturation when taking place in contexts different from those experienced in the past. To take one simple but basic example. In temperate climates the eucharistic elements became fixed as wheat bread and grape wine – at least for the canonists (the practice of mediaeval Europe was a great deal less uniform). The central Western liturgical tradition has never since compromised on these requirements. Yet, outside climates in which wheat and vines naturally grow, it could hardly be God's intention that the eucharist should not be celebrated. The culture of symbol and language lives within a culture of economics, politics, and kinship. Rice and wheat are not quite the same thing culturally any more than materially, and the difference between a society living upon the one and a society living upon the other is not just a matter of menu, but also of subtle approaches to the symbolization of food. Yet in a rice society, while rice may not be culturally identical with wheat in a wheat society, it is far closer to it than is wheat in a rice society. To insist upon a wheaten eucharist in a rice society is a great deformation of the eucharist's essential meaning, while a rice eucharist, which may seem odd to the European onlooker and invalid to the Roman canonist, is in point of fact the true and requisite translation of the old tradition in a culturally new context – as requisite a translation in a climate where wheat does not grow as was that of the words from Aramaic to Greek. The retention of a wheaten eucharist is externally faithful to the tradition, but internally a deformation of meaning. To insist upon the retention of wheat while adopting some slight Hindu-type gesture at the moment of consecration is to follow the spirit of article 38. To move to rice is the implicit agenda of article 40. For the liturgist the medium must not be the message. The message can finally be the same: Jesus Christ, yesterday, today, for ever. But that message can never be mediumless and the medium is the appropriate context of contemporary culture: yesterday, today, tomorrow, always changing. Believing that Jesus is Adam so that no human culture can finally be alien to him, we must believe that a changing liturgy, shaped and reshaped by a changing human culture, can still affirm and reaffirm, never perfectly yet sufficiently evocatively for the believing participant, a single word and sacrament of life that engaged the apostles and will always engage the community of the church.

★ 7 ★

Where Does the Ecumenical Movement Stand Now?

Fifty years ago, in the summer of 1937, the Ecumenical Movement experienced its most exciting – perhaps its greatest – moment: the decision to establish a World Council of Churches. At that time the movement consisted principally of two separate organizations. One, *Life and Work*, was more practical and socially orientated; the other, *Faith and Order*, was more theological and ecclesiastical. Each was holding its major international conference that year in Britain – *Life and Work* at Oxford in July, *Faith and Order* at Edinburgh in August. The man whose vision was more responsible than any other for a World Council was the layman J. H. Oldham, but the man who steered the decision through, despite a good many misgivings in Edinburgh, was William Temple, then Archbishop of York. It seems very unlikely that that decision would have been taken, hurriedly as it was, had it not been for the international crisis building up in Europe. It was Hitler, we may say, who pushed through the World Council, galvanizing cautious ecclesiastics to uncharacteristic boldness. The famous Pastor Niemöller, who should have been at the Oxford Conference, had been arrested just twelve days before it began, and he would remain in prison and concentration camp for the next eight years. 'The first duty of the church, and its greatest service to the world, is that it be in very deed the church'. Such was the challenging message of the Oxford Conference. For them, then, galvanized by the spirit of Niemöller, that duty entailed establishing the World Council: 'the church', a recognizably single and Christlike fellowship of witness and service, had somehow to be seen again to exist, within and above the multiple separations of history, to respond to the *kairos* of the Hitlerian crisis.

Fifty years ago the Ecumenical Movement represented the cutting edge of an embattled but forward-looking church, more sure of its mission to the world and essential unity than it had been for a long while. Where, in comparison, do we stand today? No great movement can for ever maintain the sense of enthusiastic expectation it may engender in its early triumphs. Inevitably it becomes institutionalized, commonplace, even stale. It has often been said of recent years that the ecumenical movement has run out of steam and we should hardly be surprised if there is some truth in that. If, for William Temple in 1942 it was 'the great new fact of our era', in the opinion of one recent commentator it 'has been the great ecclesiastical failure of our time'.[1] Certainly it has not achieved everything its most committed supporters have hoped for, yet – equally surely – its goals have become uncertain just because so much has been achieved. An attitude of embittered or detached belittlement would be quite inappropriate for a 1990s Christian, but so would any easygoing contentment with the old agenda, an ability to believe that things today are still going bravely forward, that we can leave matters confidently enough in the hands of Geneva and of Rome.

Let us begin by summarizing the achievements. First of all, it engendered ecumenical institutions which have, to a quite considerable extent, enabled Christians, while remaining divided into numerous churches, to act as if they were the One Church in which they all believe. The World Council, the British Council of Churches, Christian Aid – modern Christian life would really be almost unthinkable without such as these. They allow all sorts of good things to be done which, otherwise, would be impossible. They enable stronger churches to help weaker ones, first world churches to co-operate unpatronizingly with third world churches. They make it possible for Christians to face the major secular problems of today to some considerable extent as a united body. Secondly, the Ecumenical Movement has helped bring about full 'organic unity' in a few significant cases between hitherto divided denominations. The most internationally symbolic, battled-over, almost normative model was the CSI, the Church of South India. That was followed by the

---

[1]John Kent, *The Unacceptable Face*, SCM Press 1987, p.203.

Church of North India, the United Church of Zambia, the United Reformed Church in Britain, among others. Significant as these united churches have been both for their members and as realized symbols of what the movement was more or less working towards everywhere, they have nevertheless remained few in comparison with the bilateral and multilateral negotiations embarked upon which have not come to fulfilment. Of such negotiations those between Anglicans and Methodists in this country are, probably, the most memorable. Moreover, it must not be forgotten that the large majority of Christians in South India or Zambia are not members of these united churches. The search for the organic unity of 'all in one place' has been at the very heart of the ecumenical movement and more than anything else it has produced its hardest thinking and most agonized reappraisals. Yet it could be claimed that it is its very failure to establish full outward unity which has, more than any other factor, forced forward our whole understanding of what, in this still penultimate age, 'this generation', we should properly be seeking.

But, thirdly, the ecumenical movement has forged a new collective consciousness which has profoundly altered the way in which almost all of us personally experience what it is to be a Christian. 'Do you still feel yourself to be a Presbyterian?' William Paton was asked towards the end of his life. 'Well, not really', he replied, 'to be quite honest I belong to the World Church'. Paton was a generation ahead of his generation but as the years passed his new sense of belonging was to be shared by more and more Christians who increasingly realized that the names that had been adopted, and rather firmly stuck to, of recent centuries – Presbyterian, Anglican, Methodist, or whatever – while not without a justifiable meaning were, nevertheless, if used as the practically primary and almost exclusive indicator of identity and belonging, gravely misleading. In these fifty years more and more Christians have rediscovered that they actually feel themselves to belong to the 'One Church' in which they affirm belief rather than to some lesser body which they call 'church' but which at the same time has a further adjective identifying it nationally or in terms of some specific 'founder' or theological tradition. For a large part we no longer, as individual Christians, think or act – at least in what matters most – in a predictably denominational way. Even our sharpest divisions – over the interpretation of creed and scriptures, the political implications of discipleship, the ordination of women – are hardly denominational. If we were really to be divided, communionwise, according to our personal responses to the major questions which worry us, we would have to reshuffle our church membership entirely. We have, in fact, spiritually largely outgrown the historic denominations in which we nevertheless, *faute de mieux*, remain. And that can be true of post-Tridentine Roman Catholicism as well.

These three achievements were very considerable. But they were very nearly as complete by 1967 as they were in 1987, except perhaps for one important point: the degree to which ordinary Roman Catholics shared in the sense of a common Christian consciousness. At that point there had, in these twenty years, been a large advance.

The Ecumenical Movement, in truth, was in a quite fundamental way transformed by the election of Pope John in 1958, by his convening of the Second Vatican Council (1962–65) and by consequences of that Council which have affected Christians of other churches almost as much as Roman Catholics themselves. Prior to Pope John many of the movement's leaders had been anxious enough to draw Roman Catholics into their enterprise but it had proved effectively impossible. Rome had consistently refused to co-operate. Half the world's Christians were within her communion, and it was not an illogical position to argue that if at last other Christians – subdivided into so many separated bodies – wanted visible unity, then they should find it by submitting to the 'see of unity' which had argued the case so uncompromisingly for the necessity of visible unity all along. The pioneers of the movement agreed with Rome upon the vast importance of a visible, organic, international unity of Christians, but they could not agree with Rome's conditions. As there seemed not the slightest room for manoeuvre or likelihood of significant alteration in the Roman position, they had been forced to develop a strategy which simply left Rome out (though the increasing participation of the Orthodox prevented it from being – what it might in the movement's early years have looked a little like being – a strategy of Pan-Protestant unity).

Now it had all changed. At the World Council's Third World Assembly, held at New Delhi in 1961, official Roman Catholic observers were present and active. They have been so ever since. The presence, at the Vatican Council itself, of observers from other churches in quite considerable numbers probably did more than anything else to create a decisively new and hopeful atmosphere, even an unrealistic atmosphere. Roman Catholics were now actually being encouraged to pray with their fellow Christians, to share in a common work of Bible translation, to co-operate in all sorts of practical ways – even to share churches and exchange courses of theological education. Pope John may not have been a thorough- going ecumenist in his theology (though he became so in his heart) but men like Cardinal Bea and Mgr Willebrands, whom he put in charge of his newly established *Secretariat for Promoting Christian Unity*, certainly were. No church was more affected by all this than the Church of England, represented throughout the Council by John Moorman, Bishop of Ripon. As soon as the Council was over, the Archbishop of Canterbury visited Pope Paul in Rome and was received as some sort of equal with such solemnity and publicity as no one could conceivably have thought might happen only a few years earlier. An Anglican/Roman Catholic international commission began its meetings soon afterwards, in January 1967. Twenty years later its successor is still meeting.

The effect of all this was to engender an enormous hope, especially among those who had always felt a special sense of affinity with Rome. Progress on this side almost inevitably tended to put the brakes a little upon any other kind of advance which might only too easily be seen (rightly or wrongly) as impeding the delicate but exciting and decisively important business of reunion with Rome. After all, the Council had been extremely careful to avoid doing things which might dig new ditches between Catholics and others. Had not everyone else now a sort of on-going duty to reciprocate? Might not the acceptance by Anglicans of the Methodist ministry, or of women priests, of whatever, create new obstacles to unity just at the moment when something at last might be about to happen? More and more, as the years passed, the new situation became in consequence one as much of new brakes as of new hopes. At the level of ordinary people a sense of ecumenical consciousness went on growing, drawing Catholics and other Christians together more and more, but at the level of ecclesiastical authority it would be hard to point to anything very positive happening within the new frontiers after the start of the 1970s.

The ecumenical movement could now go forward neither with nor without Rome. To distance itself a little from Catholicism in order to recover the freedom to realize its own earlier objectives in a more limited framework would seem a terrible step backwards, a rejection of the new hope of the 1960s, and indeed an almost pointless exercise in a country like Britain, for it would mean seeking a unity which left out many of the most active Christians on the contemporary scene, people who are many of them individually most deeply ecumenical. But to accept Rome as effectively laying down the rules for ecumenical progress must ensure, equally, next to no ecumenical progress at all, except occasionally for a little symbolism, the excitement of the emotion-filled special occasion. The Curia desires no more. This was already true of the latter years of Pope Paul VI. It is still more obviously the case since John Paul II became Pope in 1978. As a result the ecumenical movement has been brought back, face to face, in the post-Vatican II era, with the perennial tragedy of historic Christendom: in its fullness ecumenicity means 'catholicity' – not as a mere idea but as renewal of the always recognizable, historically central tradition of Christianity, a Catholicism which is inconceivable apart from the communion of Rome, the central apostolic see. Yet, in age after age, Catholicity has been deformed by Romanism – over-bearing, legalistic, clericalist, imperialist. Historic Christianity cannot thrive and go forward globally outside the historic Catholic sacramental tradition, and it is a will-o-the-wisp to imagine that that tradition can be reconstituted without the 'great church' centred upon the see of Peter. One cannot have Catholicism without Rome but – given Roman mediaeval and ultramontane imperialism (none of which has been effectively repudiated) – one cannot have it with Rome either.

The sense of lost direction facing the Ecumenical Movement today is, however, not only due to the special quandary produced by the entry into its orbit of post-conciliar Catholicism. There was, anyway, after the broad initial achievements of the first generation which established the World Council and the rather more heady optimisms of the second generation peaking in the early 1960s, a far wider loss of momentum symbolized in this country by the failure of the Anglican-Methodist proposals to go through and, subsequently, the breakdown of the 'Covenanting' initiative, since when almost nothing has happened at a higher level. In the judgment of many a tried ecumenist, the failure of the Covenant symbolized 'the lamentable fading of the ecumenical vision in the minds of English Church people'.[2] Our present impasse, depressing as it may be,

[2]Lesslie Newbigin, *Unfinished Agenda*, SPCK 1985, p.249.

should not nevertheless be seen entirely negatively. It is not merely a matter of frustration that well-constructed plans have failed or that there is a fading of vision, or a loss of clear leadership, or – more serious still – the disappearance of any highly committed task-force, of the sort generated in the old days by the SCM. Beyond all this the plans and presuppositions of the movement require radical reappraisal. The models, even the mottos, of the earlier Ecumenical Movement should be seen as very much too simple when applied realistically within the sheer complexity of the twentieth-century ecclesial scene. Above all, the ideal of the organic unity of 'all in one place', which seemed so natural and proper an application of a New Testament vision of the church may well be judged misleadingly inapplicable to our real predicament: the size of the modern town, the diversity of long-standing ecclesial traditions, the need to retain that diversity, not merely globally but within a single area, the impossibility of retaining much diversity at all adequately with a CSI-type model of 'organic unity'. We stand in need of a far more positive sense of what Christian history in its very divergences has been all about than official ecumenism of this type has seemed to allow us. We tend far too easily to damn it all in terms of sinful divisions for which we (who were not involved in making them anyway) have to be regularly beating our breasts and declaring, dutifully, but not very convincingly, our sincere repentance.

Schism was not just sinful division but was also, again and again, the rough expression of a determination upon both sides to adhere to genuine truths and values of many sorts: to ensure or retain a necessary and enriching diversification of the total tradition in a way that could not apparently be achieved on any single model. I do not believe that the logic of either official Catholic theology or the official Ecumenical Movement has done justice to the requisite diversity of a thousand flowers both achieved and required by the ecclesiastical and theological tradition of twenty centuries. Ecumenical theology should learn from liberation theology: just as reconciliation cannot come before justice, so unity cannot come before both truth and a deep respect for the divergent traditions of truth-seeking, revelation-interpreting, *koinonia*-creating, which are what Christian history at its best are all about. They are not going to disappear. Certainly they ought not to disappear.

Do not forget the warning contained in those moving lines of David Jones, a warning as relevant for the ecclesiastical as for the political and the ecological.

till everything presuming difference
and all the sweet remembered demarcations wither
to the touch of us.

Let us not go down that road. Somehow, within the ecumene, we must discover it to be gain not loss that we retain 'the sweet remembered demarcations'. An 'organic unity' which irons them all out would be the most terrible impoverishment not only historical and cultural, but spiritual and evangelical too. It would be a unity oblivious of two thousand years of incarnation history.

What is required now is, I believe, first a truly theological re-evaluation of the multiplicity of our human traditions and present state, and, secondly, the courage for Christians to recognize the existing unity of the church within the multiplicity and so behave as to demonstrate their mutual recognition. The church upon earth is one, a fellowship whose essential unity certainly does have its visible form. It is a communion in the widest sense but also in the narrowest: the communion of faith and charity and hope lived and expressed in ever so many ways but most precisely and decisively in the sharing of the sacrament of the Lord. Eucharistic communion is less a ritual than the primary evangelical affirmation under the form of our common human culture of eating and drinking that Jesus is central to, and creative of, this community now. He is remembered and the church is made present. The body of Christ makes these believers, and reaffirms them to be, the body of Christ. The act of communion, each in ones own church, in fact establishes intercommunion and the essential sacramental unity of the church whether or not we verbally recognize it. Baptism as ecclesial initiation is precisely entry into the one communion – it gives one the right to receive the sacramental body of Christ, side by side with all other members of the mystical body of Christ, not as a private person but as indeed a living member of an organic body. Intercommunion with ones fellow baptized is the right, almost the social right *par excellence*, of the Christian.

It is, of course, very anomalous to find ourselves united in the church's eucharistic fellowship, while its ministry and organization continue divided and largely unco-operating. But a state of anomaly is no new thing for the church – we have been in it for much of our history, and quite particularly since the division between East and West in the middle ages. If the church exists at all, and if it has existed at all through the endless and frequently appalling vagaries of its history, then it has existed – and even has to exist – in modes very different from that of its ideal nature. In fact the anomaly of an experienced disharmony between eucharist and ministry is less than the situation we have put up with for so long – of disharmony between baptism and eucharist, for they are two far more important sacraments than is that of orders.

In so far as anyone, including the hierarchical authority of any church, endeavours to prevent intercommunion, its instructions should be disregarded, charitably but firmly, as un-Christian, wrong, un-Catholic and *ultra vires*. The only sound reason not to do so is a pastoral, not a theological, one – that we are as yet insufficiently conscious of being one church to be able to share communion with one another charitably and sincerely. To some extent this remains the case today. One must not force ones own conscience nor that of others. One must not offend people by making the sacrament of unity an apparent act of defiance or aggression. For many of us our sense of unity, even if much greater than it used to be, may not be sufficient as yet for eucharistic sharing. The primacy of a subjective conscience must always be respected – and that applies as well to the consciences of bishops. A mistaken conscience can, naturally but unfortunately, be much reinforced by the directives of ecclesiastical authority opposing intercommunion. Such directives should be treated politely but firmly ignored, just as it would have been right a few years ago to disregard other directives forbidding the saying together of the Lord's Prayer.

Where, however, we do not feel that we ourselves are ready to practise intercommunion or, while being ready ourselves, judge that it would be hurtful or discourteous to others and a source of bitterness rather than of unity and peace, then clearly we cannot practise it. In such circumstances, which remain common enough, we need to find other, less formally sacramental, ways of living already in principle as the one church which in faith we know ourselves to be. That is the basic point – to live spiritually as the one church which the Ecumenical Movement has re-revealed to us that we are, while accepting that we remain at the same time within a Babylonian captivity, institutional and historical, that in hierarchical terms we cannot throw off in the forseeable future. In so far as the various claims behind the institutional divisions are treated with the seriousness they ask for, they can only be destructive of the church. In so far as we are willing to see beyond them, yet not unaffectionately, we may survive.

To live spiritually as one church should not be to wish to break down all the lines of demarcation. Naturally some will fade; new ones will arise. The liturgical, theological, ministerial, structural shaping and re-shaping of the *Una Catholica* is, and always has been, a continuous movement at the level of the ecclesial superstructure. It will go on happening, formally and informally, as part of the unending business of *Ecclesia semper reformanda*. In principle the major traditions will increasingly be recognized as alternatives within the church, just as in earlier times the Western and Eastern traditions were recognized as co-existing; or, more recently, within the Roman Catholic Church, Benedictine, Dominican and Jesuit have co-existed. In the end, Methodism will be best seen as a 'society' like the Jesuits, Anglicanism as a regional tradition, Evangelicalism as a spiritual school – but all inside *Ecclesia Catholica*. This is not to say that all are equally good in every way, or that some may not be, all in all, better than others. We must share and learn and argue, adopt from each other, as we feel called to do – but not as a heavy single negotiation for organic unity, not as a precondition for church recognition and eucharistic communion, nor as part of a model whereby we will in due course necessarily eliminate all significant diversity within a single town or village.

This way forward may seem a rather anarchic and disorderly one, and it will be particularly hard for Roman Catholics with their strong inculcation in the virtue of a central system and ecclesiastical obedience. Certainly, the anarchic is not the way of ARCIC. But I do not see the slightest intention on the part of authority, Roman Catholic authority anyway, to use ARCIC as more than a talking shop through which to damp down the fires of ecumenical activism. If it is ever more than that, it will be because the respective communities have moved so far into unity that the hierarchies will then decide to lead them from behind by a belated act of authorization. In present circumstances, and the imperatives of long separated institutional history far more than those of personality ensure that they will not easily change, there is no alternative to the anarchic one other than to declare the ecumenical task to be in truth impossible and, in consequence, to abandon all that it has stood for in terms of Christianity's continued relevance to the world as a whole. If that goes, what would remain of a coherent gospel? We would be effectively abandoning the field to *Opus Dei* and the narrowest of biblical fundamentalists. It is a way faithful to the riches of history but also to both Catholic theology and the legacy of the Reformation. Little children, do not be afraid. We are free now, with the freedom of the children of God, to recognize that one church does exist, that Kenneth Slack and Donald Soper and Robert Runcie and Basil Hume are all members of it, and that we have an urgent and personal duty to act accordingly, misled no more by any mistaken theology or too restrictive tradition. Let us hearken to the words of our fathers at the Oxford Conference of fifty years ago: 'The first duty of the church, and its greatest service to the world, is that it be in very deed the church.'

★ 8 ★

Should Women Be Ordained?

Let a woman learn in silence with all submissiveness. I permit no woman to teach or to have authority over men; she is to keep silent. For Adam was formed first, then Eve; and Adam was not deceived, but the woman was deceived and became a transgressor. Yet woman will be saved through bearing children, if she continues in faith and love and holiness, with modesty.

The saying is sure; If any one aspires to the office of bishop, he desires a noble task. Now a bishop must be above reproach, the husband of one wife, temperate, sensible, dignified, hospitable, an apt teacher, no drunkard, not violent but gentle, not quarrelsome, and no lover of money. He must manage his own household well, keeping his children submissive and respectful in every way; for if a man does not know how to manage his own household, how can he care for God's Church? (I Timothy 2.11–3.5)

It is the nature of tradition to constitute a community, any community, in its specific character – its values, rules, self-understanding. Without a tradition of its own, and without the cherishing of that tradition, no historic community can exist, let alone survive. Its own tradition is what sets it apart from other communities. Human society is immensely enriched by a multitude of cultural particularities – indeed it would be quite intolerable without them. But each is a matter of tradition. Of its nature a tradition's quality is to be traditional – that is to say it is cherished, not just or even chiefly on account of hard logic, but because this is the way things have been done here over generations. That is enough. A tradition is adhered to, relished, trusted in, for its own sake, even in its oddities. That is true in general and it is certainly true for the Christian church as for particular churches. The role of tradition in the life of the church is all the more important for its being, for the most part, rather little adverted to. And while there is one bundle of traditions which indubitably goes with being a Methodist, another with being a Quaker or a Jesuit, there are of course a great many traditions which simply go with being a Christian and which take us back to the very earliest age of the church. Some are adverted to in the New Testament writings; others are not. I am thinking, to give just one instance, of the keeping of Sunday.

However, every living tradition does in fact change. It must change if it and the community it supports are to survive. For everything human changes. As the circumstances of society, culture, human self-understanding change, so must the collective tradition of a specific community. In the case of the Christian church this is most particularly true, and it has certainly been the strength of the church that its tradition has in fact been so flexible. Its tradition is not something placed in a glass case, but something continually alive, something being genuinely passed from one generation to another, one person to another, and affected by the passing, and the circumstances of it, so that many cherished items of tradition seemingly ancient enough are in point of hard history latter-day inventions. If a tradition is to live it cannot be otherwise.

Yet all change is not equally acceptable. Some alterations are better, some worse. Some may, indeed, be intensely damaging, but how are we to judge of this? It would seem to be by the way changes alter or drop marginal elements of a tradition in order to relate its central core of meaning better to a new society. Of course, this presupposes that every element of a tradition is not equally important, that within a tradition there is some sort of hierarchy of meaning. In very unimportant traditions or insignificant societies this may hardly be so, but the more a society and its traditions is genuinely meaningful, the more elements within the tradition will relate more centrally or more marginally to its principle core of meaning. It may, of course, not be possible to rescue the central core by altering peripheral elements. It may be that a given tradition and society at their very core have ceased in altered circumstances to make basic sense. They can, then, only wither away. But in regard to the Christian tradition, believers must surely hold that this is not so, that – while many things may pass with time and the transformation of culture and human self-understanding – yet there is an absolutely central element of meaning that will always remain supremely relevant. It is, however, obvious enough, both theoretically and from a consideration of Christian history, that this does not include everything in the tradition which has mattered, even greatly mattered, for former generations. Indeed the glory of Christian history has been, on a long view, its amazing adaptability, despite the respect for tradition that has marked it from the start.

Change has taken place again and again, even and especially in areas where most Christians were most reluctant to allow change to take place. And it has been able to do this because Christians have also been continually conscious that they did in fact possess a mechanism which could enable them to do so. They collectively possessed the gift of the Holy Spirit who, it was promised, would lead them into things they did not know at the beginning. Things can be decided, vitally important things, and they can be decided in such a way as to allow what was previously not allowed: 'It has seemed good to the Holy Spirit and to us'. Besides the basic mechanism, there are the examples of almost infinitely numerous changes from subsequent history. For instance, the speaking or the silencing of women in church, the marriage or non-marriage of bishops. When I Timothy insisted on the silence of women it was, almost certainly, reversing accepted earlier Christian practice; and it has, of course, been itself reversed by all the main churches. The church – and very particularly the Roman Catholic Church – has, moreover, insisted that, *pace* I Timothy, women may well find salvation precisely through a vocation which excludes the bearing of children. Then, again, take the marriage of bishops. There can be no doubt that I Timothy is here insistent that a bishop should have had a wife and children, yet the church subsequently not only allowed celibate men to be appointed bishops, but actually so far reversed tradition as to insist that only the unmarried could become bishops: foolish as such an insistance surely was.

Not only, then, does tradition alter originally uncertain areas, but even where scriptures might seem to provide a precise norm, this may in fact be reversed. Looked at as a whole, Christian experience demonstrates, not the fixity of precise norms, but an on-going confidence in the Spirit living within the community, which enables new decisions to be taken, new patterns of ministry to be embarked upon. Clearly these new patterns, these changes, are found opportune on account of new social and human circumstances, new exigencies of culture. Paradoxically, the high degree of culture-boundedness characteristic of the early church becomes the best guarantee of the church's subsequent freedom and even obligation to respond to alterations of culture. Nevertheless, acceptable changes within the tradition, while they must respond to culture, cannot – if they are to be good changes – be simply dictated by culture. Indeed if they are merely culture-controlled, they are fairly sure to be bad changes, if significant at all. The guarantee of their appropriateness must be that they express organically the central core of the tradition within an altered cultural context. The heart of the meaning within the tradition remains, the periphery changes because the old periphery would be a disservice in new circumstances to that heart.

We are faced today with the question whether a woman can, and should, be ordained a priest, a minister of the eucharist, even a bishop. It is clear that in nineteen centuries of Christian tradition this did not happen. It has still not happened within what are by far the two largest Christian communions, the Roman Catholic and the Orthodox (Greek and Russian). It does then constitute a significant change in the tradition, but is that change to be seen as affecting the core or as affecting the periphery of the tradition? To return to our text from I Timothy, it stresses that some people are to be judged suitable for the role of a bishop and/or presbyter, some are not, and that this suitability is ultimately a pastoral one. It is a matter of choosing appropriate people to 'care for God's church'. Personal desires may be indicators but they are not decisive. What decides is public need not personal vocation. I Timothy offers certain specific indicators – sobriety, gentleness, particular sorts of secular experience. As we have seen, these particular guidelines have in fact long been outdated, but if – behind such immediate and multiple indicators – we look for some basic one to separate appointable from unappointable ministers, we can, I think, say safely enough: the priest can and must represent Christ, and in suitable contemporary form. He represents Christ about as fully and as explicitly as anyone can. He has, after all, to say those most mysterious, most creative, most ecclesially and sacramentally central, words of Christ, and to say them in some way in the first person: 'This is my body', 'This is my blood'. The priest does many other pastoral and pedagogical things which lay people do too, but this at least the priest alone does. And it certainly does involve to an intense degree that representation of Christ here and now which is, of course, in a more diffused way a character of all Christian living. But because of the explicitness of the saying of the words of institution and because the saying of them is done in the very centre of the church, upon the Lord's day, and in the middle of the whole community, you may – if you like – put it this way: the priest is an icon of Christ, his living human symbol.

Here we need to distinguish at once between the Jesus of history and the Christ of faith. No one is going to argue that the priest must represent the Jesus of history in all his necessary particularity. He is certainly not intended to be some sort of one-man Oberammagau. Jesus was a Jew, of the tribe of Judah, he was unmarried, he spoke Aramaic; he had been a carpenter; he was now unemployed; probably he had a beard. Now none of this – important as all such points may be for a true historical representation of Jesus – matters at all for a true ministerial representation of Christ. What then is required for the latter, in order to represent the Word of God, incarnate, redeemer of mankind? God became man, *et homo factus est.* The representative must be what the Word essentially became, he must then be man and man committed to the essential function of God made man, to sharing in the mind and heart of the Saviour in so far as we can at all comprehend that mind and heart. The functionality of Christ was a functionality of salvation, the construction and instruction of a community, saved and to be saved. The representative must share in that community quite evidently. Someone unable to partake of the life of the salvation community could manifestly not represent the saviour to it or within it, but beyond that it is not easy to find the logic in excluding someone fully within the community from the basic capacity to be such a representative.

Only man can be iconic of God made man; only man can be iconic of the saviour of all mankind. But if we said more than this, if we said that the icon must also be a Jew, or unmarried, or poor, or a carpenter, then one is moving disastrously across to the sort of limiting, historic representation we have rejected. Moreover, in limiting those who can represent Christ, one is implicitly limiting his very salvific function and the fullness of participation in the Christ-life of those one has thus marginalized. Christ is man, saving man. No less. Not a Jew, saving Jews. Not a third world freedom fighter saving third world freedom fighters. Jews are not excluded. Freedom fighters are not excluded. But every wall of partition is broken down in the community of the saved in consequence of the very nature of the Saviour – that nature which needs must be represented in the eucharistic minister.

Man. *Homo. Anthropos.* Where does woman come into this? Is womanness alien to the representation of Christ only in the way that Gentileness or marriedness is alien, or instead as being a matter of non-manness? Once we have asked the question in this way, the answer follows obviously enough. A woman is, most certainly, a man and always has been – at least so far as the church is concerned. A woman is '*Homo*'. Greek and Latin have their words for 'male' as distinct from 'female', but *Anthropos* and *Homo* bridge the gender gap. Of course we know that the Word became a male, a *vir* (in Latin), just as the Word became a Jew; but credally it is not significant. What the creed asserts, in defining the incarnation is that the Word became human, *homo*, and the church has always recognized woman as *homo*. 'Remember man that thou art dust and unto dust thou shalt return', *Memento, homo.* So, century after century, the priest declared as he placed the ashes upon the foreheads of the faithful each Ash Wednesday, the foreheads of women no less than the foreheads of men. A male is not that much more of a *Homo* than a female and of necessity, therefore, the humanity taken by the Word at the incarnation is woman's humanity exactly as much as it is man's.

The poverty of some modern European languages (including English and Italian) which lack words to distinguish *homo* from *vir* has greatly added to the contemporary confusion. The word 'man' has an inherent ambiguity which '*Homo*' entirely lacks. Incidentally, if we were all Bantu, instead of being modern Western Europeans, we would not fall victim to this particular theologico-linguistic man-trap. Just as Bantu languages do not impute sexuality to the uncreated Word, as we do with 'Son', for all speak of the Word as '*Mwana*' (child), which is used for girls as much as for boys, so they do not impute any sort of sexuality to what the *Mwana wa Mungu* became, *Muntu*, that wonderful word for a human person, wholly non-sexual. Where in English we speak of 'the Son of God' and declare that 'he' became 'man', with a whole series of words sexually ambiguous or misleading, the Bantu declare their faith far more accurately theologically in terms which wholly avoid at any point the sexual loading.

The interpretation of *Homo* is in truth at the very heart of the meaning of incarnation and redemption, and the issue is whether God in being incarnationally particularized does or does not mysteriously break through the bonds of any and every limitation thus imposed. If the male/female wall of binary division remains operative, any more than the Jew/Gentile wall of binary division, then not all is assumed, not all is redeemed. The particularizations, including the constrictions of a binary model, must be entered into but only so as to be transcended. In regard to the male/female divide this is especially necessary, but also appropriate, in that a central religious symbolic tradition – and the one adopted by the Hebrew scriptures – saw sky as male, earth female. God in heaven was a male figure giving rain and life to mother earth. So God in heaven could in covenant comc to marry humanity on earth, and humanity's selected representative, Israel. Biblical symbolism implies a divine masculinity, a human femininity. In a very real but only symbolic way, in consequence, full incarnation signifies the male becoming female, while if – in docetic form – God only pretended to 'become *homo*' by 'descending from heaven' then the incarnated would remain in reality male only. It would still be a matter of 'he, he, he'. It is clear that, incarnationally, *vis à vis* the underlying biblical mythology of God, a female figure would actually represent 'man' more profoundly than a male. But in fact any such symbolism, if at all pressed or absolutized, becomes divisive and utterly misleading. God is not male nor humanity female. Male and female are subcategories, of finally limited significance, within the human. When God becomes *anthropos* they are wholly transcended and need to be seen to be transcended. The argument that a male is needed to represent the Word made flesh is really just a laughable failure of third class theologians to understand either the classical theology of incarnation and redemption or anthropology, the structures and limitations of religious symbolism and, even, the history of Western linguistics.

Let us return at this point to the nature of a living tradition and the way it should respond when faced with a challenge to what may or may not be a marginal element. Without any doubt, the exclusive maleness of the ministerial priesthood has been an element within that tradition. But how central an element has it been? Again and again, as we have seen, parts of a living tradition need to be jettisoned. The criteria for defending or jettisoning something remains its relationship to the core of the tradition. Does it, in new circumstances, continue challengingly to re-express that core, or does it now rather obscure it? Now what we see happening in the last few years is that, in order to justify the practice of excluding women from the ministerial priesthood in circumstances in which the wider surrounding culture no longer tallies with such an exclusion, it has proved necessary to justify it theologically in a way previously never done and in a way which affects a far more central element in the tradition – the understanding of the incarnation. In the principal Vatican Declaration on the non-ordination of women of October 1976, and in plenty of Anglican arguments too, the central argument has been put forward that as God became *vir*, therefore Christ can only be represented by a *vir*: 'We can never ignore that Christ is a man.' Consequently, 'in actions in which Christ himself is represented . . . his role must be taken by a man'. Such a shift in both language and meaning at the very heart of christology is not only profoundly untraditional, it is also destructive of the central thread connecting incarnation and redemption: the unity of significant nature between saviour and saved, the breaking down by Christ of every middle wall of partition. It makes part of Christ's significant human nature something not shared by all the redeemed. To do this is disruptive of the central principle of soteriological christology. To assert that the significant humanity of Christ for the purpose of representation necessarily includes maleness logically makes maleness also a necessary characteristic of the body of Christ, the community of the redeemable and the redeemed. The defenders of the periphery have thus been led to undermine the core.

Inability to accept a change within the order of ministerial structure, an essentially marginal part of tradition, thus not only demonstrates a failure to understand the way any living tradition, but pre-eminently the Christian tradition, functions. I say 'pre-eminently the Christian tradition' because here above all we have a community conscious from the beginning that it did not get the whole truth at the start, that the Holy Spirit is precisely there (not only in the first century but also in the twentieth) to lead it to make new decisions which are genuinely new but also reveal themselves as strangely faithful to what was there from the start. But such an inability also provides the absolutely decisive reason for not only allowing but requiring change, the reason that the refusal to change is now being justified in terms which are both disastrously untraditional and totally destructive of the innermost core of the whole tradition: the understanding of God made man. A clinging to the periphery is undermining the core. The central understanding of incarnation and redemption no less, is being destroyed by the opponents, both in Rome and in England, of the ordination of women.

A tradition, to live, like everything else, must also in part die. No true traditionalist will cling to everything traditional. Despite the formal instructions of the letter to Timothy, let women speak in church, let even the unmarried be made bishops but, above all else, let Christ be *Muntu* and let every *muntu*, male or female, be seen as potentially an icon of Christ. Amen.

9

Kairos: South African Theology Today

Political theology is committed reflection upon the social and political life of humanity in the light of belief in God and all that we believe has been shown to us of God and the mind of God. Just as personal theology must make use of all we can know, experientially and scientifically, of the nature, psychology and moral existence of the individual (Thomas Aquinas, for instance, takes that absolutely for granted in the development of the *Summa Theologiae*), so must political theology make use of all we can know, experientially and scientifically, of the nature, sociological laws and moral existence of society. Revelation reflects upon nature – things as they are, knowable in ever greater complexity – it in no way substitutes for such knowledge; and immediately theology fails to grapple with the current state of consciousness of that complexity, it ceases to be good theology. Theological advance necessarily presupposes both popular consciousness and the existence of related 'ancillary' sciences. Basically political theology is not something new. Yet in so far as political and social science is a relatively new growth within human culture, so is an extended political theology too something relatively new. A few generations ago a good theologian might have little or nothing to say about politics and seem little the worse for that; while the lack did in fact unbalance the rest, it was to some extent excusable in terms of the under-development of secular political science. But today we are both more conscious of those areas and have much better tools with which to interpret them, and a theology which now shies away from the task is simply very poor theology. The same thing is now beginning to be true of ecology.

Theology remains a committed wrestling from a position of faith with the world around us and its divine meaning. Christian theology centres that faith upon the person of Christ, illuminating its reflection through the long and complex paradigm of biblical history. Certainly theology is unable to draw its understanding either scientifically or experimentally simply from contemporary reality, interpreted however sophisticatedly with the tools of social science, or however participatorily with the experience of a costly involvement. But it cannot draw its understanding apart from either of these. It is the interaction of faith, experience and science, and that alone, which produces theology and only if there is plenty of experience and plenty of science as well as plenty of faith will it be very good theology.

It is of the nature of the political to be continually changeable and it needs to be of the nature of political theology to be – not a new dimension of idealized, essentialist, ahistorical and uncontextualized moral theology – but a wrestling within the historical here and now of politics by the faithful disciple committed to the service of a God of love, mercy, compassion, justice, truth and beauty, so mysterious and bewildering that he can be believed in despite the perennial misery of human foolishness, cruelty and underneath it all sheer lack of sense of direction, and can be so in the mind of the Christian because the surest sign of his love and presence has not been power, success, victory in war or revolution, but the symbolic form of an instrument of execution and oppression. A Christian theology of politics dare approach the task only with such equipment, equipment that can pass the philosophical challenge of the denial of God grounded upon the existence of such a mass of evil as we perceive around us, and the historical challenge that the institutional church and its leaders have times past number shared in the oppressing of the poor and taught authoritatively the most morally repugnant of doctrines. But in necessarily repudiating large chunks of past Christian history and traditional teaching, political theology has to avoid leaping into the arms of yet another one-sided *theoria* or *praxis*, for that would be to do just one time the more what the Christian tradition has done too often in the past. Contemporaneity is well aware of the faults of our fathers but only too blind to its own temptations. The details would be different but the underlying betrayal – likely to be only too evident to a generation soon to come – depressingly the same.

In approaching a political theology for South Africa when one is not a South African, one has evidently first to ask: what am I doing here at all? If theology must come out of experience, don't I lack the one essential ingredient in the whole business? Yet, extra cautious as one must be, there really is no alternative. In reality the South African experience is not, and cannot be, that of a self-contained society. All significant human experience challenges all other significant human experience. The rest of us are involved in South Africa, as members of political groups who have contributed to make South Africa what it is, as human beings challenged in our own racial consciousness and attitudes by so strident an example of racialist theory and practice; and we are involved because South Africans of every hue and viewpoint do in fact appeal to the rest of us to be involved in one way or another – by investing or by not investing, by sharing sport or by not sharing sport, by entering or refusing to enter into shared academic enterprise. It is today really not possible not to be seriously involved, and overt non-involvement is as morally significant as overt involvement. But we cannot be morally involved without being intellectually involved and – in so far as we are theologians – without being theologically involved; without, then, endeavouring to construct for ourselves a political theology relevant to South Africa. It is not possible, and would not be responsible or helpful, simply to take over the political theology of South Africans. And which South Africans should we then borrow from? No. In dialogue with those far more totally involved than we can be, yet independently too, we have to shape as British Christians our political theology of South Africa, contextualized both by as sensitive an awareness as we can manage of South Africa as it truly is, and by the inescapable existential fact that we are somewhere else – not subject to the truncheons of the South African police, not restricted by South African censorship laws, moderately uncomfortable and disturbed within our own moderately racialist and very unequal society, but – despite or even because of these impediments – able also just conceivably to contribute some wider gleam of wisdom discernible on account of that very degree of remoteness and drawing on whatever additional insights may be available to the sympathetic but partially non-participant observer.

It is fair to say that for me this is very much not a new position to be in. Most of my adult life I have, *vis à vis* South Africa, been a semi-participant, the person on the touch line who has occasionally run a little desperately on to the field trying to get a point across to one of the players or even to kick the ball, but has then quickly enough retreated, recognizing that the part he has properly to play is within a larger international and ecclesial game, of which the South African is an absolutely crucial part, yet still only a part. The point is that there is more than one game, but if one is really inside any one of many, many, inter-locked games, then one is not just an observer of all the others but has also – as long as one is moderately circumspect in exercising it – a catholic *droit de cité* in them all.

Anyway my first little book on the subject, *White Domination or Racial Peace*, was published by Michael Scott's *Africa Bureau* in 1954 (two years before *Naught for your Comfort!*). I suppose there are not many people involved in the struggle today in or out of South Africa who can claim a thirty-five year record of published commitment! It was followed in 1961 by my first visit to South Africa – from Uganda. I remember arriving in Pretoria and walking the very next day in the suburb of Waterkloof, where I was staying, and being both startled and amused to see before me a vast poster with the words written upon it 'Fools' Paradise': the advertisement for a local theatrical, it seemed to be rather more than symbolic, at least a sort of collective Freudian slip. In the mid 60s I wrote my 'Theology of Race'.[1] It was followed in 1970 by 'The Moral Choice of Violent Revolution'. By then I had been again to the Republic (this time from Zambia) at the request of *Pax Romana* to take part in the annual general meeting of the UCM (University Christian Movement), held, in semi-secret, in some tents on the coast at Stanger. 'The Moral Choice', with its conclusion that the decision of Christians in southern Africa to join the armed struggle 'must be recognized as coming within the mainstream of authentic Christian response to abominable tyranny', appeared in *Mission and Ministry* which was being sold openly in South African church bookshops during my third and final visit to the Republic to lecture at the Theological Winter School in 1971 (it was on sale too at Dar es Salaam airport – doubtless because of the photograph of Julius Nyerere the publisher had placed on its cover!). Someone remarked that they had lost confidence in BOSS for admitting me to the country (and my book for sale)! I have not been

[1]*Race – A Christian Symposium*, ed. Clifford Hill and David Matthews, 1968, pp. 135–50. A small part of my chapter was recently reprinted in Robin Gill's anthology *A Textbook of Christian Ethics*, T. & T. Clark 1985, pp. 526–31.

allowed in again. In 1973 came the long campaign over the massacre of Wiriyamu and Portuguese atrocities in Mozambique more generally, followed by the publication of *Wiriyamu* in 1974, together with my first Cambridge Ramsden sermon 'Called to Liberate: mission and South Africa'[2] and the CIIR booklet *Southern Africa and the Christian Conscience* in 1975. Five years later Andrew Prior invited me to be the one non-South African contributor to his symposium *Catholics in Apartheid Society* (Capetown, 1982) which produced my essay 'Why the Church in South Africa Matters'.[3]

I say all this because it may help to locate my own 'contextualization'. I too have a history in this regard and my own practical theology of it has developed just as my own mind has changed in other ways too and the situation I have continually tried to relate to has changed as well. *White Domination* was written in the age of Malan and Strydom, *The Theology of Race* in that of Verwoerd, 'The Moral Choice' in the reign of Vorster, and 'Why the Church in South Africa Matters' in that of Botha. Today, as Botha has given way to de Klerk, I find myself moving on from judging things quite as I did in the time of Verwoerd or Vorster. It is not that it was wrong then, but something other may be more appropriate now. I believe with the writers of *Kairos* that the moment of liberation really is at hand, and that political theology of South Africa if it is to be truly creative, prophetic and useful, may need to reconsider many things and to be immensely much more supple than was appropriate in the years of unswerving repression. Moreover, a prophetic theology needs to speak directly to the church as much as to the world (though it will, of course, speak to the church about the world and about how to be truly a church in the world) but it has then to speak to the church as it is today and the church in the age of Desmond Tutu (while doubtless not a fully reformed church) really is rather different from the church in the age of Geoffrey Clayton.

Political theology is not concerned with essences, with 'apartheid' or 'racism' or 'oppression' as abstractions, so much as with creative moral guidance to a historical community in a given situation. That is what the 1985 Kairos Document is all about: a response to a moment of truth, a reading of 'the signs of the times' for *now*. With manifest

[2]Adrian Hastings, *The Faces of God*, Chapman 1975, ch. 10.
[3]Reprinted in *African Catholicism*, SCM Press and Trinity Press International 1989, ch. 11.

power, conviction and clarity of analysis its writers challenged the churches to see both the situation of South Africa and the point of the gospel in a less fuzzily mellow light than they had, mostly, been accustomed to. The critique of 'church theology' was sharp, came close to the bone, but was also, in its analysis, a shade too simplistic. There was, one thinks, rather more of 'prophetic theology' of the sort Kairos sought already present in some of the church theology of its predecessors such as the 'Message to South Africa'. What was wholly new in Kairos was not just the note of deliberate confrontation, the refusal to sweeten the message at any point, the sharp clarity of a militant bugle call, but the nature and authority of the statement itself. It was not sent out by the formal leaders of the churches but just by 152 committed Christians, black and white, women and men, lay and clerical, professors and sisters, Dutch Reformed and Roman Catholic, Lutheran, Methodist, Anglican. It was indeed, as almost all other ecclesiastical statements have not been, a message of the church in its realized catholicity. The power of Kairos lay as much in this ecumenicity and the commitment of its signatories as in the verbal message it gave. It called for a changed church but it already represented a church that had changed. Beyers Naudé had been a marginal outcast for twenty years, but now the outcast was central to a new consensus able to speak not only to the church but for the church. The rest of the world has rightly responded to it with such great attention for the good reason that it is in consequence, possibly more than any other church document of the 1980s anywhere in the world, deeply authoritative because genuinely consensual and derived from a consensus attained through suffering and faith at a time of unusual crisis. It is not a theological set-piece put together in the comfortable quiet of some high-class conference centre in Windsor or Venice. It is done in the heat of the struggle, hammered out by people many of whom had been in prison or banned, whose very names are a roll-call of honour: Mkhatshwa, Chikane, Naudé . . .

Yet simply to laud and repeat Kairos would, for a concerned theologian elsewhere hardly be helpful to the cause or appropriate as a response from one theologian to others. Accepting its qualities of power and authoritativeness and, indeed, precisely because of those qualities, it would seem to be the only possible honourable role for the outsider to retain his independence and endeavour to see dimensions of a complex whole possibly undervalued in a necessarily simple and militant document and – in particular – to press the vision onwards. Prophecy must consider the 'now, now' but it should also be brave and free enough to look further ahead (and further back too), standing away just enough from the immediately necessary task – without denying in any way the rightness of involvement within it – to chance its luck, you might say, by speaking of the future.

The Kairos document lays its finger again and again upon the necessity of sound 'social analysis' and of the weakness of much church theology in this regard. It is undoubtedly true. The question is whether Kairos is not itself too open to judgment on this very count. For instance: 'The conflict is between two irreconcilable *causes*, or *interests*, in which the one is just and the other is unjust . . . This is our situation of civil war or revolution. The one side is committed to maintaining the system at all costs and the other side is committed to changing it at all costs. There are two conflicting projects here and no compromise is possible. Either we have full and equal justice for all or we don't' (4.1). Yes and No. Either we do or we don't. That would seem to be logically the case, but in reality the first comment has to be 'no one ever has', and that alters the matter a lot. There never has been a society, so far as one knows, which could boast 'full and equal justice for all'. And there won't be this side of the kingdom of God. It is one thing to struggle for it as an ideal. It is quite another to use it as a tool of analysis of a yes or no variety. It is the very nature of the human condition as it now is to be living not only with personal sin but with collective sin, the absence of 'full and equal justice for all'. This does not mean we should not be committed to a heart and soul struggle against both personal sin and collective sin; it does mean that we cannot usefully analyse situations in terms of a factor common to them all. One can end organized apartheid in South Africa and communist rule in Poland (and one probably will do both soon enough) but one cannot bring about full and equal justice. Injustice will be relocated, it will not disappear.

Again, 'Reforms that come from the top are never satisfactory. They seldom do more than make the oppression more effective and more acceptable . . . True justice, God's justice, demands a radical change of structures. This can only come from below . . .' (3.2). I don't think this is good socio-political analysis either and it is very unhistorical. Perhaps no reforms are or can be fully 'satisfactory', but reforms that come from the top – whether they be the current changes in Gorbachev's Soviet Union or the series of Reform Acts, Education Acts, Factory Acts and so forth in nineteenth-century Britain, or the establishment of the Welfare State in twentieth-century post-Second World War Britain – can achieve a very great deal, arguably more than most reforms that come in more revolutionary dress 'from below'. However, adequate historical analysis would, I think, demonstrate that it is a false dichotomy, that almost all reforms come from both above and below and that it is seriously to misinterpret the whole process of realistically diminishing oppression and increasing justice to contrast the two in a sharp, almost apocalyptic way. Sound political theology may be temporarily boosted by apocalyptic, millenarian and revolutionary rhetoric, but it won't be assisted on the long haul by unsound analysis.

There can be no question but that the present state of South Africa is one of blatant, cruel, prolonged and ideologized oppression; it is not small scale; it really damages and destroys people, huge numbers of people, in a grossly unnecessary way; it has been like this for a very long time; it is as it is for the gross material benefit of fifteen per cent of its population, its white ruling class; finally, it is all the worse for being theoretically grounded and defended by the academic and even the cleric. It most certainly has to be fought very hard indeed and Kairos has proved a splendidly strong statement of just why it has to be fought, by Christians especially, and a splendidly strong denunciation of the tepid inadequacy of many Christian responses in the past. Yet today the state of South Africa can also be seen as one, beneath the inevitable bravado, of a bevy of white rabbits scurrying around in a situation that even they increasingly recognize as an impossible one, yet too deeply terrified, bewildered and intellectually numbed quite to understand the pass they are in; it is one in which the majority, the democracy movement, is now certain to win – it may not be so near to victory as is the Polish majority, but it may not be so far behind either; it is one in which, despite appalling on-going injustice, there has in point of fact been a really immense structural, educational and psychological change over the last twenty years; it is one in which – I believe – it is fast becoming time for the future victors and their intellectual and spiritual allies to pay a good deal more attention than hitherto to finding ways to allow the defeated to surrender with a minimum of indignity and some security. It is a time, then, in which strategies of post-liberation reconciliation (very different from pre-liberation reconciliation) need to be thought about and, indeed, entered into.

'There are conflicts in which one side is right and the other wrong . . . that can only be described as the struggle between justice and injustice, good and evil, God and the devil.' Again, yes and no. There are undoubtedly conflicts which cannot be seen otherwise. Stand in Auschwitz, within the torture chambers of any tyrannical government, South Africa included, and there is simply no possibility *hic et nunc* of moderating the moral and metaphysical absoluteness of the struggle. That *hic et nunc* may be extensive enough and it may not be easy to say just where its borders lie. Nothing could be much more theologically and morally inept than to relativize the meaning of such conflict. Nevertheless, attractive as the rhetoric of absolutization often is even to the theologian, it would seem to me that it is one principal task of the political theologian to work for the narrowing of such areas rather than for their theoretical enlargement, to relativize rather than to absolutize human division and disagreement. In one way it was the theorists and practitioners of Apartheid who wanted to absolutize racial and cultural divisions, but in another way it may now be the theorists and practitioners of a form of neo-marxist liberation theology who are in danger of doing so. In dogmatic and denominational matters theologians have tended to move these last twenty years from a more either/or to a more both/ and stance; it would be a pity if in the newer area of political theology the older, more temperamentally confrontatory, mode of analysis were allowed to prevail unquestioned. Kairos rightly pillories a rather fundamentalist type of Christian political theology grounded upon Romans 13, but it then proceeds to use Exodus 3 and Luke 4.18–19 almost equally fundamentalistically. 'Throughout the Bible God appears as the liberator of the oppressed' (4.2) – certainly not, though this is the implication, by simply replicating the Exodus mode. The Bible might indeed be seen en bloc as endless subtle re-interpretation of that theme across kingdom, war, exile and cross but if there is one thing the Bible is not, it is the extension of the Moses-Pharaoh paradigm *tout court* as a valid interpretative model for human history, the relationship of God and humanity, or moral and political obligation. It really is not feasible to construct a viable Christian practice of politics out of two or three chosen texts, selected attractively for their revolutionary any more than their stabilizing connotations, any more than it is by focussing upon the antithesis of God and the devil as incarnate in human beings. Reconciliation is something relative to human beings and when you declare that reconciliation is out of place because you cannot 'reconcile good and evil, God and the devil' (3.1), you cannot 'sup with the devil', you are in danger of transforming human relations into metaphysical ones. This has often been done by Christians in the past and almost always disastrously.

What I am really suggesting is that the political theology implicit in the Kairos document involves a fusion of what one could call, a little unkindly, a simplified, vulgar marxist, kind of social analysis relating to the functioning of 'justice' and 'oppression', 'the top' and 'below', revolution and *status quo*, with a no less simplistic and fundamentalistic type of biblical theology. I don't believe that the resultant mix is likely to be either good theology or good historical-political analysis, though it may be good rhetoric. Political theology in South Africa needs rhetoric and it needs to be able to appeal to lots of rather unlettered people in comprehensible and action-orientated words – and Kairos is doing both very well while theology elsewhere largely fails to do either – nevertheless it also needs to be able to do rather more than that, to be more supple and perceptive, more profoundly liberating in its concepts because also more consistently reconciliatory.

Current theology tends to contrast liberation and reconciliation (I have done so myself) and to see the latter as characteristic of liberal, bourgeois 'church theology' of the recent past: reconciliation can only rightly follow after the primary task of liberation is accomplished. For Kairos 'reconciliation' is indeed the key word within the fallacy of 'church theology' and it is pilloried as becoming in reality a matter of 'reconciliation with sin and the devil' (3.1). 'Reconciliation, forgiveness and negotiations will become our Christian duty in South Africa only when the apartheid regime shows signs of genuine repentance' (3.1). But can we ever say that forgiveness is not our Christian duty *now*, but only 'afterwards'? True Christian forgiveness is not soft forgiveness. It does not leave things unchanged. It does not imply any glossing over of injustice, structural or personal. It does not leave out issues of the repayment of ill-gotten gains, even tenfold. It is not an alternative to liberation but rather is each internally part of the other. There is a current wisdom which divides situations of conflict into those which call for reconciliation rather than liberation (e.g. Northern Ireland) and those which call for liberation rather than reconciliation (e.g. South Africa). Certainly there is some truth in that analysis. The weight of objective one-sided injustice can be far, far heavier in some situations of conflict than in others. Yet too sharp a contrast is likely to become over-simplistic socially, analytically and theologically. It is very doubtful whether there is any serious situation of human conflict which does not involve oppression and need liberation. There is also certainly none in which reconciliation is not needed. To argue that liberation must come before reconciliation is as one-sided as to argue that reconciliation is possible without liberation, just as it is over-simple to distinguish change 'from above' (bad) from change 'from below' (good). Reform has always to come in many, interwoven ways, just as reconciliation and liberation will be intertwined in many forms. It is perfectly true, and a very valid criticism, that in the past a great deal of liberal and Christian approaches to such problems were a matter of 'reconciliation' only or almost only, and reconciliation of an unstructural and very superficial kind. But such approaches were invalid in genuinely reconciliatory terms. Yet, to put the Southern African church record straight, it is also true that there has been a strong tradition of Christian action which has been at least as liberating as reconciling (the tradition of Van der Kemp, John Philip, Colenso and Shearley Cripps) even if it has been very much a minority tradition and one of ecclesiasticals not born in South Africa.

If reconciliation does not involve liberation, it is fraudulent – it will not genuinely reconcile; and if liberation does not involve reconciliation, it is fraudulent – it will not genuinely liberate. Reconciliation is *with*, liberation is *from*. Each in its way must, theologically and pragmatically, have the primacy – reconciliation in relationship to people, liberation in relation to the impersonal, to situations of sin and oppression; but as people have primacy over things so does reconciliation finally take precedence over liberation. The reconciliatory model is a unitary and unifying one, the liberatory model a dualistic and divisive one. In Marxist praxis it may be that the class struggle is effectively the most decisive of norms, but in Christian praxis the underlying norm is the 'all in all' of Christ, a unifying one from which no one is excluded. Hence, greatly as liberation is required in a sinful and oppressive world, it must remain in principle the handmaid of reconciliation, not the other way round. Again, one could say, reconciliation in itself is the thesis, liberation the antithesis, a truly, fiercely liberatory reconciliation the synthesis. A theology of liberation so much in tow to Marxism that it could not recognize this hierarchy of values would be sub-Christian, but that is not at all the way most theologies of liberation in fact operate, and in the immediate terms of an appropriate strategy in situations of great oppression it is absolutely right to keep the word 'liberation' right in the middle of things. Anything else would be profoundly misleading.

There are circumstances in which a liberating attack on unjust structure and policies must take the most absolute priority in terms of action over attempts at social and personal reconciliation – such is certainly the case in regard to the rights of Amazonian Indians today. And it is indeed arguable that in almost all circumstances of conflict, the strategy of effective action should be liberating more than reconciling – and this holds for Northern Ireland. Yet, at the same time, the strategy of intention not only for the future but actually for the present, should be no less primarily a reconciliatory one. And this must involve the avoidance, so far as is possible, of the diabolization of the other side – a diabolization, of course, which happened in the First World War in Europe, frequently in Ireland, just as in South Africa. Indeed it may well be that the Kairos use of the devil model is in part an unconscious take-over and inversion of the disastrous nineteenth-century missionary approach in Africa seen as the 'dark continent' in the possession of the devil.

It is certainly true that human beings can be exceedingly wicked as well as being exceedingly foolish and that the structural system of South Africa – political, economic and educational – has been an expression of collective and sustained wickedness, blindly upheld without doubt by many mediocre people who are far from personally wicked. But while a bad case of wickedness it is, in world-wide terms, today (or in the past) not so unusual a one. Christian tradition is right in stressing the ubiquity of original sin and it would be gravely mistaken and profoundly misleading to suggest that such a condition is exceptional or has anywhere been genuinely overcome. There are, of course, different types of structured and organized wickedness (and South Africa is a bad case, though not the worst) and the greater the depravity, the harder we must fight against it. Recognition of original sin is not a reason for quietism, though many on the Right would have it so. On the contrary, it simply provides the backdrop to the challenge human and Christian life is faced with, and a large part of the challenge for the Christian does actually consist in fighting injustice without diabolizing the apparatchiks, sycophants, informers and running dogs who are used and consumed by it. The recognition that they, above all, require liberation; the ability to look into the eyes of the police informer and see there not only a despicable wreck of humanity but also a brother in Christ, to see the liberatory struggle in all its fierceness as already now, and not only hereafter, a work of reconciliation: all this is not a secondary and additional but a primary and essential moral dimension of the task. I was in the past surprised on my visits to South Africa to be struck by how much more happy and humane ordinary blacks actually looked in their faces than did whites. I should not have been so. Anything else would be very surprising.

In the First World War, anti-German bellicosity was propagated by publicists (including ecclesiastical ones) at home. On the front line there was little room for it, rather an immense compassion for common humanity. So it should be in the current war against racial oppression. What the world needs most from the South African church and South African theology – and to an exciting extent has been getting – is a living theology from the front line of how to cope with injustice, personally and collectively, in a truly human and Christian way. It is obtaining it from South Africa because for a tough minority of South African Christians, black and white, the real issues of Christian and human living in today's world would seem to be more genuinely perceived as important theologically than almost anywhere else in the world. There actually is a lot of theology in South Africa. It is not that tyranny in South Africa is necessarily now worse than anywhere else in the world (it is not) though South Africa does particularly well encapsulate many of the wider world's modern woes. Nor is it that the church in South Africa is mostly so much more Christian or less Christian than the church anywhere else. But there is a certain matching of living church to tyranny which enables it to function as one of the principal forging grounds for a new Christian consciousness, a new theology, and South African theology is mostly healthily less academic (though not deprived of academic assistance) than most European theology. Almost certainly there is nowhere else in the English-speaking world where there is today so seriously committed or living a theology outside the university. It is the very significance of South African theology for the rest of the world that makes it appropriate for someone elsewhere not only to support but also, to a degree, to criticize and try to stimulate it still further.

I always think that 'only' is likely to be a dangerous and misleading word for theologians. Kairos is rather fond of it: 'Reconciliation, forgiveness and negotiations will become our Christian duty in South Africa *only* when the apartheid regime shows signs of genuine repentance' (13.1). 'True justice . . . can *only* come from below' (3.2). 'A regime that is in principle the enemy of the people cannot suddenly begin to rule in the interests of all the people. It can *only* be replaced by another government – one that has been elected by the majority of the people' (4.3) (italics mine). Yet Brezhnev was replaced by Gorbachev, the Hungarian government has rehabilitated Imre Nagy: we cannot so narrow the options of either history or theology, let alone the working of the Spirit of God. Not by one way alone can humans come to a measure of either justice or of truth.

Yet South Africa is today not really the world's starkest paradigm of injustice. If you look for that, look to the Kurds in Iraq or the fate of the Amazonian Indians. And in such cases it is infinitely harder not to feel the need to diabolize the oppressor. Yet how much has the church to say about either? Undoubtedly, the particularly close involvement of the churches in South African society and history do mean that here there is a special responsibility, and it is not one that is over yet. The struggle against racial oppression in South Africa has been long and honourable with many lost battles, many martyrs, a few prophets. But today, I believe – and I think it was part of the point of Kairos to affirm – the struggle is entering upon its final act: and still more so in 1989 than when Kairos was written in 1985. Across the world today the big battalions, marshalled in the past to uphold white domination, are in fact shifting their ground. I am glad they are, but it has ceased to be very prophetic to call for change. It may soon be a matter more of negotiation: a Lancaster House type of conference is not so very far beyond the horizon. Even in New Haven the main corner of the Green beside Yale, George Bush's university, has been renamed Tutu Corner by the municipal authorities. The prophet, I believe, had to stand up for black rights in South Africa for very many years; while the struggle is not over by any means, while police brutality can be even worse when a tyranny is losing its grip than in the days of its confidence, while more martyrs will doubtless have suffered in the cause before victory is won, one has also now to look ahead, even to recognize that there were some things of value, not so much in the implementation of apartheid as in its pluralist theory.

The implementation of a unitary cultural and political model could be even more disastrous for South Africa than it has proved elsewhere on the continent. In practice, and even in theory, *Apartheid* (separation) has never in South Africa been separable from *Baaskap* (domination). Though it may well be too late in the day after decades of a foolish and cruel tyranny masking under the pretended pursuit of positive values of separation, what is greatly needed remains the recovery of a sense of the honourableness of a moderate separateness – respect for all the diversities of a particularly pluralist society – with some sort of structured federalism (the effective whittling away of the degree of federal freedom that did formerly exist in South Africa in order to ensure the universal dominance of the Afrikaner tribe has been just one of the many foolishnesses of the Nationalist Party). It should be a task of the truly liberated and far-seeing theologian today not to dismiss such concerns as the hesitances of an outmoded liberalism but to speak out for them as long-term requirements for the freedom of an infinitely pluralist humanity, needing protection as much from the tyrannies of the future as from those of the past.

A way forward consonant with their history, their identity and their very Africanness has absolutely to be found for the tribe of the Afrikaner: it too has had its ten just men – Albert Geyser, Bram Fischer, Beyers Naudé . . . Mugabe's amazingly successful use of the theme of Reconciliation in Zimbabwe is becoming ever more relevant south of the Limpopo. Reconciliation should not be seen as almost a dirty word by the South African radical theologian but as the very keystone of the arch of the future. Mother Africa, so open, so forgiving, so accepting of diversity – so different from the harsh ideological character of the European fundamentalist, Christian or Marxist – will not, I dare to trust, fail in her wisdom to offer forgiveness here too, a forgiveness as vast as her land mass, as unconditioned as the heart of Christ, as genuine and as undeserved as the welcome whites have received from blacks across her continent time and again. Liberation still has far to go but reconciliation cannot wait.

Postscript: February 1990

In South Africa, as in Eastern Europe, events have moved of late with bewildering rapidity. It is hard to be either a political theologian or a prophet when what has long been a very static situation suddenly becomes extraordinarily fluid. I wrote this paper in June 1989. As I correct its proofs Mandela has been released from twenty-seven years of prison. In 1975 I ended my pamphlet *South Africa and the Christian Conscience* with the words: 'Be not deceived . . . into participating in the guilt of phoney reconciliation . . . Remember Nelson Mandela . . . Not until oppression ends can reconciliation begin.' Some people felt last year I had forgotten this message. I thought, on the contrary, that things had at last begun to change irrevocably and that a political theologian had a new duty – to reassert, once liberation begins to work within what remains a highly oppressive situation, the theme of the ultimate priority of reconciliation. I think so even more today.

10

Newman as Liberal and Anti-Liberal

John Henry Newman has to be recognized as, without possible comparison, the most powerful English theological thinker of the nineteenth century: the most sustained, the most systemic, in the long run easily too the most influential. The paradoxical character of that fact may have helped to impede its clear recognition – thus English departments of theology almost wholly ignored him, except as a figure of church history, at least until the 1950s. Paradoxical it certainly seems – for England in the nineteenth century can be characterized by all that Newman was not. It was both Protestant and Liberal and highly successful in both. It may be that, in the course of the century, it grew somewhat less Protestant; it certainly grew a great deal more liberal. The Oxford Movement itself began as a counter-attack against the advance of liberalism, but ended as an almost revolutionary attack upon Protantism. Liberalism seeped deeper and deeper into the intellectual, cultural, political and religious ethic of the land.

Late Victorian England was a liberal England in which rights were guaranteed regardless of beliefs, in which the universities ceased to be educational wings of the Established Church, in which there was a general acceptance that reason and social utility should prevail over tradition and authority. Freedom of conscience and of expression was the presupposition of this society as it never had been of pre-nineteenth-century England. When Newman was born in 1801 England was not a liberal society. When he died, in 1890, it was.[1]

The young Newman saw the way things were going clearly

---

[1] 'In my own lifetime has that old world been alive, and has gone its way', *A Letter Addressed to his Grace the Duke of Norfolk*, ch. 6.

enough. He did not like it. He set himself against it. Liberalism was the enemy. The aim of the Tractarians had been to awaken and arm the church to fight back against the liberal erosion both of its institutions and of its beliefs. To make that fight possible a new ecclesiology had to be hammered out to replace the soft erastianism which could no longer effectively underpin a Christian society or protect a national church from a liberal tide. Newman hammered it out but then found his creation unconvincing and, in 1845, left the church of England for another church, far more consistently illiberal. Even in old age his conviction remained – expressed most strikingly in the *biglietto* speech of May 1879 – that his whole life had been one long battle with liberalism. There can be no doubt that, in his own mind, Newman was an anti-liberal and that, moreover, in being so he consciously and systematically challenged the dominant orthodoxy of his country and his age.[2]

It may, then, seem strange to find Newman so often proclaimed, to the contrary, the chief nineteenth-century prophet of liberal Catholicism and the veritable father of the more liberalizing developments of the twentieth-century Catholic Church as centred particularly in the Second Vatican Council. How could the English anti-liberal, one might ask, be also the Catholic liberal? Yet Bishop Butler, summarizing the effects of the Council, could write shortly after its close 'The tide has been turned, and a first, immensely important, step has been taken towards the vindication of all the main theological, religious, and cultural positions of the former Fellow of Oriel'.[3] He has been echoed by many. Derek Holmes sees 'something of a liberal temper' in Newman's writing[4] and recognizes that he was 'the symbol of the hope of English Liberal Catholics'.[5] Owen Chadwick, perhaps the wisest of living Newman scholars, has summed up the issues in chapter 7, 'A fight against liberalism', of his

[2]The view of Newman as anti-liberal has recently been restated by Mark S. Burrows, 'A Historical Reconsideration of Newman and Liberalism: Newman and Mivart on Science and the Church', *Scottish Journal of Theology*, 40, 1987, pp. 399–419.
[3]B. C. Butler, OSB, 'Newman and the Second Vatican Council', *The Rediscovery of Newman: an Oxford Symposium*, ed. John Coulson and A. M. Allchin, Sheed & Ward and SPCK, 1967, p. 245.
[4]J. Derek Holmes, 'Newman and Modernism', *Baptist Quarterly* 27, 1972, p. 337.
[5]J. Derek Holmes, 'Newman's attitude to ultramodernism and liberal Catholicism on the eve of the first Vatican Council', *Bishops and Writers*, ed. A. Hastings, A. Clarke Books 1977, p. 16.

classic miniature study *Newman* in the *Past Masters* series and comes down, gently but firmly enough, upon the liberal side. Like Gladstone, Newman may have begun as an out-and-out Tory but we may be led to surmise that, despite protestation, he was in point of fact far too deeply immersed in the contemporary movement of thought to have ended as he began. Like Gladstone, then, we could conclude, Newman ended as a liberal. But, of course, unlike Gladstone, he did not admit to having done so or see himself as having done so; rather – as again Chadwick stresses – he was 'a man with the same mind all his life'.[6] Moreover, Newman was not only the greatest English theologian of the nineteenth century, he was also its greatest Catholic theologian – again there is really no one with whom one can plausibly compare him in Germany, France or Italy. And, despite earlier suspicions, he ended his life ecclesiastic- ally acclaimed as a cardinal in a church which – under Leo XIII – was only marginally less illiberal than it had been under Pius IX. So, if Newman is after all to be judged a liberal, we have yet further paradox upon that side.

A first conclusion we may well come to is that it is idle to put names upon the great. Newman was simply too large and profound a mind, too deeply concerned with a great range of issues and – one might add – at work over too long a period (his major writings cover no less than fifty years from the publication of *The Arians of the Fourth Century* in 1834 to 'On the Inspiration of Scripture' in 1884) for it to be conceivably reasonable to interpret him in pre-packaged terms. Liberalism itself has meant many things both in our century and in his. Newman meant, maybe, one thing by it, his contemporaries meant two or three others (and his contemporaries of the 1830s were by no means identical with those of the 1870s), while we may be meaning something different again. 'What Newman denounced as liberalism, no one else regarded as liberalism' remarks Chadwick (74). He could then be an anti-liberal in his terms but a liberal in ours. In fact even at the time, he was being classified as a liberal precisely while classifying himself as an anti-liberal, and both could make sense.

I, nevertheless, dare at this point to attempt a working definition of the liberal, broadly usable both for its originating locus of the

[6]Owen Chadwick, *Newman*, Oxford University Press 1983, p.5.

nineteenth century and for its twentieth-century sequel and roughly applicable in both the secular and the religious arena. Liberalism meant a commitment to personal, intellectual, social and economic freedom within a world in which the apparent unity of church and society, backed by the authority of a simple supernatural religion, was breaking down under the pressure of rational enquiry, political efficiency, and *de facto* pluralism. It was opposed to a Tory or traditionalist commitment to maintain the unity of society and control its life on the basis of authority, including religious authority, as hitherto exercised. Liberalism went with a practical acceptance of social and intellectual pluralism. It dethroned the public authority of religion. It did not renounce the concept of truth but it did renounce the right to impose truth other than through conviction, or on the basis of rational, empirical evidence, and it had absorbed a new approach to history such as to recognize that the formulation of truth must in part at least be historically conditioned. The liberal, then, stood for freedom where the anti-liberal stood for a unity of public order not wholly other than that of *cuius regio eius et religio*; the liberal stood for as wide an appeal to reason as in given circumstances seemed practicable where the anti-liberal stood for authority whether it be natural tradition, supernatural revelation or simply absolute monarchy; the liberal was likely to be influenced by a sense of history, of evolution physical and social and the measure of relativism which must derive from it, the anti-liberal held rather to a sense of permanence, a non-historical unchanging orthodoxy or order or ideology. The positive name for an anti-liberal was a Tory.

Newman's long-held, rather self-conscious, anti-liberalism was both an inheritance of his early Tractarian and pre-Tractarian period, the youthful commitment of a Tory (and as he said, 'Toryism was the creed of Oxford', *Apologia* Note A) out to fight every rationalizing reform of the church deriving from German Protestant theologies or English Whig government, and a link of on-going empathy between him and the church he had later joined. He knew well enough under how much suspicion he laboured in the church of Pius IX. At least he would not be under suspicion when he declared his anti-liberalism. Yet perhaps for that very reason he at times, with his extremely sensitive conscience, held back from what was sure to please, but was also likely to be misunderstood. It is only when this suspected liberal is actually so fully vindicated as to be created a

Cardinal that he feels free – and judges it appropriate – to pull out the stops in his *biglietto* speech in denunciation of liberalism as the enemy of dogma.

But what did he mean by it? For that one can best turn to the *Apologia* of 1864 and its account of his early intellectual history. Around 1827 he was, he tells us, 'drifting in the direction of the Liberalism of the day', partly under the influence of Dr Whately, Principal of Alban Hall, where Newman was Vice-Principal. Indeed, the first of his university sermons, preached in July 1826, is very much of a liberal temper and even in passing makes use of the word appreciatively. But by 1828, under the influence of Keble and Froude, he was moving sharply in a quite opposite direction and Liberals were now the enemy. 'The Great Reform Agitation was going on around me as I wrote. The Whigs had come into power; Lord Grey had told the Bishops to set their house in order, and some of the Prelates had been insulted and threatened in the streets of London. The vital question was, how were we to keep the Church from being liberalized? . . . I felt affection for my own Church but not tenderness; I felt dismay at her prospects, anger and scorn at her do-nothing perplexity. I thought that if Liberalism once got a footing within her, it was sure of the victory in the event' (*Apologia*, Chapter 1). That represents his position in 1832 (the year of the Reform Bill) as seen by Newman in 1864. Liberalism meant at once the suppression of Irish bishoprics and the slightly latitudinarian views of Dr Arnold on the interpretation of the Old Testament, but it basically meant playing down dogma and substituting for it a vague moralizing religion and no more. It might be represented by Peel, leading the new Conservatism, as much as by the Whigs. It was an assault upon the old orthodoxy of Oxford and England. Against all this Newman had 'fierce thoughts' and so did Keble. On July 14 1833 Keble preached his university sermon on 'National Apostasy'. That was, for Newman, the start of the Oxford Movement and it was, quintessentially, anti-liberal. 'My battle' he wrote, 'was with liberalism'. Liberalism he defined as 'the anti-dogmatic principle and its developments' but in practice – in spirit and sympathies – anti-liberalism meant taking 'its developments' pretty widely. It meant abhorrence for the Irish bishoprics bill. It meant dissuading a lady from attending the marriage of another who had seceded from the Anglican Church. It meant saying such fierce things as writing to a friend, of liberal and evangelical opinion, that 'we would ride over him and his, as Othniel prevailed over Chushanrishathaim, king of Mesopotamia'!

Newman further defined liberalism as 'false liberty of thought, or the exercise of thought upon matters, in which, from the constitution of the human mind, thought cannot be brought to any successful issue, and therefore is out of place. Among such matters are first principles of whatever kind; and of these the most sacred and momentous are especially to be reckoned the truths of Revelation. Liberalism then is the mistake of subjecting to human judgment those revealed doctrines which are in their nature beyond and independent of it, and of claiming to determine on intrinsic grounds the truth and value of propositions which rest for their reception simply on the external authority of the Divine Word' (*Apologia*. Note 1).

This lengthy quotation from Note 1 on Liberalism of the *Apologia* may be excused on the grounds of its importance, if also of its obscurity. But let us remember that Note 1 is explicitly a note about Liberalism as Newman conceived it in the 1830s and 1840s, not as he conceived it in the 1860s when he wrote the *Apologia*. In chapter 2, where he defined liberalism as 'the anti-dogmatic principle and its developments', he went on to assert that his position over this had never changed:

> From the age of fifteen, dogma has been the fundamental principle of my religion . . . What I held in 1816, I held in 1833 and I hold in 1864. Please God, I shall hold it to the end. Even when I was under Dr Whately's influence, I had no temptation to be less zealous of the great dogmas of the faith, and at various times I used to resist such trains of thought on his part as seemed to me (rightly or wrongly) to obscure them. Such was the fundamental principle of the Movement of 1833.

On this basis of dogma, the Movement developed as 'a second proposition' the re-assertion of the Church and the Sacraments. The first proposition (the fundamental principle of the Movement as he saw it) put it against liberals; the second proposition would in due course both put it under suspicion in the eyes of traditional churchmen and in the decades subsequent to Newman's conversion to Roman Catholicism, effectively transform the Church of England. It is with the second proposition that, retrospectively in most of our minds, the Tractarian Movement is chiefly associated; it was, however, with the first – the anti-liberal proposition – that it was above all associated by Newman. Indeed he saw the movement as successful in that it had – at least for some years – held 'liberalism' at bay and still toward the end of his life, years after writing the *Apologia*, he continued to interpret his own life struggle in the same terms.

Yet it seems a strange interpretation, at least quite in the form he offers it. If the mere exercise of rational thought about dogmas instead of their simple acceptance upon authority constituted liberalism, was not Newman by all his activity essentially a liberal while Keble equally clearly was not? Newman himself recognized the difference between them clearly enough. Keble, Newman tells us, in that same note on the nature of liberalism, 'was a man who guided himself and formed his judgments, not by processes of reason, by inquiry or by argument, but, to use the word in a broad sense, by authority'. Keble was then in Newman's view, and surely correctly, the quintessential non-liberal. But Newman? He remarks at one point of himself what was profoundly true at every point: 'I felt then, and all along felt, that there was an intellectual cowardice in not finding a basis in reason for my belief, and a moral cowardice in not avowing that basis' (*Apologia*, chapter 2). Or again: 'Few minds in earnest can remain at ease without some sort of rational grounds for their religious belief; to reconcile theory and fact is almost an instinct of the mind' (*Apologia*, chapter 5). Was that not indeed the motivation of *The Via Media*, the *Essay on Development*, the *Grammar of Assent*? What on earth was he doing in Chapter V of the *Grammar of Assent* if not 'exercising thought' upon the most basic 'truths of the Revelation' – the Unity and Trinity of God? All his life he was seeking 'a basis in reason' for his belief, as Keble (at least consciously) was not. And that was the very badge of the liberal. Of course, Newman did not see the 'basis in reason' as proof, as a determination 'on intrinsic grounds' of the truth of revelation in a formally precise logical way. But how many 'liberals' did either? One cannot but conclude that, to defend a high view of the content of dogma against liberals who had a low view of its content, Newman himself increasingly became a 'liberal' (even in his own theological sense of the word). With his kind of intellect he could not have been other despite a certain temperamental conservatism, and his brief, almost explicitly, liberal period with Whately was far more permanently significant than he ever recognized. Yet it was – again paradoxically – after, not before, he became a Catholic that the rational and potentially liberal dimension of his thinking really became plain. Part of the problem was that he had early developed a phobia for the word which was as much political as theological. Thus about 1840 he was making it a point against Rome that, in the politics of the time and particularly their Irish dimension, Catholics and liberals were standing together. So, he commented, 'the alliance of a dogmatic religion with liberals, high or low, seemed to me a providential direction against moving towards Rome', and again 'Break off, I would say, with Mr O'Connell in Ireland and the liberal party in England, or come not to us with overtures for mutual prayer' (*Apologia*, chapter 3). He can hardly have been thinking at that point that Rome was imperilling the dogmatic principle by an alliance between Irish Catholics and the Liberal Party. However, by the 1860s he could see that the liberal society had come to stay, that there was no conceivable alternative consonant with justice, and that the principles of the *Syllabus of Errors* were not so much wrong as just completely anachronistic. He was far too pessimistic about this world to share the political enthusiasms of a Montalembert or an Acton, but he did not disagree with their conclusions. His political anti-liberal phobia had almost completely disappeared: it might remain as a verbal whimsy but in practical politics he now normally preferred the liberal option.

Maybe one must return to Chadwick's comment that 'What Newman denounced as liberalism, no one else regarded as liberalism'. One feels that, drawn from his youth – and reinforced by the terminological preferences of Rome in the latter part of the nineteenth century – he allowed this term to continue to function in his thought, inadequately analysed, as the shorthand for a sort of anti-religious conspiracy in modern society – at first more political, then theological, finally just the way the world was going, the 'deep, plausible scepticism' (*Apologia*, chapter 5) which he saw spreading everywhere around him. In the eyes of an Augustinian, it had come to mean what 'the World' meant for the writers of the New Testament. In the last of all his publications, when he was now 84, *The Development of Religious Error* (The *Contemporary Review*,

October 1885), his view of a world increasingly rejecting dogma and succumbing to liberalism was sombre enough:

> If, as I believe, the world, which the Apostles speak of so severely as the False Prophet, is identical with what we call human society now, then there never was a time since Christianity was, when, together with the superabundant temporal advantages which by it have come to us, it had the opportunity of being a worse enemy to religion and religious truth than it is likely to be in the years now opening upon mankind . . . Not, of course, that I suppose the flood of unbelief will pour over us in its fullness at once. A large inundation requires a sufficient time . . .

Newman's use of 'liberalism' as a word has most surely to be understood within the context both of an Augustinian theology and a perception of nineteenth-century history at once pessimistic and perspicacious. While it would be hard to fault the correctness of his judgment upon the wider social and intellectual movement of his age in relation to religion, it may well be said that such a profoundly negative judgment upon modern culture and society is not only verbally anti-liberal, it is also substantially very far from being that of a liberal. That is fair enough. Yet in point of fact Newman fully recognized and appreciated 'the superabundant temporal advantages' of the nineteenth-century liberal state. Politically he had moved far from old-fashioned Tory views and Roman ones too. He had little sympathy for either the defence of the Papal states or opposition to an effectively secular, religiously neutral society. Still more, educationally, was he a liberal. ('From first to last education has been my line.') Now what is probably his most widely influential work, *The Idea of a University*, is quite explicitly a defence of liberal education. Here he repeatedly uses the word 'liberal', in the Preface, the Introductory chapter and, especially, in Chapter 5, on 'Knowledge its own End'. Liberal is here seen to stand for something entirely desirable in human life – for freedom, equitableness, moderation, wisdom, courtesy. There seems a remarkable contrast in tone between the Newman of *The Idea* on the one hand and the aged Newman of *The Development of Religious Error*, or the young and newly converted anti-liberal of the University sermon on *The Usurpations of Reason* (December 1831) upon the other.

Or consider the contrast between rival passages even within a single work, that wonderful final chapter 5 of the *Apologia*. On the one side there is, for the liberal, the following undoubtedly painful passage:

There is a time for everything, and many a man desires a reformation of an abuse, or the fuller development of a doctrine, or the adoption of a particular policy, but forgets to ask himself whether the right time for it is come: and, knowing that there is no one who will be doing anything towards its accomplishment in his own lifetime unless he does it himself, he will not listen to the voice of authority, and he spoils a good work in his own Century, in order that another man, as yet unborn, may not have the opportunity of bringing it happily to perfection in the next. He may seem to the world to be nothing else than a bold champion for the truth and a martyr to free opinion, when he is just one of those persons whom the competent authority ought to silence . . .

It is not surprising that Mark Burrows, for instance, in his recent restatement of the case for Newman as an unwavering anti-liberal, quotes that in full.

Yet consider it within the context of passages both before and after, together with the ecclesiastical atmosphere of 1864 and it becomes, I believe, little more than the statement of an opinion once held, trundled out to soften the impact of the message he is now trying continuously to put across. It is, after all, preceded by the words 'In reading ecclesiastical history, when I was an Anglican, it used to be forcibly brought home to me'.

Turn a couple of pages back and we get Newman in a very different mood:

It is the custom with Protestant writers to consider that, whereas there are two great principles in doctrine in the history of religion, Authority and Private Judgment, they have all the Private Judgment of themselves, and we have the full inheritance and the superincumbent oppression of Authority. But this is not so, it is the vast Catholic body itself, and it only, which affords an arena for both combatants in that awful, never-dying duel. It is necessary for the very life of religion, viewed in its large operations and its history, that the warfare should be incessantly carried

126   The Theology of a Protestant Catholic

on . . . : Catholic Christendom is no simple exhibition of religious absolutism, but presents a continuous picture of Authority and Private Judgment alternately advancing and retreating on the ebb and flow of the tide.

Add to that the later lines about the importance of the theologian not feeling that authority was 'watching every word he said . . . then indeed he would be fighting, as the Persian soldiers, under the lash and the freedom of his intellect might truly be said to be beaten out of him'. (Compare with this his letter to Miss Bowles the year before in which he complained, bitterly, that he was in just such a case: 'How can I fight with such a chain on my arm? It is like the Persians driven to fight under the lash'.[7])

Verbally, he is consistently an anti-liberal in the *Apologia* as he is not in *The Idea of a University*. The dates of the two books account for this well enough. In the 1850s, when *The Idea* was written, the Liberal party seemed still the natural ally of British Catholics. On the Continent too there were Catholic liberal stirrings. Newman, detached from the defence of the Established Church, was reshaping his mind in more liberal terms. The *Rambler* years still lay ahead. By 1864, when the *Apologia* was written Newman had been badly burnt in his attempt to help English Liberal Catholics over the *Rambler* while liberal Catholicism on the continent was now being ruthlessly condemned. Lacordaire had died in 1861, 'a penitent Catholic but an impenitent Liberal'. 1863 represented the movement's most outspoken moment: at a Congress of Belgian Catholics Montalembert had delivered two major speeches on 'A Free Church in a Free State' and on 'Liberty of Conscience'. A little later in Munich Dollinger addressed a Congress of Catholic scholars as its president, on 'The Past and Present of Catholic Theology': 'Christianity is history and in order to be understood it must be studied in its development'. Here we have the central characteristics of liberalism: the assertion of the value of freedom, personal and social, and of the necessity for the understanding of Christianity of a historical and developmental approach, with all of which Newman could not now but be in sympathy. Yet by 1864 all this lay condemned, first by the Munich *Brief* and subsequently by the

[7]Meriol Trevor's biography of Newman, vol. II, *Light in Winter*, Macmillan 1962, p. 298.

Encyclical *Quanta Cura* and the *Syllabus of Errors*. The *Apologia* was written and published between the *Brief* and the Encyclical. It would have been near suicide at that point for Newman to admit himself in some sense a liberal. It is not surprising if he continues to take such trouble to distance himself from the word, even mildly reproaching Montalembert for using it. Perhaps Newman's caution was over-great, but it is rather too easy in retrospect to blame him. It would be quite unrealistic to evaluate his usage of the word in the *Apologia* without reference to the high tide of anti-liberalism flowing through the Catholic church at that point and brooking at least no clerical disagreements. Newman may well have been losing his old antagonism to the word but it would have been tactically absurd to show it at that point. Tactically his record of anti-liberalism was, on the contrary, one of the few cards he had to play in the church of Pio Nono but if he played it, it was in point of fact within a defence of the substance of Catholic liberalism – of the need to cultivate Private Judgment as much as authority, and to take history seriously.

In the early *Usurpations of Reason* we do not find any stress upon the value of the 'intense and varied operation of the Reason' or 'the freedom of the intellect' of the sort that we do find in the *Apologia* and which do provide adequate practical basis for the expansion of a liberal Catholic theology. What had grown in him between the 30s and the 60s, and particularly since becoming a Catholic, was a pervading sense of the importance of both reason and freedom. Newman's position could never be identified with that of anyone else – and certainly not with the 'liberal Catholics' who rather clung to him in the *Rambler* period, people like Simpson and Acton. Edward Norman, in his discussion of Newman and liberalism, remarks 'he was certainly close to positions also occupied by the liberal Catholics, but his reasons of arriving at these attitudes were far from theirs'.[8] Indeed they were not identical but their reasons were not as different as one might easily think. Given Newman's lifelong anti-liberal protestations, what seems remarkable is how close he came to the avowedly liberal. In fact, as Altholz remarks 'Newman's intellect was liberal, his instincts were conservative'.[9] This is certainly true of

[8]Edward Norman, *Roman Catholicism in England*, Oxford University Press 1986, p. 99.
[9]Joseph Altholz, *The Liberal Catholic Movement in England*, Burns & Oates 1962, p. 20.

the Catholic Newman in his maturity and is borne out by the most controversial writings of his middle period, 'On Consulting the Faithful in matters of doctrine' and the *Letter addressed to the Duke of Norfolk on the occasion of Mr Gladstone's Expostulation*. We find in these the clearest theological expression of his commitment to the Christian need for freedom in the life at once of the individual, of the church and of society. It is not without significance that instead of going to Rome to attend the Vatican Council as invited, he stayed in England to write *The Grammar of Assent* which, while undoubtedly a defence of dogma, was very much a book about reason. This did not demonstrate his being out of line with the Council which also had a good deal to say about reason but it does suggest, I think, how distant he actually was from either the anti-liberal theologian of his own formulation or the typical Ultramontane of the time. In his defence of conscience and civil freedom in his *Letter to the Duke of Norfolk*, in his defence of the role of the laity in 'On Consulting the Faithful', of the need for theological freedom and Private Judgment in chapter 5 of the *Apologia*, and of course of the absolute necessity for looking at historical evidence honestly and recognizing the necessity of change in the *Essay on Development*, 'On Consulting the Faithful' and elsewhere, in all this Newman was undoubtedly aligning himself with theologians and lay people who at the time did call themselves liberal Catholics and struggled against the narrower ultramontanist tendencies dominant in the church of Pius IX. He was also laying foundations for much of the theological development in and around the Second Vatican Council. The objective liberalism of Newman within a Catholic context in these terms is hardly disputable.

Yet we still seem faced with the apparent paradox of the *biglietto* speech. After the long years in which he was under a cloud in Rome substantially as a liberal, here he was in old age created a Cardinal in the first consistory of Leo XIII and taking the opportunity precisely to reassert his opposition to liberalism. A very old man, nearing 80, at the greatest moment of his ecclesiastical career, the wholly unexpected moment of vindication, he rises from his seat to declare 'I rejoice to say to one great mischief I have from the first opposed myself. For 30, 40, 50 years I have resisted to the best of my powers the spirit of liberalism in religion . . . an error overspreading as a snare the whole earth'.[10]

[10]*The Times*, 13 May 1879, p. 5, reprinted in Wilfrid Ward, *The Life of John Henry Cardinal Newman*, Vol. II, Longmans 1912.

It is as if, with the world listening – for every word of his speech was printed in full in the British daily papers next day – he wished to summarize, from his own viewpoint, the central struggle of his life: 'Liberalism in religion is the doctrine that there is no positive truth in religion, but that one creed is as good as another, and this is the teaching which is gaining substance and force daily. It is inconsistent with any recognition of any religion as true'. Religion has ceased to be the bond of society and is becoming no more than 'a private luxury' where – when Newman was young – 'Christianity was the law of the land'. The Liberalism here denounced is, obviously enough, quite other from the liberalism he was suspected of advancing and yet the two were not *wholly* unrelated either in the minds of his adversaries or his own mind or indeed in the objectivity of things.

The opening sentences of Newman's *biglietto* speech have been a great deal more quoted than the latter parts of it, but to understand his thought upon the subject, the latter parts are at least as important, and for them to be interpreted aright, they need comparison with another slightly earlier writing which in many ways duplicates the argument: chapter 6 of the *Letter to the Duke of Norfolk*, entitled 'The Encyclical of 1864'. Here, five years before the speech, Newman was explaining to a critical British people the true meaning of *Quanta Cura*. What is striking about Newman's position in both is that he sees the intellectual advance of liberalism as being a necessary consequence and aspect of a vast social change (what we might call secularization consequent upon the spread of pluralism) which was both inevitable and actually right. 'The liberal principle is forced on us', he declares in his speech 'through the necessity of the case'. And he means it. The advance of nonconformity, a far wider pluralism of religious belief even than that, together with all that is 'good and true' in 'the liberalistic theory' have left no alternative. 'We cannot help ourselves.' Newman does not pretend that, personally, he likes the change. He confesses himself 'an admirer of the principles now superseded'. 'No one', he says, 'can dislike the democratic principle more than I do'. He far preferred the Tory England, the Tory world, of his childhood. When he defends *Quanta Cura*, it is largely in terms of its being quite in line with the way things always were in England up to a couple of generations ago. The Pope he admits is behaving entirely anachronistically but, he says, don't be too hard on him: he is only saying in Italy in the 1860s what was the common mind of

England sixty years earlier. 'Men of the present generation, born in the new civilization, are shocked to witness in the abiding Papal system the words, ways and works of their grandfathers' (*A Letter*, chapter 6, 263). 'Englishmen, who within fifty years kept up the Pope's system, are not exactly the parties to throw stones at the Pope for keeping it up still' (*A Letter*, 269). Yet what is striking in both the Letter and the speech is Newman's stress upon the inevitability of what he calls 'the new civilization', 'this great revolution' – the ascendancy of liberalism, an ascendancy intellectual and religious as much as social: 'When the intellect is cultivated, it is as certain that it will develop into a thousand various shapes, as that infinite hues and tints and shades of colour will be reflected from the earth's surface, when the sun-light touches it; and in matters of religion the more . . .' (*A Letter*, 267). The consequence he sees as clear and inevitable: 'The whole theory of Toryism, hitherto acted on, came to pieces and went the way of all flesh. This was in the nature of things. Not a hundred Popes could have hindered it.' (Ibid, 268).

Let us recapitulate: Newman meant by liberalism the vast revolution of the nineteenth-century whereby society accepts its pluralism and was secularized in consequence, so removing religion's public significance. His heart, as he freely admitted, was with the Christendom world of the past, but he wholly recognized the inherent inevitability and indeed appropriateness of the liberal and secularizing revolution. He lost any sympathy with the desire to reverse it by political or ecclesiastical power and he considered any such attempt futile. But he saw too that as religion lost its public and political position, it seemed also to lose its sense of objectivity, its dogmatic quality. In so far as it survived, it did so as 'a private luxury', controlled by all the quirks of subjective sentiment. I find it hard to disagree with Newman's analysis or to deny that it was a fair use of the word 'Liberalism'. It was a very holistic use and a very far-seeing one – in many ways, perhaps, a case of Bryan Wilson's secularization thesis propounded a century prior to Bryan Wilson. I am not sure that one should really say with Chadwick, 'What Newman denounced as liberalism, no one else regarded as liberalism'. Rather Newman so summarized a vast process which he had actually been closely observing across an unusually long life-time in such few words that the resultant shorthand was almost unintelligible.

But what was to happen next? Newman believed in Christian

dogma in an essentially traditional way. He recognized that the liberal revolution was inevitable, concurred profoundly with human nature and yet was necessarily undermining church and dogma in the form they had long taken. The final lines of the speech are, I think, too seldom considered:

> Christianity has been too often in what seemed deadly peril, that we should fear for it any new trial now. So far is certain; on the other hand, what is uncertain, and in these great contests commonly is uncertain, and what is commonly a great surprise, when it is witnessed, is the particular mode by which, in the event, Providence rescues and saves His elect inheritance. Sometimes our enemy is turned into a friend; sometimes he is despoiled of that special virulence of evil which was so threatening; sometimes he falls to pieces of himself; sometimes he does just so much as is beneficial and then is removed. (*Biglietto* speech)

Or to quote *A Letter*, 'in centuries to come, there may be found out some way of uniting what is free in the new structure of society with what is authoritative in the old . . .' (286).

Newman recognized that the system was collapsing. In his twenties he had, briefly, partially shared a liberal view. He had then fought it fiercely as a Tory anti-liberal, but the more he fought the more he found himself sharing a great deal of what he had first set out to fight – the importance of freedom, and the use of reason, and the implications of modern historical science. He realized, as a Catholic, separated from the state church, that the old system in England or elsewhere was socially an anachronism. Liberalism had become part of the air which later nineteenth-century man could not but breathe.

He saw even that his own Catholic church greatly needed this air. In the 1850s and 1860s he was becoming, in many ways and always rather *contre-coeur*, a liberal, but in moving with the world and with the living mind of the nineteenth century, empirical and evolutionist, he was moving against the leadership of the Catholic Church in the later, highly embattled years of Pio Nono. And no one of high intelligence had ever believed more in respect for authority than Newman. Far more of a theological liberal than Pusey, just as he had his finger far closer to the pulse of the secular world, yet aware of his responsibility to an Acton or to his own priests around him in the

Birmingham Oratory, he had somehow to salvage in the anti-liberal atmosphere of the Ultramontane high tide not necessarily the word 'liberalism' (which he temperamentally never did and never could like) but the positive substance behind it. The strain upon so sensitive and far-seeing a person was very great, but the strain was borne across forty years and a future for liberal Catholicism, which would be of enormous value in the next century, was salvaged by the integrity of his faith and the profundity of his judgment. It is paradoxical that the very edition of the *Times* which carried his anti-liberal *biglietto* speech also carried an article stressing the significance of Leo XIII's creation among his first Cardinals of not one but several 'Liberals' – including Newman ¬adding, fairly enough, 'the term Liberal must here be understood in the sense Roman Catholic churchmen of enlarged minds give to the word'. The details of Newman's mode of reconciling the claims of dogma and the supernatural with the claims of the nineteenth-century liberal intelligence may in many ways be *passé* for us now, but if he had not consistently, profoundly and painfully battled with the need for such a reconciling, he would not as a theologian matter to us very much today. He would remain a fascinating figure of past ecclesiastical history, but if beyond that he is almost the only English and Catholic mind of the nineteenth-century that continues to act upon us, to influence religious thought today, and almost to persuade us to reconsider issues of our own age, it is because he was himself a mind of quite exceptional force and clarity caught up upon both sides 'in that awful, never-dying duel . . . of Authority and Private Judgment alternately advancing and retreating as the ebb and flow of the tide'.

★ 11 ★

The Church of the Future[1]

The Christian community has always been in principle though not always in practice a future-orientated one. Of course it is, no less, present orientated, it is now that matters. And it is past orientated too, centred in its worship and ordered life, indubitably, upon a memory; the recollection of Jesus, and of much else too. Certainly we look back. Certainly we live for 'the present'. Yet, equally certainly, and unlike some other traditions of meaning, we are committed to the future, even to a series of futures. It was so from the beginning. Jesus spoke of his coming death. He spoke of a catastrophe which would engulf Jerusalem. He spoke of the coming of the Spirit. He spoke of a future day of judgment. 'When that day comes . . .' Through the symbols, the religious experiences, the historical events these various sayings refer to, we can spell out the structure of a multiple future: an ultimate and a series of penultimates. From then to now the Christian church has been living with both. Of course it has often looked back rather than forth: back to the Apostolic Age, back to the high days of the Christian Empire, back to the Middle Ages, the age of faith, back maybe to the Reformation. Yet however much we may feel at times of depression (and our predecessors certainly felt the same time and again) that we are living in some sort of sunset epilogue, with the great Christian experience far behind us, the title deeds of our existence point, of necessity, onwards along a pilgrim road into the future, rather than backwards to any known domain.

The virtue most evidently to be related to this commitment to the

[1]With particular reference to the Church of England. This paper was originally given as a lecture for the centenary of the Diocese of Wakefield, 1988.

future is hope: hope in God's ultimate future, but hope too in the immediate future. Hope is a natural virtue as well as a Christian one. Few of us could go on without it. In human terms, there seems often enough little to hope for, yet hope wells up again and again in humanity's consciousness. Humankind wants a future and Christian hope insists that in wanting we are not deluded for all that is ahead lies within the hands of God, as all that is past – hard as it is to see what that implies. He has made us beings of hope, hopefulness is at the heart of humanity's very nature and the hope that is offered us in Christ responds to all the natural hopefulness within us; not only a hope for the ultimate, it includes the penultimate as well – our immediate future, the church's own immediate future. The church remains the community of Christian hope, and the sustaining of hope implies the sustaining of the church: the church must itself have a future. The church is then not only the subject of hope, a community of the hopeful. It is also an object of hope: it will still be present in every penultimate age, able to witness to a future beyond whatever point mankind has then reached. Christian hope goes far beyond any concern with the church of the future, yet it always includes the confidence that the church will go on. While then we may feel sure of relatively little about the church of the future, we should be sure that there will be one, and this is already something. It is of course an assurance of faith, not of reason. When we were young, my generation probably still thought the British Empire would go on and on. If the sun could not set on it, that was a matter of time as well as of space. Doubtless little children in Londinium, 1,600 years earlier, had thought the same about another empire. Perhaps even Alban thought it as a child, but both empires have gone and many others too. Yet the Christian church does go on: 'we never closed'. That is not a small claim after 1,960 years, give or take, and there is surely no intention of closing now even if other empires come and go, so if we cannot prove that the church has a future, a sober view of past and present does nothing to dissuade us from that affirmation.

But what sort of a future? When one starts to try and answer that question, it is I believe essential to remind ourselves that the future is not fixed. For Christian faith, human freedom is essential and if we are free, our future is not determined. A study of history confirms this. There is absolutely no reason to think that things had to be as they have been. Not only have almost accidental factors significantly affected the human story, but so have the decisions, the faith, the courage, the obstinacy, the prejudices of thousands of people. Christian Egypt or Syria did not have to go Muslim; Christian Spain could have gone Muslim; there did not have to be two world wars in this century; there did not have to be a holocaust of six million Jews. These things were not inevitable. Just as William Temple or Dietrich Bonhoeffer or John Wesley or John Henry Newman were not inevitable. The Christian Missionary Movement of the nineteenth and early twentieth century was not inevitable, nor its consequence that the southern half of Africa is today a largely Christian continent. It did not have to be. Things could have gone quite differently. If they went as they did, for good or ill, it is due to an immensely complex combination of human choices together with other more apparently chance-like factors. There are always alternative futures, in our own personal lives, and in those around us. There is no way with some super scientific insight we could see inexorably the future before us in all its fullness. We make our future and we are making it now by our present. Doubtless there are limits to our power, yet the history of Christianity, full of implausibilities as it is, should make us beware of overstressing the limitations upon our freedom to make our future. Indeed, it may well be that mankind today is more radically free to shape its future than it has ever been. The immediate future possible at any given time was to a greater degree determined in the past than it is today or ever will be again. This is, in point of fact, clearly so. Today we are free to destroy the planet as a place of life, and we may well do so. In which case, the ultimate for humanity will have arrived, and any penultimate future for the church, or anyone else, will be no more. It is a genuine possibility but not a certainty. It is one of our futures, but there are others.

This example demonstrates at once that one cannot speak of the future of the church without speaking of the future of society, and of the world. The church and its character cannot be discussed apart from the world, church history making no sense at all upon its own, divorced from the context of total human history. The future of the church is inextricably linked up with the future of the world.

What sort of a world will there be in the twenty-first century? What sort of a society in Britain? What sort of a relationship between the Continents? What sort of ideology will be motivating the powerful?

Will technology have brought a good life to all, or will it rather immensely enhance the power and the pleasure of a few while subjecting tens of millions to powerlessness in a divided world? We do not know. But we do know that there are huge choices being made by our society today by its political, economic and cultural leaders, and that the future of the church can only make sense in the context of those choices and of the sort of world which comes out of those choices. We cannot even begin to imagine a church apart from them, a church for which these things are irrelevant. The church could not be the same after printing as it was before; after universal education as it was before. We can imagine more or less pessimistic scenarios for the future of human society in the next hundred years; the range of alternatives, each with a measure of plausibility behind it, is very great. And this is not just a matter of peace or war (the multiplication of wars of the Iran-Iraq type for instance), ecological pollution, the collapse of whole societies in the third world, and so forth. It is also a matter of basic understanding. As the hegemony of Christianity in the Western world has receded, it has been replaced by a number of battling ideologies of which, for a time, Marxism in one of its forms seemed to be the most socially challenging and potentially hegemonic. But it, too, is now in sharp decline and it is perhaps harder to predict the ideological future that faces us than any other aspect of the future. Perhaps, except as a subject of after-dinner conversation, ideology, philosophy and religion will all publicly atrophy and what we will be facing is a society in which fundamentalisms may thrive in the margins but whose central core will be characterized – in contrast with all previous societies – by the prolonged absence of any publicly recognized value other than that of what is demonstrably useful to those who already possess the elements of power.

All these are likely questions of the future, still more than they are questions of the present, though really we can only project them as the former because they are already in part the latter. If you think of the world of the future as a sort of ever-enlarged world of yuppies, or if you think of it as an ever-enlarged world of famished Ethiopian refugees, you have indeed two very different models, and the churches that exist within them will be very different churches too.

If the church is part of the world, sharing every characteristic of contemporary society, its true vitality and justification in terms of its own faith must still be seen in its ability not to be enslaved by contemporary society but to speak and minister to the world critically but positively in both its failings and its strengths: to take each world as it comes and see it through Christ's eyes. The church is in some ways the extension of the incarnation: Jew with the Jews, Gentile with the Gentiles. Incarnate but not immersed. The savour of the salt must still be there. The light must still shine but always within a society it is part of. If too immersed, it loses its *raison d'être* and becomes a mere religiously validating guarantor of the secular with all its current structures of untruth, injustice and selfish meaninglessness. If not immersed enough, it is to a given group of people an alien and itself meaningless intrusion.

The ability of Christianity to identify, participate, move on with human culture is the ground of its continuing changeableness. Of all the great religious traditions it has best demonstrated its vitality by its openness to change, to become different. This was so from the start. The relationship of Jesus to the church is very different for instance from that of Mohammed to the Umma, just as his relationship to the New Testament scriptures is very different from Mohammad's to the Koran. Jesus did not preside over a functioning church, just as he did not write even one book of the New Testament, central as he is to both. His distance from both has always allowed a quite extraordinary freedom to change and to diversify. The diversity already within the New Testament is often seen as a weakness, a ground even of attack. It is in fact quite the opposite. It allows space for unending diversification. There is a very great temptation for Christianity to try to re-establish a first-century church, or, say, the church in its imagined thirteenth-century glory. It is of course profitable to look to the past for hints on how to cope now. But the models of the past as a whole are forbidden us. We have no more reason to follow the model of the Twelve peripatetically traversing Galilee around Jesus, the early post-Easter Jerusalem community, the first communities in Corinth or Rome, the more ordered shape that we find in the Pastoral Epistles or such early post-New Testament writings as the Letters of Ignatius. Change (and that has meant loss as well as gain) has been a principal mark of Christianity's existence in history. It is, one should claim, a necessary characteristic of a truly incarnate religion. Without it and its genuine theological justifiability, it would be quite impossible for a faith alive in the culture of two thousand years ago to be still alive today – genuinely alive, intellectually and socially.

But clearly all this adds immensely to the difficulty of our subject –
the Church of the Future. In a time when human society is changing
more rapidly than it has ever done, the church has to change, not just
to keep up with the Joneses, but because it is the Joneses. It has to
change to keep up with itself and its own really quite odd ability to
adapt despite its very heavy luggage of history. We are feeling that
luggage in the West particularly heavily at present. Take the matter
of buildings. Buildings just weren't part of the business in early
Christianity. and the church throve without them. There were
doubtless by the late third century a few smallish, specifically
ecclesiastical buildings here and there, but absolutely no equival-
ence in meaning between community and building, Church and
church. It really was Constantine and his great Basilica building
programme that changed all that. Of course it is very convenient to
have buildings, and edifying and instructive too, and in some
circumstances socially constructive. So every mediaeval town and
village became dominated by spire and tower, nave and aisles,
transepts and clerestories. Society has changed but the buildings
have remained in all their splendid cultural and historical richness,
presenting all the same a massive problem for the late twentieth-
century church: not a problem one encounters in the grass-roofed
chapels of African villages! The Christian church is not just a
present, living with its hope on the anguished frontier of the future.
It has to be faithful to its past too: it has such an immensely rich
memoriale at its heart, not only of Jesus but of a human tradition of
saints, without whose inspiration we certainly could not face that
frontier with the degree of confidence we have. We cannot then cast
aside the great legacy of past centuries and yet only too easily we
could be crushed by it, unnecessarily crushed. In coping with it, so as
not to be crushed, we need again and again to remind ourselves of
how very changeable our long history has been. What we must not let
happen – though there is at present some danger of it happening – is
to see the church sink into being a sort of religious dimension of the
National Trust, a heritage body taken up with the myriad cares of
Durham Cathedral, York Minster, Westminster Abbey, and ever so
many more historic shrines of national or local interest. That is
indeed one not impossible scenario for the church's future in this
country, but clearly we cannot and must not be satisfied with it. The
trouble here is not so much that it is chosen as a deliberate option as

that it could simply be the one thing left if every other public role be taken away, the final amiable rump of an established church which has lost both political authority and spiritual purpose.

A contrasting and equally dangerous scenario, containing within it a more subtly attractive temptation, would be to settle on the freedom of a sect and, socially, nothing more. It is conceivable that the Church of England, to preserve its freedom over against the state – perhaps in regard to some relatively secondary point of difference – would finally reject any Establishment status at all; perhaps even reject the use of many of its greatest buildings, and at the same time be increasingly rejected by society. The separation in this country between the Church of England and the secular Establishment has, after all, grown fairly steadily and considerably. Part of that separation of recent years has been due to the church's insistence upon its social responsibilities in ways that some people in government in a Thatcherite age have not at all liked. But separation, if it goes too far, and if the church should come to be dominated by a rather different sort of theology from at present, might lead to the church's withdrawal, not just from its last flimsy hold on secular power, but precisely from that sense of responsibility for secular realities which at present irritates. Instead it would turn in on itself, as a gathered community of the committed – sacramental, charismatic or scripturally fundamentalist – a community with a clear identity and frontier, far removed intellectually and in its daily concerns from the greater part of the rest of society. To take such a direction would be, I believe, un-Catholic and un-Anglican, though it could claim New Testament credentials and to seem an almost necessary response to an increasingly Godless world. What has Athens to do with Jerusalem? Back to the Catacombs. It is a tempting stance and one which appeals to the all-or-nothing enthusiast in many of us, particularly if we are young. For the Church of England this was, hitherto, not an option. Today it is starting to become one. Yet tempting as this could seem, I believe the church absolutely must avoid the Scylla of sectarianism at least as much as the Charybdis of heritageism.

Against heritageism the Church must remain first and foremost an *Ecclesia*, a fellowship of loving care, of people bound together, not by the care of buildings but by a common spiritual purpose. It has no future without a faith focussed upon the memory of Jesus and a hope in the Living God; a faith and a hope which still provide a way of life and a pattern of values which say something to the world which the world needs but does not of itself accept, a way of life sacramentally shown forth by the celebration of the eucharist and its sharp concluding 'Ite, missa est': Go forth, out of this supportive atmosphere of congregation and (maybe) building, back to society.

Against sectarianism the church must go on hearkening to that 'back to society'. However hard the times may be, however low its membership may fall, however little society may care to heed it, the church for its part cannot abdicate the sense of public responsibility it has borne for so long. It is not just a matter of the historic church of this country rightly turning away from a millennium or more of public and political concern, the role for which St Dunstan exactly one thousand years ago may stand, perhaps better than anyone, in the binding together of the ecclesiastical and the civil. It is rather that while Christianity in its origins stood remarkably free of political structure, it never stood for the outright rejection of political concern as unworthy of the religious. You must not give too much to Caesar but you must not give him nothing either. You may look on the Empire with the eyes of Romans 13 or with the eyes of Revelation 13, but probably best with a bit of both, for both are canonical. The story relates Jesus to Chief Priest and to Herod, to temple, to tax, to the killing of the prophets; above all to a judgment upon the crying contrast of rich and poor. To the form of public concern appropriate to a particular situation, we can sit easily enough: many forms have existed and been appropriate in different ages, but over the continuance of that underlying concern itself, one cannot compromise. The Christian tradition does not separate the religious from the secular. It claims its right and duty to prophesy across the board. Everything in culture and in politics, in economics and sex is part of God's world. Nothing is irrelevant to the New Adam.

We do not know the shape of the future. It would be foolish to prognosticate rather specifically that Britain and the world will be such and such by the year 2010 and then to lay plans for the church accordingly; so many buildings, so many archdeacons, so many bottles of altar wine! What matters most are the concerns that should remain dominant and one thing which, for the church, should never be dominant are concerns about itself and its own organization. Yes, there may be far fewer full-time priests. Yes, something may have to be done about financial responsibility for a great many buildings before then. The Christian community which has been through so many centuries and phases of clericalization is moving back into a more and more laicized form. It has for so long been effectively identified with the clergy that a vast decline both of the clergy and of the clarity of any sort of clergy-laity divide must inevitably look like a decline, almost a disintegration, of the church. Yet it may well be that the decline of the clergy is the *sine qua non* for the rebirth of the phoenix. The more the church hangs on to a mediaeval concept of clergy the more it must decay, the more it recognizes the theological groundlessness and modern social irrelevance of the clergy/laity distinction, the more it may live. Probably the church really will be more a matter of basic communities – worshipping and thinking groups, far smaller and more intimate than most present parishes, meeting less formally, sharing ideas more deliberately. How far is the present parish a genuinely thinking group at all? Many more parish churches may become redundant, but cathedrals, I suspect, may still be very useful – precisely as a counterpoise for sectarian tendencies. The cathedral, hopefully conceived in its functions far more ecumenically than at present, should stand as focal point for the visibility both of the wider church and of the church-for-society: the integration in its still central grandeur within the modern city of the religious with the socio-political.

All this, however, presumes that society itself proceeds onwards on a more or less even keel. Will it? Maybe not. Maybe a Russian-American entente will not really bring peace to the world, or prevent some tiny fanatical group from setting off a nuclear holocaust, or again prevent a more extended, but irretrievable, ecological collapse of the planet. Maybe we are, very nearly, the last generation. It could be. In which case, if the world is to go down into darkness, it still needs in its last hours a soothing hand, a voice that still speaks in faith of the possibility of hope. It will still need a caring church.

Maybe, to the contrary, the yuppies (and we have most of us, these days, in the West, a lot of the yuppy in us) are here to enjoy a long dazzling summer. If so, there is need more than ever for someone to speak out prophetically the deception of the image, the hollowness of this never-had-it-so-good view of human beatitude. And there will be those around us who are not yuppies. The poor will always be with you. It is better to give than to receive. It is very hard to see how there are not going to be a great many people here and abroad who are blatantly left out from the Big Deal of tomorrow's affluence. The church is for all, but Christ's preference and its preference is not for Dives but for Lazarus. If the world of the future is to be ruled by yuppies for the sake of yuppies but increasingly populated by Ethiopian famine victims and the homeless of our own inner cities, then the future of Christ's church within such a world ought to be far more in terms of the latter than the former. A yuppy world does not really want to know about a non-yuppy world. It will be, perhaps, the chief public duty of the church of the future to ensure that it should not plead ignorance.

Perhaps. It could be. It is not determined, not externally. The church will be what the church – under God, strengthened by the spirit, in fidelity to the memory of Jesus – makes of itself day by day. It may again and again be swimming against the tide. It may be easier far just to give up – to settle for heritageism or sectarianism, or just to believe no more. But it would be sad if that happens, very sad indeed for our great-grandchildren, a loss irretrievable.

Cities and Gods: On Faith in the City

> Great is the Lord and greatly to be praised
>   in the city of our God!
> His holy mountain, beautiful in elevation,
>   is the joy of all the earth,
> Mount Zion, in the far north,
>   the city of the great king.
> Within her citadels God
>   has shown himself a sure defence.
>
> Walk about Zion, go round about her,
>   number her towers.
> Consider well her ramparts,
>   go through her citadels;
> that you may tell the next generation
>   that this is God.   (Psalm 48)

It might not seem too misguided to look upon the whole vast biblical narrative, and much subsequent Christian writing as well, as one stupendous epic, a Tale of Two Cities: Jerusalem, the holy city of God, upon the one hand, 'Babylon the great, she who made all nations drink the wine of her impure passion' (Revelation 14.8), upon the other. Long after the historical Babylon had ceased to matter in the least to Jew or Christian, and long after the historical Jerusalem had ceased to matter all that much to Christians at least, the symbolism of the two cities lives on, and new Babylons continue to be denounced, new Zions, new Jerusalems continue to be built in Europe, America, Africa and elsewhere. The names have come to symbolize a warfare of the spirit, a vision of the end-time, the security of a spiritual home, a model even for ethical and political interpretation, always seemingly renewing a sense of warfare, a dichotomy, a dualism between heavenly and earthly, good and evil, the holy and the profane.

Yet the Bible is not in its vast complexity really as simplistic as that, and in the perplexities of our own time – in which we still, albeit a little desperately, seek for faith in the city, yet sense that towns, in which we once thought maybe we had gone some way towards building Jerusalem around spires and towers, have instead more the appearance of Babylon – it may be helpful to begin by exploring a little the deep ambiguities that have always existed in the city/God relationship. When occasionally some harassed citizen of the late twentieth-century world looks again at the Bible – could there, after all, be guidance, there? What is most important is that she or he should not be offered a cop-out, a credulous escape-hole – whether nostalgic or millenarian – from today's predicament.

The city is mankind's characteristic home and achievement – not where we start but where we arrive. As humanity congregates together, shaping and reshaping a vast civic artefact, domestic, commercial, artistic, academic, pleasure-seeking, the myriad expression of our collective industries, imaginings, whims, aspirations across generations, it can only integrate the endlessly diverse through men and women sharing something of a common understanding of themselves and their destiny, a sense of good and evil, a common will, an ideology. It is inconceivable that such a subtly inter-involved complexity, a bubbling organism like a hugely diversified ant-hill or bee-hive, could shape itself in all its uniqueness and come to greatness without the unifying and urging-on force of a shared and imaginatively creative belief system. That is as much a Durkheimian conclusion as a religious one.

The odd myth of the building of the city of Babel to be found in Genesis 11 is not a bad point at which to begin. The supposition of the story is that the city was a human achievement made possible by a great gathering of people in one place with a common purpose and a single language. Should such a great leap forward be pleasing to God? The city's building ends when they are scattered geographically and linguistically. A single language is not far different from a single religion – each provides a common medium of meaning, interpretation and communication. Out of the intensity of such intelligent sharing grows a city.

Of course, one biblical theology might be that man in his pride makes the earthly city – Babel, Babylon or whatever. Only God makes the heavenly city, his city, Jerusalem. The dilemma 'God *or* man' is one which the Bible wrestles with continuously and only with 'God made man' will it in principle be resolved. Nothing is made only by God. Jerusalem is, after all, David's city as well as God's, and the building of the temple comes quite late in its history. Like every other city, it has to be a place of buying and selling, of a diversity of trades, of rich and poor, of public work and private enterprise. In point of fact it is also a city of sin, in which temple and holy law can themselves become tools of exploitation, so that the historical Jerusalem turns out to be only too like other cities – Tyre, Moab, Edom, Damascus: whatever sins can be found elsewhere, are to be found here too. Amos makes the point with painful explicitness. That winsome city of God, the subject of so many passionately devoted psalms, is a city in which justice is not done, in which shady deals are the order of the day, in which the rich grow richer and the poor poorer.

So Jerusalem, whose towers and ramparts seemed the very proof of God's power and presence, the unique city of God, standing up in glorious contrast with all other cities, becomes in the grey light of day, an unholy Jerusalem, as condemnable as any. But then – if still more tentatively – they become as Jerusalem. Even – and especially – Babylon, the most infamous of all. It seems to be Jeremiah who here pioneers the intellectual revolution: a faithful, good-living Jew can inhabit Babylon much as he inhabited Jerusalem. Thus Jeremiah wrote to the exiles: 'Build houses and live in them; plant gardens and eat their produce . . . seek the welfare of the city (Babylon) . . . and pray to the Lord on its behalf, for in its welfare, you will find your welfare' (Jer. 29.5–7). A very basic step in the secularization process is taken at that moment, and with it a step towards the acceptance of pluralism and away from too close an identification of faith and the city. The real city in which one lives and the mystical city to which one spiritually belongs can henceforth be divided, despite many subsequent attempts of Jewish nationalists – or later again Christian or Islamic nationalists – to reunite them. From now on one may be a Jew in faith but live in Babylon and pray for Babylon. One may preach to Ninevah. God may send prophets to them all. He may forgive them all. He may punish them all. He has, clearly, distanced himself from any one. The 'City of God' is ceasing to be localized – that is, then, already true for post-exilic Judaism as well as being, of course, a taken-for-granted presupposition of Christianity: 'Not on this mountain, nor in Jerusalem, but in spirit and in truth' (John 4.21–23). Not in Rome, then, nor Lourdes, nor London. Of course the Christian world could not quite live up to that. The mediaeval ideal came very near to re-identifying kingdom and church in a very precise territorial and institutional way. And we have never quite got over that either, which makes it all the more important to insist as we struggle with the debris of too many legacies, that the mediaeval one is not in fact the biblical and Christian one, but just a bewitching misreading of the former.

And yet, wholly to dissociate the city of faith from the temporal/ physical city could not be biblical or Christian either. The kingdom of God is not just in the future, it is here with tares in it. The kingdom of God is not wholly different from the church. The church is not wholly different from the political community. There must at least be a continual sense of provisional symbolic sacramentalizations of a reality far beyond them, and these sacramentalizations need to be as much political, civic and artistic as ecclesiastical or self-evidently religious. So long as we recognize their provisionality it is not wholly wrong to re-erect our pilgrimage centres, to build our new Jerusalem again and again in Rome, in Lourdes, in England's green and pleasant land, in strange little villages up and down Africa. But these, of course, derive their symbolic validity not just, or chiefly, from ecclesiastical ownership or liturgical cycle, but from the experience of a living community of faith and love and hope: that is what makes Iona or Taizé or some house of Mother Teresa's nuns a new Jerusalem set in space and time. So too, at the other end of human experience, there are, in an equally recognizable way, new Babylons – a Devil's Island, an Auschwitz, a Gulag Archipelago.

Between Taizé and Auschwitz there is an immense distance, and one may argue that the ends of this spectrum are so remote, the large intervening area so vast, that one can hardly throw light upon the middle by consideration of the extremes. I am not so sure. The message of Babel is that one cannot have a city without a common language, a shared ideology – even if that ideology be an evil one. Try as one may to stimulate a wider appreciation of the values of pluralism, unless beneath the pluralism there be a sense of common human community, a sharing of values which transcend the pluralism, will the city not inevitably go the way of Belfast or Beirut? The idea that such a sense just naturally and inevitably exists is simply incorrect. Certainly our western and English culture traditionally strove to see its city as, in a unified way, a city of God – the cathedral spire in its midst. The city of London makes no topographical sense without St Paul's at its focal point. There was plenty of place too, pluralistically, for subordinate gods, like Lord Nelson on his high pillar, or the Stock Exchange, or the corpse of Bentham in University College – though the effort was made too to draw these minor deities where possible together within the walls of Westminster Abbey. This was no very pure religion but a strange mix of Bible and mediaeval inheritance, the monarchy, Scrooge, Dick Whittington; and it could as well be a cruel and perverted religion, when it isolated and exiled the Jews, or turned on Lollard, Papist or witch. But it did follow the law of Babel in linking human achievement with civil community held together by a common language and blessed, à la Jerusalem, with a central temple served in their different ways by priest and merchant alike, and it included the alms house and the jury of common men to judge even the poor. The Christendom ideal, the concept of the Established Church of the nation providing a broad authenticating framework of belief behind public action and civic organisation, that ideal was wobbling unhappily for long but it has only completely and manifestly crumbled as a working reality with our time, whether that crumbling be judged liberating or disastrous. It was seen as a glorious liberation in the characteristic thinking of the sixties, the optimistic lauding of the arrival of *The Secular City* by such as Harvey Cox. In San Francisco California offered the world a new, uninhibited model. Not, of course, that this new model did not carry with it something of a new language, the very ideology of Western secularism in all its glitter, the vision of Hollywood – the saints replaced by stars, perfect in health, beauty and the attainment of happiness. Evelyn Waugh's biting account of it, *The Loved One*, was a prophetic little book. The revelation of the pathetic life and death of Marilyn Monroe betrayed in due course the truth of that pseudo-gospel and today San Francisco is, to its misfortune, more than any other place, the city of AIDS.

The ideology of the Hollywood of Marilyn and Ronald Reagan and their colleagues, even supplemented by Disneyland, Melodyland, and what have you, is only too obviously inadequate to reflect and cement, à la Durkheim, the city of today. It is a solvent of more serious ideologies but does not replace them. For a little while the new secularist ideology of beautiful affluence might make almost enough sense in Los Angeles, but it can make very little in Brixton and still less in Cairo, Calcutta or Beirut. The modern city may be mobilized effectively enough for a moment or two by Marilyn here, Hitler there, the Ayatollah somewhere else, but in most places and times one is conscious on the contrary of a cumulative disintegration: the collapse of cheaply-built multi-storey blocks in Cairo or Mexico City; the million strong prostitute trade of all the great towns of the third world; the dread of being out at night in almost any major American city; the way town houses are being turned into mini-fortresses in places like Lusaka; the riot at Broadwater Farm; the sheer uncontrollability of a modern city; the ever more obvious absence of an appealable-to common belief system.

No large city can operate healthily without a very real measure of pluralism – the refusal to admit that led straight to the Inquisition. Even the empires of the ancient world saw this – as did, of course, the British Empire. One sees it in the letter of Cyrus, King of Persia, at the beginning of the Book of Ezra, ordering the rebuilding of the temple in Jerusalem. What had been *the* faith of the city becomes *one* faith in the city and the city – logically at least – becomes in principle itself tolerant but faithless. Yet if the city wholly submits to that logic, its own survival is bound to be in question for it will have lost its principle of unification and cohesion. Its very existence requires at least some sort of acceptable umbrella above the pluralism. That really is the nub of the modern problem. The modern city has privatized faith, but without a living civic faith things fall apart. In our apparently post-religious, post-Christian, even post-Marxist age, the gadgets of society, ever more bewilderingly potent silicon chips, are in seemingly inexhaustible supply, but the glue to hold society itself together is almost visibly disintegrating. The option of the urban guerrilla, undividedly committed to some essentially private faith or ideology or minority cause, whether tragic or potty, is proving more and more appealing, because there is less and less of a shared language in which to communicate the folly of such ways. The umbrella – even Mao's umbrella – is today exceedingly leaky.

It would be foolish to consider this country's problems of both city decay and the decay of faith in the city without continually relating them, as I have been trying to do, to a far vaster and more horrific panorama of civic geography. Consider Bombay or Manila, Kinshasa or Nairobi. In sheer human terms they – not London or Leeds – are the focus points of humanity and its predicament today. The drama of faith and pluralism is being fought out most evidently at this moment in Beirut. Such cities have, all of them, taken over a Western civic model and various layers of Western culture, religion, political ideology – all more or less in tatters. But they have not much else to work with other than a resurgence of one or another bitter fundamentalism or equally bitter nationalism or some maimed splinter off the Marxist tree, together, of course, with the gun.

When Augustine, in later middle age, faced the collapse of ordered imperial civilization around him in the years subsequent to the sack of Rome in 410, he had to deal with the charge that all this was due to the abandonment of Rome's traditional gods: they had seen Rome safe and glorious through centuries of crisis and expansion, the mediterranean-wide pursuit of law and order. Now they had been abandoned, Christianity hurriedly adopted, and ruin had followed. It was to face such a charge that Augustine wrote the twenty-two books of *The City of God*. Here again was a tale of two cities – the city of God and the earthly city, but he wished to detach them both from any too precise historical incarnation. The rise and fall of empires is not to be explained, he argued, by religious but by secular causes. Rome was not protected by its gods, nor abandoned by Christianity's, that is not how things work. The city of God is identified with no state and will subsist through all. Augustine is here clearly in the line of Jeremiah. Each was facing a crisis of his state and each responded by a measure of disentangling of the religious from the secular. He was right, but was he not wrong too? A Durkheimian perspective might make us suspect that the abandonment by Rome's emperor of Rome's traditional religion must almost certainly have had a far more disruptive effect than Augustine was willing to admit. The religious, in fact, is a decisive part of the secular. Again, Augustine is misleading in suggesting at times that the earthly city can be explained in merely selfish terms. No, even temporarily abiding, city can be. The more a city sees itself in merely self-seeking, market economy terms, the more danger of disintegration must it be in. The earthly city is intrinsically required, for its very existence, to seek peace, the best peace it can, and no such peace is conceivable without conviction and faith that go far beyond the immediately self-seeking. Augustine recognized (again not unlike Jeremiah) that the peace of the two cities actually overlaps (*De Civitate Dei* XIX.17) and this is important for them both. Those who believe in a city of God cannot ignore the need for peace of the earthly city. They cannot collectively withdraw from the responsibility of pursuing the latter into cave or monastery. They share an obligation to be concerned with the state, with justice, with the common pursuit of peace. But those who see themselves as primarily concerned to build up the earthly city – and, quite especially, the earthly city in its most complex forms – can equally not ignore the relationship between what they seek and the pursuit of higher things only possible in terms of a common language of meaning and value. If they do ignore these things, they are cutting their own throats.

This, of course, does not and cannot imply a return to the sense of a sacred city. All our history bars the way to that, including our religious history. Jeremiah and Augustine point towards a far more complex theology of the provisionality of all temporal forms. Nevertheless, within a perspective of the provisional, we have still – especially in a time of marked disintegration – to remember that every city stands willy-nilly somewhere on a line between Taizé and Auschwitz. Whatever we do in regard to the city will move things, just a few inches, in one direction or the other – towards, or away from, a civilization of love. And that movement will depend at least as much upon the engendering of a sense of collective civic faith as of the material provision of particular resources. It is only too clear that our age is as far as can be from one of large public religious commitment. The vast erosion of confidence in priest and belief system of any sort is obvious – as clear as the need of it. We cannot think today of even provisional cities of God, only perhaps of stimulating into new life some sort of anonymous Christianity, stimulated and led on by quite little groups of faith, 'basic communities' of believers not closed off from the mass of the city but rather wombs of a new wider consciousness. We can all of us look into the sky and see Lord Nelson far above us, now nicely cleaned and newly photographed. His symbolic value – the sense of history and place and the sheer particularity of all that is on earth worth loving – is certainly not to be spurned; but at least some of us need to be able to look up, at least in our dreams, and still see far beyond Nelson, 'the traffic of Jacob's ladder, pitched between Heaven and Charing Cross', or look down and see 'Christ walking on the water, not of Gennesareth but Thames'.

The prophet Jonah was sent to preach not to Jerusalem, but to London, that is to say Nineveh. It was a great and wicked city, but Jonah was reluctant to take on the job and fled away. The Lord seized him, arranging for a whale to swallow him up, until he agreed to do as he was told. So Jonah proclaimed, walking through the city streets, 'Yet forty days and Nineveh shall be destroyed'. The people listened. They put on sack cloth and ashes, God relented, and Jonah was annoyed. 'Did I not say this would happen? I knew you were a soft and merciful God and would never really do it. Why have you put me to all this trouble?' To which God replied, 'There are more than a hundred and twenty thousand persons in Nineveh who do not know their right hand from their left'. Now if Jonah's swallowing by the whale is no more than a pleasing story, so is his preaching to the city of London, and its repentance. What stands is the final message – Nineveh is a mess, but behind the sin is an abysmal ignorance. They know not their right hand from their left. That really is God's comment upon us all: Nineveh and Jerusalem and Rome, mediaeval London and modern London, San Francisco and Beirut. It is no new predicament. Never identify the city of God with any earthly city, but never quite separate them either. Never wholly sacralize one spot, nor wholly secularize any other. Pray for the welfare even of Babylon. Even in Dachau find Christ. Realize that the peace of the one city is not separable from the peace of the other, that every sort of real peace depends upon the pursuit of truth and justice, and that both heavenly peace and earthly peace will be best authenticated by nothing more sophisticated than the sound of cheerful laughter. In the words of Zechariah, 'Old men and old women shall again sit in the streets of Jerusalem, each with staff in hand for very age. And the streets of the city shall be full of boys and girls playing in its streets' (Zech 7.4–5). The very old and the very young will be there in the streets, relaxed and playful. Yes. Even in Broadwater Farm. That is what concerned the prophets, what concerned Augustine, in the grimmest of times. It is what faith in the city is all about.

★ 13 ★

On Overcoming Binaries

Set your minds on heavenly things, not on earthly things . . . but
Christ is all, and in all (Colossians 3.1–11).

One aspect of the resurrection faith, stressed both biblically and
liturgically, is that of victory in a two-sided battle. There is here a
conflict of opposites brought out by a binary pattern of symbolism:
life and death, light and darkness, Heavenly things and earthly
things. *Dux vitae mortuus regnat vivus* – as the old Latin sequence of
Easter affirms: the Lord of Life, once dead, now reigns living. Life
has overcome death; the Light has overcome darkness. There was
indeed one form of redemption theology which saw it in terms of a
quite personal battle between Christ and the devil. Faith in the Risen
Christ is the very heart of Christian believing and it remains faith in a
victory of this sort, of the prevailing of good over evil – despite all
appearances to the contrary; and the appearances of Calvary were
convincing enough.

The resurrection faith entailed from the start an on-going
commitment to a struggle of the same sort – a religious and moral
struggle within a world seen in the strongly binary terms required for
battle and victory.

We have seen it expressed very forcibly – and for us perhaps even
somewhat awkwardly – in this text of ours from the Letter to the
Colossians. We must set our minds on the things that are above, not
on the things of earth. We must put to death whatever is earthly in us
– and Paul provides a number of examples: impurity, covetousness,
anger, malice, slander. Only through killing these things will Christ
live in us. Yet one can hardly help thinking that 'the things of earth'

cannot all be so easily dismissed. The binary model is forcing Paul, here as elsewhere, into a rather rhetorical type of simplification.

We should certainly not underestimate the sharpness of conflict which cross and resurrection impose on us. Christianity *is* a very conflictual thing, with this strongly binary sense of good and evil, of acceptance and rejection. The working out of that faith in other lives has stimulated a sense of conflict again and again.

Take some events of just one hundred years ago: the weeks after Easter 1886 in Buganda, the run-up to the great persecution by Kabaka Mwanga. The princess Nalumansi was baptized and married at Easter, though as a princess of the blood she had no business to marry at all. But worse was to follow. She was appointed – as was customary for princesses – guardian of a royal tomb, in this case the Kabaka Jjumbe's. She promptly burnt the traditional relics she found in the guardian's house as 'works of Satan'. Worst of all, when her mother brought her her umbilical cord, something she was traditionally supposed to guard and reverence most devoutly – symbol of the womb she had come from, the whole sacred past of Ganda society – she cut it in pieces and cast them away. That was in May. Hardly three weeks later the bodies of Christians were burning to death on the fires of Namugongo.

Doubtless the princess may appear rash in this stark symbolic repudiation of the beliefs which hitherto had led her and her society, yet sudden conversion from darkness to light, from the Ganda gods, the Balubaale, to Christ, seemed to her to require sharp, symbolic expression. Christ, dead and risen, is set starkly against the kingdom of Satan. If that was battle, so also must our sharing in the faith be.

Or go back three hundred years further, to 1586, and Yorkshire's own most lovable, if obstinate, woman martyr, Margaret Clitheroe, pressed to death in York this very year, four centuries ago – a centenary that Archbishop Habgood and Cardinal Hume have recently been celebrating. Margaret Clitheroe, a butcher's wife, and immensely loved by him as 'the best wife in the world', was killed for giving hospitality to Catholic priests and, at her trial, refusing to plead. So she was pressed to death with the child within her. Remember how clergy of the established church tried to pray with her before her death and she answered them with an absolute 'No': 'I will not say Amen to your prayers and you will not say Amen to mine.' That famous answer has been quoted times without number to justify the refusal of Catholics to pray with Anglicans – and equally has doubtless time and again proved embarrassing for many an ecumenist.

It should not be embarrassing. The resurrection faith requires separations and in those circumstances it seems to me absolutely right in Christian terms for Margaret to refuse to pray with the clerical lacqueys of her persecutors. Set your minds on things that are above, not on earthly things. You have put off the old nature, you have put on the new.

And yet, would it really be right in other, all, or even most circumstances to imitate the Princess or the butcher's wife? Were not the things the former felt compelled to burn in fact worthy objects of reverence, symbols of piety, instigators of a genuine morality? Were not the Anglican prayers, rejected by Margaret Clitheroe, Christian prayers – largely indeed but translations by Cranmer and others of the very prayers of the Roman missal used by the priests she harboured? I recall some twenty years ago in Africa how at one time I used regularly after Sunday Mass on returning to my room to turn to the Book of Common Prayer to read the prayers and lessons of the day – and how often I found they were the very same as those we had just read – still at that time in Latin – in our Tanzanian chapel. For four hundred years the two churches had in fact held to the same collects, and this I found rather moving – especially as almost no one in either church was aware of it. The prayers we were refusing to share nevertheless bound us together in their very objectivity.

I am suggesting then that behind a binary pattern of confrontation which at sharp moments, so reminiscent of cross and resurrection, is certainly required of us, there is at a still deeper level again and again, a unitary pattern, which embraces both sides of a conflict. It is expressed by the final words of our text, 'Christ is all and in all'. We cannot, and often must not, avoid the pain and the struggle of conflict, which a very real actuality of evil requires of us – as it does today with torture, terrorist murder, governmental retaliatory murder and so much more. Faced with all that, we absolutely must not say just 'Tut, tut', be gentlemanly and uncommittal. We have to take sides. We have to say 'I will not say Amen' to the prayers of torturers and bullies. Yet we have also to see that in the longer vision it is equally important to escape from a rigidly confrontatory pattern

– to see how again and again there is an ultimate unity, able to embrace things far more widely than at a time of conflict seems possible. No temptation can be more damaging, or perennially more seductive, for the religious mind than an unrestrained reincarnation of the conflict of good and evil within some current large divide of human loyalty, power and perception: West versus East, capitalism versus communism, even a moralized Marxism versus an immoral capitalism.

I find G. K. Chesterton's *The Man who was Thursday* a pleasing parable of this predicament. It is, you may remember, the story of a policeman who gets into the inner ring of anarchists committed to the overthrow of law and order, named by the days of the week and presided over by the mysterious Sunday. Slowly he discovers that all the other members too are secret policemen and what begins as a terrifying conflict between the forces of anarchy and the forces of law ends when Sunday is revealed as the power who both commissioned the policemen and created the Central Anarchist Council. 'When I saw him from behind I was certain he was an animal and when I saw him in front I knew he was a god' (302). 'It seems so silly', someone complained, 'that you should have been on both sides.'

I am alpha, I am omega – the beginning and end of all things. The immediate sense of enlisting in an army and for a battle engendered by the sharp actuality of the resurrection faith has time and again, and inevitably, produced a sense of sectarian exclusiveness, and of binary values: Puritan versus Cavalier; Evangelical versus Catholic; the religious versus the secular; and on and on. We hardly seem able to cope with issues, even to grow in truth and love, except through taking sides as if we can each only manage a fragment of the truth at any one time, and that in controversial mode. Yet in retrospect we see again and again how the taking of sides, the conflictual element, can narrow the truth for everyone and straighten all our fellowships.

The great moral and spiritual dilemma for us today is how to be ecumenical without being soft, how to take up a position very firmly – and at personal cost – against torture, the bomb, the barrage of official lies to which we are increasingly subjected, racialism . . . and yet to escape yet another holy, sectarian huddle, another captivity within a too binary model of human experience. One of us is a Catholic, one an Evangelical; one a politically minded Christian, one interested in little beyond the parish; one is a Quaker, one a Jesuit.

We must not devalue any of this even though each necessarily involves its own horizons, its limiting frontiers. Without a hard particularity we can each lose our cutting edge. Yet finally we have somehow to see that God, silly as it may seem, is time and again upon both sides, including the apparently less heavenly side. He is even with the old Ganda pagan priest or the erastian York chaplain in 1586; the risen Christ has one body but many members, and the earthly things as well as the heavenly things have to be caught up in him who is all and in all.

⋆ 14 ⋆

Your High Priest, Melchisedek

Quod tibi obtulit summus sacerdos tuus Melchisedech,
sanctum sacrificium, immaculatam hostiam.

That which your high priest Malchisedek offered to you,
a holy sacrifice, an immaculate offering.

Thus does the ancient Roman Canon refer to the mysterious figure
of Melchisedek, king of Salem, described in Genesis in his
encounter with Abraham as 'priest of God most High' (Gen. 14.18).
In later times the author of Psalm 110 referred to him in the context
of what may be seen as a messianic prophecy: 'The Lord has sworn
and will not change his mind, "You are a priest forever after the
order of Melchisedek".' Centuries later again the author of the
Letter to the Hebrews applied these lines to Jesus. Melchisedek, he
declares, was king of peace, he was a priest for ever and superior to
Abraham himself for Abraham offered him tithes. What is clear is
that he stands in principle outwith the Abrahamic tradition and
community of faith. The Roman liturgy canonizes this view just as it
hails Abel – still further back in humanity's common history – as
'your holy servant'. Abel and Melchisedek here stand for human
religion and holiness outside either the Christian or the Jewish
covenant, but both scripture and tradition in the most central and
authoritative of texts recognize them as paradigmatically fully within
the history of salvation. Nothing could be more removed from a
narrow 'salvation by explicit faith in Christ alone' view of the matter,
nothing more symbolic both of the realizable and realized truth of
the assertion that God 'desires all men to be saved' (I Tim. 2.4) but
also of the complexity of the existential and religious model required

to make any real sense of such an assertion when coupled with the claim that 'there is one mediator between God and man, the man Jesus Christ, who gave himself as a ransom for all' (I Tim. 2.5).

The most sensitive, vital and form-deciding issue in Christian mission today, but also maybe in Christian theology and in any formulation whatsoever of Christian identity and self-awareness, is that of the relationship between Christianity and other religions and faiths. We have of late very frequently been told, first, that Christianity was, until recently, utterly exclusivist in regard not only to the uniquely significant position of Jesus within the history of the God-humanity relationship but also in regard to the necessity of personally believing in that position to be 'saved'; second, that a recent breaking out from an 'exclusivist' position into some sort of an 'inclusivist' but still Christ-centred one, constitutes no more than the attempt to rescue a now unbelievable doctrine by a series of increasingly unconvincing 'epicycles' – additional devices thought out to prop up the original, but now tottering doctrine; and, third, that the theological issue of the relationship between Christianity and other religions can now only be convincingly resolved by jettisoning the 'myth of Christian uniqueness', leaping across a (perhaps only recently discovered) Rubicon in a Copernican manner and thus coming to hold, instead, that Christianity is, in John Hick's words, but 'one of a plurality of contexts of salvation – contexts, that is to say, within which the transformation of human existence from self-centredness to God – or Reality-centredness is occurring'.[1] That sounds a sensible enough hypothesis from a religious studies standpoint and – in a rather more watered down form – from a wholly secularist standpoint. The continual Christian claim to 'absoluteness' is, and must be, a scandal to the non-believer and an impossible ground-ethic for any 'neutral' department of religious studies. But it is not from such standpoints that we have here to evaluate it. Hick's starting point, both personally and by continued necessity in the formulation of his argument, is that of Christian theology, and it is by the latter's internal criteria that the plausibility of his appeal for the crossing of a Rubicon must primarily be examined. It is, after all, only the Christian believer and theologian

[1]John Hick, 'The Non-Absoluteness of Christianity', in *The Myth of Christian Uniqueness*, ed. John Hick and Paul F. Knitter, SCM Press and Orbis Books 1987, p.23.

who can cross this particular Rubicon, everyone else having done so long ago without probably ever even noticing that the river actually existed! Should we do so? I am myself doubtful whether, if Christianity did in fact adopt his approach, it would really have any intellectual justification for surviving at all. It would certainly have abandoned that which has always been most central both to its theology and to its worship and wider life, especially its missionary activity (and Christianity has always been, par excellence, a missionary religion), the assertion of a universal and ultimate significance in religious and moral terms of the person of Jesus of Nazareth. Is there, however, some internal necessity within the structure or on-going thrust of Christian belief to either require or at least render underlyingly consistent and appropriate such a revolution? Or again – as Christian belief is purportedly an interpretative key to the whole of reality, and especially all human experience – are there significant elements within human experience hitherto overlooked by Christian theology which – when properly appreciated by the latter – simply fail to be plausibly interpreted by a more traditional Christian model and almost require reinterpretation in this way? Only too clearly, a positive answer to that question is easy enough to give: Hindu, Buddhist, Sikh, Muslim and much other religious experience was indeed negated, treated as worthless and even diabolical, or at least ignored, by a vast amount of exclusivist Christian theology and the common beliefs of numberless Christians, mediaeval or Victorian. It still is by many. Anyone brought up within such a tradition and then coming face to face with something of the riches and depths of non-Christian religious experience, will rightly revolt against it and while probably continuing to believe it to constitute the undeniable central attitude of Christianity *vis à vis* other faiths, may only too sensibly and easily conclude that the one honourable way to escape from an intolerably smug and ill-informed judgment upon the religion and morals of the majority of humankind must be to leap into a full-blooded pluralism.

It is at this point that Melchisedek comes into his own, for if, on the contrary, exclusivism of the sort we have been concerned with, while exceedingly wide-spread within both Catholic and Protestant traditions, represents in truth by no means the central and normative Christian understanding of world religions, but rather a mediaeval aberration taken over and hardened by classical evangelical Protestantism, then that which has a better claim to be central and normative should at least be seriously pondered before it be cast away. If one starts with a cut-and-dried exclusivism as normative for Christianity and then sees it as having been rather hastily modified in quite recent times by an 'inclusivism', formulated perhaps rather individualistically in such terms as those of Rahner's 'anonymous Christian', then one may well judge both the norm and its latter-day modification so profoundly unsatisfactory, that there appears no alternative other than one of instant immersion in the waters of a newly discovered Rubicon and emergence from the waters blessed with the vision of ultimate pluralism.

But if, instead, one starts with an integrally inclusivist model and inclusivist not so much of individuals as of priesthoods, religions, faiths, covenants, then one may well judge the honest believer's present predicament rather differently. The foundational model – though, admittedly, it is one which almost every Christian theology has failed to analyse with adequate seriousness or subtlety – is the relationship between the Abrahamic-Mosaic covenants upon the one hand and the 'new' covenant in Jesus upon the other. One type of Christian, the Marcionite, has always wanted to reject the former completely, thereby insulating Christian faith within a revelational vacuum; the opposite type has wanted instead so to identify the two, effectively imposing upon the former covenant the notes claimed for the latter that a very simplistic notion of a unified 'Bible' is created, thereby eliminating the inherent tension between two dispensations and two scriptures. A sound theology needs rather to assert an ongoing distinction between old and new, the authenticity of the old as divine revelation and road to holiness, truth and salvation, and nevertheless the power of the new to subsume it into a definitive dispensation which surpasses without condemning it. Diversity cannot finally be defended in terms of an unordered pluralism but rather of a structured pattern of multiple fulfilment which, within the onward trajectory of history, can both affirm and deny elements of earlier systems, upon which it profoundly depends but beyond which it is enabled to advance.

One of the most decisive insights of early Christians was, not any invalidation of the central Jewish tradition of salvation, but the recognition that this tradition – while in many important ways unique

– was yet at the same time a paradigm for innumerable other localized experiences of salvation. Thus Peter perceived that 'God shows no partiality and in every nation any one who fears him and does what is right is acceptable to him' (Acts 10.35). 'What you do not know and yet worship' declared Paul, 'this I proclaim to you' (Acts 17.23). Doubtless they did not greatly enlarge upon this recognition of the universality of contexts of salvation prior to the 'new' covenant, so excited were they by the proclamation of the latter, but indubitably it was there. And that is what the canonical status of Melchisedek and Abel is all about. The great church of the people of God did not begin with Jesus, as it did not begin with Abraham. It begins with the beginning. It is an 'Ecclesia ab Abel', an almost infinitely varied 'ecclesia ecclesiarum' of beliefs and traditions.

Is this not, after all, the religious pluralism of Hick, simply poking its head up rather earlier in Christian history? I do not think so. You cannot conclude with an assertion of pluralism in this or in any area of genuine seriousness. Once you insist that Thomism, Cartesianism, Marxism and Logical Positivism are all to be hailed as simply different ways of expressing philosophical conviction, you reduce the lot to insignificance. Once you declare that as between the physics of Aristotle, Newton and Einstein, it is wrong to assert any absolute superiority, you stand outside the whole exercise of the physicist and, in terms of contemporary significance, you trivialize it. At the very least, you move from the role of participant to that of an external historian and phenomenologist. Philosopher and physicist has each in the end to be committed to a unitary view, not closed but equally not functionally pluralistic, in terms of which other views as well as the phenomena investigated must be explained. The believer and the theologian cannot function otherwise. Christian faith and its interpretation is not a closed, unchanging system, but it is not a basically incoherent system either, despite never excluding massive use of non-Christian insight, experience and text. On the contrary, while never, from apostolic times on, hesitating in its commitment to preach a universalist rendering of Jesus, it has both treated the Hebraic scriptures as its principal written source of divine inspiration and immediate context for that rendering, and yet further contextualized the Mosaic covenant within a still wider pattern of Christianity's religious continuity with the experience of humankind.

We are not able to formulate Christianity quite as our parents, still less our grandparents, formulated it. But in reality that has always been true of Christian faith and may well be seen as strength rather than weakness. We may, of course, find the pressures of our own age too great and abandon the Lord Christ, as Thor and Woden, as Mithraism, were abandoned. We may do it regretfully but inescapably, as altogether too inadequate to cope with today's intellectual and moral needs, unable to offer any more a coherent and believable account of either beginnings or endings, creation and its inner logic upon the one hand, an intellectually convincing human eschatology congruent with gospel and creed upon the other. In which case we may replace it, explicitly or implicitly, by some form of Buddhism, by a liberal Judaism or Islam, or – still more probably – just by a secular, materialist agnosticism, a little nostalgically sympathetic to the values and rituals fostered by religion in more 'primitive' times. But it is simply not intellectually possible to replace it by a non-judgmental pluralism. In terms of seriousness that is not on. Once we do so we are reducing the whole thing to the level of eating leeks on St David's Day and haggis on St Andrew's. And behind such trivializing one will inevitably detect the covert form of a new, essentially single model of interpretation – for pluralism is always ultimately justified in terms of some higher non-pluralism.

Yet it may also be that, undaunted, we do remain convinced that Christianity retains resources, human and divine, beyond any other deposit of received wisdom, and this not accidentally but from the very being of the Lord we reverence. We may remain convinced that no other world religion has ever equalled its intellectual and rational flexibility, its capacity to stimulate both mind and heart, philosopher, ascetic, social worker, its capacity to be all things to all men, its geographical but also spiritual universalism. These are large claims and here unprovable. They are in part, I would hold, demonstrable to the sophisticated historical mind, part more a matter of a believer's vision. They will not facilely convince the outsider, nourished by some other tradition, but they may none the less be morally adequate to undergird the knowing, loving and living of the thoughtful believer. Christianity may still – for the philosopher, the physicist, and the social scientist alike – provide the least flawed and most creative of spiritual interpretations of the predicament of existence. If that is so, and for those of us for whom it is so, it remains as necessary as it ever did, faced with a world often near despair, the aimlessness of unmeaning, to enunciate our *evangelium*: good news as unexpected and implausible as it ever was. But it is never, never an *evangelium* of the straight denial of any good, created by God or fashioned by humankind beyond the ecclesiastical and Christian frontier. Any such Barthian or Kraemerian denial, if such has been made, must be profoundly repudiated as essentially sub-Christian. The Christian covenant is not to be set against the covenants humanity in its great need has forged or been granted as tools of hope, meaning and moral support. It is, instead, supremely a covenant of covenants, embracing all that is good, from the rainbow covenant of Noah on, a rainbow unified yet crossing the sky of hope and faith in varied colour, a vision briefly glimpsed but potent in memory.

If, amid the myriad problems of a Christian believer in today's world, we are still able to hold to this view of things comprising both finality and comprehensiveness, then we will I think be helped in doing so by pondering the insistence of scripture and canon that Melchisedek, priest-king of some remote, long-lost little middle eastern society should be placed beside Abraham 'our patriarch' as nothing less than God's 'high priest'. To his name, Father, Son and Holy Spirit, be all glory and praise. Amen.

15

Theology and Praxis

I am sending you out like sheep among wolves (Matt. 10.16).

Faith by itself, if it has no works, is dead (James 2.17).

It seems appropriate that an end of session service of the Divinity Faculty should somehow turn on the hinge that relates theory and praxis. An academic faculty cannot but be immediately preoccupied with theory – with the examination, elaboration and discussion of ideas, of books and their contents, the rational analysis of extended systems of thought: all of which can function, and even apparently flourish, just about as well whether or not those involved are actually doing anything about it outside the lecture room and the magic circle of debate.

Yet all this is strangely paradoxical in that the method of the theological faculty has by doing this effectively turned the central content and thrust of its very subject – Christian belief and commitment – on its head. For in Christianity both as a matter of historic fact and as a matter of on-going dynamic necessity, praxis comes well before and above theory. This is obvious enough if you consider how relatively late in the life of the early church came the writing of any sort of Christian scripture, and still later the elaboration of that scripture into any more formal system of theology. At the start there was quite clearly a doing: a sequence of events handed on in memory, so that at the heart of Christian life is the celebration of a memorial, itself a doing and a reminder of something done – 'Do this in remembrance of me'. Not a theology of the eucharist but a doing of manual actions: Eat, drink and remember what I have done. As often as you eat this bread and drink the cup, you proclaim the Lord's death.

At the beginning of it all then there was a praxis – actual concrete liberating behaviour, not an idea, not a philosophy. This concrete liberating behaviour was even, we claim in faith, no less than divine: The divine praxis of merciful salvation made human, made historic, made singular in time and space in Jesus. It all begins in particular events – passion, death, resurrection, singular moments of teaching – not in theories and philosophies, and if one departicularizes, demythologizes, those events into general theories and spiritual philosophies, they may remain interesting enough but they must lose their character of historic decisiveness, their complete moral compulsion for the individual. Ceasing to start with the authority of praxis, they cease to require imperatively the praxis of response. What is crucial to Christianity and to its specific claim upon mind and heart to absolute allegiance is precisely this: the historic and singular incarnation places praxis first. It asserts that the most absolute norms available to man are to be found not in law nor in philosophy but in historical factuality, once for all normative events to be gripped by that most characteristic human faculty, the memory. Christian faith is not commitment to a timeless theoria, it is commitment through a vivifying memory to a historic praxis such as must produce in its holders a comparable contemporary praxis. A faith, as James so rightly said, that 'has no works, is dead'.

Such must be the case and such was the case. The challenging memory of eye-witness to particular Acts of God and its passing on in 'tradition' to later generations, person to person, is primary, a theoretical elaboration of that remembered praxis is extremely secondary. The early Christian certainly applied the doctrine of Karl Marx well enough: the point is not to understand the world but to change it.

Nevertheless neither the Christian nor the Marxist can banish 'theory' – both indeed have shown extreme susceptibility to its attractions. And not really surprisingly. It is human nature to think, analyse, interpret; the more important things are, the more we are committed by an imperative of our nature to think them out in all their pros and cons. We cannot as men claim supreme significance for the praxis we believe in, and not submit it to every discipline of the intellect we can bring to bear. The Word of God commands our all: we do not respect it if we do not bring all our intelligence to bear upon it. The Divinity Faculty is intended to do just this, a fitting labour of love for the thinking disciple, a necessary fruit of human fidelity to the seriousness of faith. Its temptations are no less grave for being almost built-in to an institution itself so obviously right. The more we take academic theology with due seriousness, the more likely that it subvert the intrinsic relationship between theory and praxis, in quietly assuming primacy for the former, in relegating the latter to a distinct and rather technical department. The speculative study of theology may come to patronize or just render insignificant the actual business of discipleship – or the two become so separate that it no longer signifies anything to the academic that the Kittel of the Wörterbuch may have been an anti-Semitic Nazi or Tillich an irresponsible womanizer. The world of speculative, scholarly, academic theology becomes an independent self-justifying entity with its own rules, its discreet silences, its in-games to control the behaviour and value judgments of those belonging to it.

Participation in a world dominated not only by the academic in-game but also by the class structure which almost necessarily goes with it, is not likely to prepare one for mission; for witnessing to and serving a freedom and a fellowship which must always be breaking beyond the structures and frontiers of society; for setting off in fact as sheep among wolves, somehow as classless as Christ. A submission to the divine praxis of redemptive liberation which overturns all the categories and cosy respectabilities of this world, which challenges class stratification and the primacy of theory over practice, and thus sets out constitutionally against the accepted order of this world, is exactly that which establishes one as a sheep among wolves, for wolves are really those committed not so much by malevolence as by a sheer state of belonging to the structures of oppression, alienation and cruel behaviour in the world around them.

When James distinguishes faith and works he is really contrasting a religious relationship which does not bear secular fruit but is justified simply in its own terms, with a living commitment which overturns the classifications of this world, which treats the poor man in shabby clothing as it treats the Executive Director and the Cabinet Minister, which actually does feed the hungry rather than invite the already well-fed to an extra helping of caviare.

A theology which does not feed the hungry and protect the oppressed is profitless and indeed positively destructive of the gospel, however many Wörterbuchs it produces, however many distinguished chairs it fills.

By your fruits you will be known. Those who leave the Divinity Faculty this year and go in some way into the ministry of the church should ask themselves with great seriousness 'Are we going as wolves or as sheep?' And if you are a sheep, don't put on a wolf's clothing – for what you appear to be you will become.

The world is a world of wolves, that is the point of the verse, and it is very hard to be a sheep in it – to be something so vastly different, so unprotected, so vulnerable. Personal and public commitment to the priority in understanding, and importance over all else, of the divine praxis with at its heart the trial, cross and resurrection of Our Lord Jesus Christ does indeed render one very vulnerable. And yet singularly strong too. It is not a theory, not a theology, and if we put it forward as a theory we might rightly dismiss it as improbable and implausible and unacademic because unscientific – academically respectable theses are not built on single events of the remote past and such events, when they appear, are politely demythologised. But we do not move from theory to praxis, but from a praxis which has gripped us precisely in its singularity, through its understanding and back to its implementation, and it is here and only here that we have to start.

Certainly four years in a Faculty of Theology are not too long to spend, if they enable us not to succumb to the primacy of theory and an orthodoxy of demythologization, but confidently to throw the ball back, to face the world with the awkwardness of the gospel in its own terms not the world's, to rejoice at the sheep's clothing we still have on our backs. A Faculty which embraces the truth of its own evangelical insignificance as academe, but – while robbing the Greeks of their theories – still points not to theory but to praxis, to the deeds of God; a Faculty which then refuses to justify itself in terms of what seems most specific to it, will indeed be justified a hundredfold. We have, as inhabitants of academe, to take each sophisticated distinction with the utmost seriousness, and yet allow the academic to wither within us before a greater reality. Unless the seed going into the earth die, itself remaineth alone, but if it die it can bring forth rich fruit. Fascinating as theology may be, it must die as theory through the conviction of its insignificance as such in relation to the praxis of God's revolutionary love revealed in Christ and in relation to the praxis of our revolutionary responses in love and service.

All that sounds naive enough, I am sure; it is, in the particularity of its certitude, rather unscientific. Its confident assertion is likely to leave us quite out of step with the world around us – the world often at its most cautious and indeed humanly worthy. To accept the gospel, to return time and again to the memory of cross and empty tomb as seriously decisive for our thinking and acting, can be in truth a shattering experience – an experience almost at times too hard to be bearable. The gospel did after all shatter its first bearer upon a hill of execution and what else can one expect, if in response to his call, one agrees to be sent forth again as a sheep among wolves?

16

Jesus and the Scribe

You are not far from the Kingdom of God (Mark 12.28–34).

For many of us, the most decisively compelling and universally authentic characteristic of Christianity as a religion and of the teaching of Jesus its originator and abiding focus is at once the primacy of love and the integration of the two loves – God and neighbour – into one. Love of God is love of neighbour 'as yourself'. Such is the message of many of the parables, of the great Pauline hymn to love in I Corinthians 13, of the judgment scene in Matthew 25. It is too the recurrent theme of the Johannine epistles: 'This is love, that we follow his commandments; this is the commandment, as you have heard from the beginning, that you follow love' (II John 6). Matthew, Paul, John – wherever you look the message is the same, different as are the ways in which it is formulated – in the story of prodigal son or Good Samaritan, the hard practicality of 'I was sick and you visited me', the lyrical poetry of John or Paul. Ritual, religion and dogmatic formularies are not meaningless but they are wholly secondary, dependent upon their organic relationship with love and damaging if they escape from that relationship.

It is the absolute integration of the divine with the human love, the first and second commandments of our text, which seems most characteristically Christian. The king will answer, You did it to the least of my brethren – not seeing me explicitly at all – but you did it to me. There is no way to God, no service of God, no love of God, no true religion outside the brethren of our secular and daily life, our society, our world, its needs.

Yet this was not just an invention of Jesus of Nazareth. Rather, in this originating text of the series, Jesus is quoting lines which were already central to Jewish religion and experience. It is true there was a great deal else in the books of Deuteronomy and Leviticus from which he takes them and much of that else looked less loving, less forgiving, harder than this inmost pearl he draws out and offers to his hearers. It is also true that the veritable identification of the two commands (not in fact quite shown here but in due course the true theme line of Christianity) is new – at least in the degree of emphasis given it. Nevertheless, the Christian primacy and centrality of love remains essentially a Jewish message, perceived, sharpened and reinterpreted by Jesus the Jew. And he is doing it, of course, as a first-century Jew, sharing in the living consciousness of the Jewish religious community of his time, a community which has in many ways advanced beyond the world for which Deuteronomy or Leviticus was actually written. However much he is effectively going beyond that consciousness to weave a new whole, he is doing it from within and out of a living religion, and a living religion at its contemporary best.

Mark makes this absolutely clear by the dialogue in which he sets our quotation. A scribe has questioned Jesus and immediately comments upon his reply 'You are right, Teacher; you have truly said that he is one, and there is no other but he; and to love him with all the heart, and with all the understanding, and with all the strength, and to love one's neighbour as oneself, is much more than all whole burnt offerings and sacrifices'. What a wonderful response! Yet Mark does not even leave it at that but continues 'Jesus saw that he had answered wisely and said to him "You are not far from the Kingdom of God"'.

There is no suggestion here that the scribe was a follower of Jesus or other than a wise and sincere Jewish scholar. He commends Jesus' teaching and Jesus commends his sincerity. There is a meeting of mind and heart, a dialogue which may be seen as providing a model for religious encounter and particularly for the relationship between Christian and Jew. Of course, the gospels give us a great deal of encounter of a different, more confrontatory sort, and we must not overlook that either. Jewish religion at the time, like Christian religion since, was not a morally unified thing. There were, and are, good priests and worldly priests, good scribes and worldly scribes, good theologians and worldly theologians. Religion can liberate. It can also oppress. It nearly always in point of fact does both. A prophet must not fear to denounce the one, but a denunciation of worldly, oppressive religion – of the blindness of the sadducee and pharisee of tradition – will be misleading, if it makes one fail to discern that there was – and is – much else there too.

By and large in subsequent history Christians have lamentably failed to see the on-going goodness in Jewish religion and sadly one has to admit that a verbally anti-semitic element already discernible in the gospels is partly responsible. Of course, if the gospels were written by Christian Jews and largely for Christian Jews, that note of denunciation sounded in its original context very differently – just as denunciations of Britain and the British government made by British people to British people are not anti-British but could seem that way if written down and read and re-read later in some other land and age.

So this story which, instead, demonstrates mutual respect and profound agreement upon the central obligation of religion between Jesus and the scribe has a quite special illustrative importance. Sadly, it almost wholly disappears in Matthew's account of the incident and is much weakened even in Luke's. What is absent in the latter is the absence of any positive word of his own on the scribe's side or of explicit recognition by Jesus of the scribe's own wisdom. We have to be all the more grateful to Mark for giving us the story and all the more determined to hearken to its inner points.

There has in fact been a continuous ambiguity within Christian faith in regard to the relationship between it and the Old Testament. There are those who have effectively, and rather simplistically, identified in authority the two sides of our Bible and all its parts and even allowed elements of the old most remote from the spirit of the new to exercise a predominant influence. But there are others who have, on the contrary, effectively abandoned the rich root of hebraic religion in a narrow 'Jesus only' doctrine and piety. The true strength of Christianity lies, instead, in the recognition of a range of related, all historically conditioned, revelations. Jesus himself, the Word incarnate, indeed writes nothing – save on sand. He as Word is not to be equated with the words written around him, sacred as they are, a generation later by many people in many places. The model here is one of the necessary diversification and interpretation of incarnational wisdom, a process that does not stop with the writing of the New Testament, but does not start there either. Jesus is not a new beginning, but a newness within all that is old: new Moses, new Israel, new Adam. The scriptures of the early church are, primarily, the Hebrew scriptures. Its prayers are, primarily, Hebrew prayers – the psalms. There is no 'Christus solus' here – rather a new ray of light, blinding maybe in its brilliance yet still illuminating an ever so much vaster tradition of revelation, holiness and sin – a human tradition that is an ongoing human community too. The new covenant does not negate, reject, contradict or despise the old: rather in the way of all sound human history and learning, it grows integrally out of it, shedding bits here and there, seeing afresh the wisdom and power of other bits, returning again and again for renewal to its ancestral roots, never fundamentalistically frightened to disagree, but always reverent, always grateful.

That is the way the Christian-Jewish relationship should have been, but too seldom has been. In fact it developed across a bitter schism, recriminations, distrust, at times almost total misunderstanding. Religion (like all human things) has got to advance and new religious movements to come out of religion as it has been. It is in the nature of things that this happens, but as it happens the adherents of an old order are almost inevitably embittered by the seemingly unquestioning enthusiasm of the new group just as the innovators become contemptuous of the seeming apathy, conservatism, evidently conformist ways they perceive in the other. Schism follows. We have lived with a Jewish-Christian schism ever since, and subsequently with a Greek-Latin schism, and then a Catholic-Protestant schism, and still there are more.

Each time this happens there is the strongest temptation utterly to condemn the other side and, of course, to a large extent that is what happened. The Jews were damned by Christians as God-murdering unbelievers, whereas in fact they shared with and had given to Christians the central conviction, in the words of our scribe, that 'He is one and there is no other but he', and is to be loved with all our heart and understanding and strength: and that remains the heart of it all for both our traditions. One can look across every schism of mind and fellowship and see upon the other side a brood of vipers, or one can look across and see instead a scribe, attentively listening and able then to say those healing words; 'You are right, Teacher! It is love alone that counts'.

In no society, no part of the world has God left himself witness-less. He would not be the loving father of all mankind if he had done so. It is part of the universalist logic of our own Christian faith to assert that the other great faiths are not empty, valueless things, bowing down to wood or stone, devil-worship or whatever – but in their own way covenants of grace and love, ways to the Father. It must be so, if God is God. How can that be reconciled with the centrality of Christ? How could one fail to do so? That should rather be the question. The interlocking model of Old and New Testaments provides the paradigm. The New Covenant nullifies no old covenant but fulfills it, and throughout the world there are old covenants: every culture has had its own. With each Christ must dialogue. For that to be possible, both a depth of spirituality and the presence of the sincere scribe must be recognized and respected in each so that to each we are able to say 'You are not far from the Kingdom of God'.

17

Jimmy and Joan

James and Joan Stewart died following a car crash in Lesotho on the 11 July 1984 and are buried there at Roma. At a requiem mass in Harare, Zimbabwe, 27 July, I preached the memorial sermon:

Jimmy and Joan Stewart are dead. That is why we are gathered here, gathered to celebrate a glorious memory and to pray with their family for them and – shall we not say too? – to pray with them for their family. We are praying in the way they themselves would certainly want. We are celebrating Mass, something which was absolutely central in their lives. The eucharist is the memorial celebration of a dead man whom we believe not to be dead, and when we recall Joan and Jimmy in this context we are affirming as emphatically as we can that they too are not finished, but in many different ways still living and with us in example and inspiration. Their memory will remain like a strong tower in years to come for those of us who were privileged to know them.

I first met Jimmy and Joan almost exactly thirty years ago. It was in Rome on their honeymoon in June, 1954. They had been married in Oxford, in fact from my brother's house, and Fr Gervase Mathew, the friend and counsellor of so many of us Africanists, had preached their wedding sermon. I was then a seminarian in Rome and they had written to suggest our meeting. They had let me know the *pensione* where they would stay and I went there one hot Mediterranean afternoon, was told their room, knocked on the door and entered – to find them lying naked on the floor together. I retreated hastily and they dressed. I think that none of us was too embarrassed. I tell the story now – it has never been mentioned before – because for me it is so extraordinarily symbolic of the way they always were. No other couple I know has been always so manifestly and so deliberately united. It remains for me almost inexplicably fitting that I met them first at a moment of such unity. And in Rome. That too was symbolic: a honeymoon in Rome with the blessing of Pope Pius XII. Jimmy was already by then a lecturer in English literature – the first layman to be appointed – at the Catholic University College of Pius XII in Roma, Lesotho. Their marriage pilgrimage of thirty years was to start in Rome and end in Roma. Two more loyal – though never uncritical – Roman Catholics it would be hard to find, in this very much like their close friends, Frank and Maisie Sheed. They were much more than just zealous Catholic laity, but they were never less than that. Rome, the Mass, the Mystical Body of the Church meant so very much to them, and it is right that we recall this here. Turn the letters of Roma backwards and you have AMOR, the Latin for 'Love'. For Jimmy and Joan Roma in Lesotho and the Roman Church and love – love for one another and for all the rest of us – went very close together.

In fact it was in Roma that I next met them, then at a December Group conference at Spode House in the heyday of *Slant* in 1965, then in Cambridge, in Nairobi, and lastly here in Zimbabwe. South Africans in a long self-imposed exile, they were in some way always homeless; in another way they were so committed to Africa, east, central or south, that many, many places were truly home. Seven more years at Roma in the later fifties and early sixties were followed by six in Nairobi as Senior Lecturer in English and then four as Professor in the University of Malawi – all this interwoven with periods at Harvard and Cambridge. Then in 1976 came a bolt from the blue, one of President Banda's sudden arbitrary decrees, and Jimmy was deported from Malawi. Despite the cushioning of two kind years of a fellowship at the University of Notre Dame, this ended Jimmy's academic career. In 1978 came the decision to return to Lesotho and to work directly for church and society through setting up the group called *Transformation* to prepare people through processes of a conscientization for a more Christian and socialist society in southern Africa.

In the long central years of university life one saw in Jimmy first of all the struggle for professional academic excellence. His standards were of the highest and perhaps for that reason he found it desperately hard to write anything which satisfied him. The long

agony of completing his PhD thesis on D. H. Lawrence for
Cambridge was shared and supported by Joan. The tortuous
struggle for the right word which could be so difficult a part of his
conversation effectively prevented him from publishing. But his very
commitment to Africa may also have, in its way, impeded the full
flowering of his academic career in a conventional form. Immensely
important as good prose and poetry were for him, there were still
more important things. Jimmy and Joan were both wholly committed
to the struggle for justice on this continent, for an inter-racial and
caring society. As a very young man in South Africa, Jimmy was at
one time chairman of the Catholic Students organization. Upon his
committee were Robert Mugabe and Bernard Chidzero. Friendship
with them was a good beginning. From later on we may recall just
one small but significant action: the sending of their sons, John and
Peter, to be the first white students at Alliance High School, Kenya.

Yes, they now had a family: two sons and three daughters. This
too was absolutely central to their life. In a strange but unmistakable
way it became all of a piece – this peregrinatory exiled life, the
commitment to Africa, Catholic Christianity, socialism, the family. It
was a lot to try to hand on to one's children. Yet how well they
succeeded! I have friends with high ideals whose children, to their
grief, have hardly at all been able to enter into the parental vision.
The generation gap has cut too sharply between them. It was,
perhaps, the most lasting achievement and source of happiness of
Joan and Jimmy, Joan especially, that in this often extremely
worrying and exacting way of life they carried the family with them:
not only the most united of couples, but also of families. It was, for
the observer, quite natural that though, when the accident occurred,
no member of the family was in Lesotho but all were scattered across
the world, at the funeral no member was absent.

But they were wanderers and that was hard – for all of them. The
word of God to Abraham 'Go from your country and your kindred
and your father's house' applied very really to these two South
Africans spending all thirty years of their married life outside the
country they both immensely loved. There was not in them the
beginning of a belonging to Britain or America, despite the happy
years of study spent there. To be on pilgrimage, somehow homeless,
is deep within the spirituality of Christianity, but to make of it the
spirituality of one's own family must impose a very great strain on all

its members, and the children of Jimmy and Joan who – unlike their parents – had never known South Africa as home must often have found it exceedingly hard. They should not feel that loyalty to their parents requires its permanent continuation. I am sure it has been a great joy and privilege to be in the Stewart family, it has also demanded a great deal.

And so we come to the last six years: the return to Lesotho and the setting up of *Transformation*. Plenty of people have been enthusiastic about the quality and spirit of the workshops it organized in Lesotho, here in Zimbabwe and elsewhere. Jimmy's academic life was past, the family were grown up and gone. They were alone to work together, in a way more equally than before. Joan's quiet strength had always in truth been the basis of the family's survival, but publicly she had seemed the almost silent partner. Now in *Transformation* she was able to show in their joint work the great clarity of mind and sureness of purpose which she had had too little opportunity to use publicly in earlier years. Liberation. Inter-racial peace. Socialism. The Poor Christ. *Transformation* was well backed by the Catholic bishops, but it was also a highly ecumenical team: the Stewart way of embodying the Vatican II spirit at its best.

In many ways Joan and Jimmy hardly changed at all: always enthusiastic and hopeful, real perseverers in the ideals of their youth, very consciously radical yet a bit old-fashioned too. They went on their way to that last moment, undeviating. And then it came, like the knock of a stick bringing two ripe apples to the ground, perfect in the completion of their life's cycle. No decay, nor decline, no period of uselessness, of self-questioning, of being on the shelf. If that did happen it had been earlier, after the expulsion from Malawi. Now they had given their last years wholly to the struggle for the central things they believed in. They had fought the fight, they had finished the race, they had kept faith. And they had done it together. United in life as few ever are, their consciousness on this earth was ended at the same instant. Two years before, celebrating a wedding anniversary, they had said together these lines from the Book of Ruth: 'Where you go I will go, and where you lodge I will lodge; your people shall be my people, and your God my God; where you die I will die, and there will I be buried'.

And so God permitted it to be. Jimmy and Joan are buried together in the graveyard at Roma where they spent so many years, in the midst of the mountains of Lesotho, and close to that little college started as a Catholic initiative and now the national university, where Jimmy had been the first lay lecturer. Could it really be better done? Let us as we feel a quite numbing absence still thank God for the whole of their lives and their exceptional wholeness. It is hard, very hard, to come to this ending but we can, I think, still see the point in it.

⋆ 18 ⋆

Flavia and Nicholas

We are here today, gathered in this delightful but slightly odd place, to support, encourage and celebrate with Flavia and Nicholas in what may be the most important decision of their lives. We both witness the event of their marrying and take it into our own lives too.

Marriage and family remain for most of us the most shaping element of our personal worlds – the worlds of homes and children and hospitality, of in-laws and mortgages and names, private worlds yet social and public too, the world we relate to mostly in others. Now this public, still almost institutionalized, thing can be personally – as all of us know – almost heaven or hell. What makes it one or the other – or a bit of both – is a very simple, but very, very, difficult and inward thing: love or the lack of it.

Love is kind, forgiving, supportive, thoughtful. Love goes on forever.

The awkwardness of marriage is that it is both a social, public thing – on account of which we all dress up in a very special way and assemble on a February Saturday here in Fleet Street (what strange behaviour) – and an adventure of two human hearts, a pretty risky adventure.

Is it really sane for Flavia and Nicholas (or any other two mature, awkwardly angled, individuals) to think they can seriously commit themselves to this, for life? For richer, for poorer. All those days and nights together, long years of sharing coffee and marmalade, fidelity, the hassle of children and illnesses, of coming home tired and irritable, growing old and dull?

It's not *quite* sane, as no great adventure begun in faith and courage and high heart ever is. But it's a risk gloriously worth taking.

Nicholas and Flavia know as well as any of us that one and one normally make two: each one is lost but their power is thereby doubled. However, it is also good to remember that one and one can also make eleven. In that case each one is not lost but, so long as they do stick side by side, their power grows more than tenfold. That better illustrates the creativity of a love which respects the individuality of each. Perhaps it is the symbolic model you should go for.

Flavia and Nicholas, as you enter today upon this great adventure, we simply – all of us – have come to wish you well. For us of course it's clear gain: another son or daughter, niece or nephew, cousin, a friend the more. Another house in which to cadge a bed or a meal when in London.

For you, it's so much more. In life there's nothing much worth winning but the love of friends. Married love is at the centre of it all, not a separating love but a great shared well of affection which will, we hope, flow out again over us all. Nor should it separate you from the 'mental fight' you are both already engaged upon, rather may it be a 'golden chariot' to carry that fight forward together.

It's difficult. There will probably be times when each of you thinks it was just a ghastly mistake. It comes to all of us. But true love can grow through those times, even gaining from them in depth, sensitivity and realism, learning from them not to take oneself too seriously. In human life, tears and laughter always will go together. May it be so with you.

All of us, who are here today to celebrate with you, would say 'thank you for asking us to do so' and 'may it go very well'. Find your own ways of making one and one eleven. And may God bless you too, today and always.

Fifty Years of Theology at Leeds[1]

In September 1931 the University of Leeds learnt that it had been left £20,000 in the will of the late Mrs Emily Fawcett of Bramhope for the endowment in perpetuity of a Chair of Theology. The legacy was at once gratefully accepted by the Vice-Chancellor, Sir James Baillie, who even observed, in his earliest letter on the subject,[2] not only that this would meet 'a long felt want' but also that it 'will make possible the institution of an entirely new Faculty – a Faculty of Theology – and will thus mark a new stage in the progress of the university'.

Others felt less happy with a development which seemed about to breach the rather deliberate secularity and non-sectarian character of the university. It was, almost certainly, to placate opposition that the Senate decided in the course of 1932 that the new chair should not, strictly, be in Theology at all but in the more neutral-sounding 'Philosophy and History of Religion'. The £20,000 was paid in full in October,[3] the appointment committee first met in November and the following June, of 1933, Edwin Oliver James, the Vicar of St Thomas', Oxford, and President of the Folk-Lore Society, was appointed the university's first Professor of the Philosophy and History of Religion and – apparently – head of a department with the same title. Three years later, 1936–37, the title 'Theological Studies' first appeared in the Calendar, so we may fairly claim that

[1]I am most grateful for help received from Mrs Cooksey of the Brotherton Special Collection, Mrs Forster and Mrs Stephens in the University Archives, and the staff of the central Filing Office.
[2]Letter to J. Hurworth Esq, 23 September 1931, CFO/T.
[3]See *Annual Report*, 1931–32, 75–6 and letter of Scott, Turnbull and Kendall to the Vice-Chancellor, 14 October 1932, CFO/T.

we are, in December 1986, entitled to celebrate pretty precisely fifty years of Theology at the University of Leeds. The background to these developments is, however, a complicated one and we need now to turn back a little if we are to understand both the appointment of 1933 and the subsequent history of our subject.

Article X of the Charter of the Yorkshire College which, in 1903, became the University of Leeds forbade its Court 'to adopt or impose on any person any test whatsoever of religious belief or profession in order to entitle him to be admitted as a professor, teacher, student or member'. This clause enshrining the principle of non-discrimination in terms of religion was in reaction to the discrimination which for long characterized the universities of Oxford and Cambridge. It represented a consensus of liberal secularists, Free Churchmen and – in so far as they mattered – Roman Catholics and Jews. It was a principle basically accepted by all the modern universities of Britain, reflecting particularly the mood of the great northern industrial cities and nowhere more than Leeds, a city which – by the late nineteenth century – had developed a notably tolerant and open character. Article X will provide one decisive point of reference throughout the story we are to consider.

But non-discrimination can be understood in different ways. For the last twenty years of the nineteenth-century the Yorkshire College formed part, with colleges at Manchester and Liverpool, of the Victoria University. Despite having so much in common, the approach of the three to the introduction of Theology into the university proved strikingly diverse. Owens College in Manchester, the senior partner, had a strong Free Church background and well before 1903 Manchester had twice unsuccessfully proposed that it should be done. Once the three separated, Manchester hardly delayed at all before establishing a Faculty of Theology in which, for the first time in England, a Free Churchman – A. S. Peake, a Primitive Methodist and a very distinguished New Testament scholar – was appointed Professor.[4] The attitude of Liverpool, on the contrary, was absolutely opposed by its very charter (until

[4]William H. Draper, *Sir Nathan Bodington*, First Vice-Chancellor of the University of Leeds, Macmillan 1912, 160–6, 241–8; for the Manchester Faculty see: Manchester University: Faculty of Theology, *Theological Essays*. In Commemoration of the Jubilee by L. W. Grensted et al., 1954, in particular that of T. W. Manson, 'The First Fifty Years: A Sketch', pp.7–18.

revision in 1961) to any theological teaching.[5] It may be surmised that it was the rather bitter sectarian divisions in Liverpool which made this necessary. Leeds was different. Its concerns were markedly earth-bound. Less Free Church than Manchester, less sectarian than Liverpool, it was neither as sympathetic to theology as the one, nor as hotly opposed as the other. Sir Nathan Bodington, the Yorkshire College's first Principal and Leeds' first Vice-Chancellor, declared indeed when the idea was mooted within the Victoria University that he was not opposed in principle. 'No one would be more glad to see . . .' What he could not accept was the Manchester-proposed model, whereby the teachers within the Faculty would be the existing members of staff of Theological Colleges in the vicinity appointed inevitably, as a consequence, subject to a test of denominational acceptability. That – as he saw it – would go clean against article X. If the university had the money to draft in 'learned men, appointed without any test of membership of any particular communion, or any test of the exercise of any religious profession' this would be fine, but of course it had not the money and, moreover, as both the students and the teachers were in a way already there in the colleges, it would be pointless as well. 'To link a College to this or that Theological School . . . seemed to him to be a very grievous thing.' So, while both Manchester and London went forward with the development of Faculties of Theology, despite their commitment to the principle of non-discrimination, Faculties which consisted almost entirely of staff co-opted from a range of Free Church and Anglican Colleges, Leeds felt unable to do this and so, for a time, did nothing yet without adopting the 'no Theology in principle' position of Liverpool.

It is, I think, clear enough that Bodington was genuinely not opposed to Theology as such. Nor, presumably, was the Marquis of Ripon, the university's first Chancellor. He took an extremely active role in regard to the young university until his death in 1909 and Bodington, his biographer tells us,[6] developed toward him 'an almost feudal and filial attachment'. Ripon was one of the most powerful and able of Liberal statesmen. He had been born in 10 Downing Street, was a member of cabinet after cabinet, yet had at one time seemed willing to sacrifice absolutely everything in public

[5] Thomas Kelly, *For Advancement of Learning*, The University of Liverpool 1881–1981, Liverpool University Press, 1981, pp.119, 130, 311.
[6] Ibid., p.111.

life on account of religious conviction when, in 1874, he became a Roman Catholic. The *Times*, voicing as it thought the opinion of a horrified nation, declared in an editorial that 'Such a step involves a complete abandonment of any claim to political or even social influence in the nation at large and can only be regarded as betraying an irreparable weakness of character'.[7] Only eight years later the Council of the Yorkshire College unanimously invited him to become its President. He was by then an outstandingly forward-looking Viceroy of India, from where he returned to be a member of further Liberal cabinets until the time of Asquith. For our story it is, I think, helpful to recall that the University of Leeds came into being under the patronage of a man of particularly intense religious conviction, but also – in Britain – of a minority conviction. The secularity of Leeds university, we may conclude, could never have been intended as in any way an anti-religious one, but as a conscious determination in no way to discriminate, even within the field of theology, against minority convictions. Indeed we find Bodington, at the end of his life, actually writing in 1910 to the Vicar of Leeds to express his worry that teachers coming out of the university and expected to give biblical teaching in the schools, had had no training for the work, and suggesting that if the churches could nominate lecturers, the lectures might be given within the university.[8]

Already by 1919 the BA course did include options in both Hebrew and Ecclesiastical History to be given at Rawdon Baptist College, so some slight co-operation with denominational Theological Colleges, whereby the university recognized and made use of their lectures to a limited extent, had been accepted during the vice-chancellorship of Sir Michael Sadler. But that was not much, and as Leeds developed further and seemed set to become Yorkshire's major university, it was natural to press for more. In the early twenties, in fact, the Archbishop of York, Cosmo Lang, 'chided' the university 'for the absence of theology from its faculties',[9] but it was – I suspect – with the arrival of James Baillie as

---

[7]The *Times*, 5 September 1874, First Leader. For Ripon's return to public life see John P. Rossi, 'Lord Ripon's resumption of political activity', *Recusant History*, 11, 1971–72, 61–74.
[8]Draper, *Sir Nathan Bodington*, p.242. It is, perhaps, also worth noting that Bodington's biographer, W. H. Draper, was himself the Rector of Adel.
[9]A. N. Shimmin, *The University of Leeds, The First Half-Century*, Cambridge 1954, p.50.

Vice-Chancellor in 1924 that the scene was really set for the ending of that absence. Baillie was a masterly if unpopular Scot with large plans and a very considerable ability for realizing them. He had been Professor of Moral Philosophy in the University of Aberdeen for more than twenty years, for most of which George Adam Smith had been its Principal and Vice-Chancellor. Adam Smith was both an outstandingly gifted Old Testament scholar and a Principal of exceptionally wide influence. Moreover, the Faculty of Divinity in Aberdeen was an ancient and assured part of the university. Baillie was hardly a religious person but I cannot help thinking that for him, coming from the Aberdeen of George Adam Smith, it seemed more obviously correct than to Sadler or Bodington to establish a Theology Faculty here too. A Scottish mandarin, he tended to be patronizing about what he termed 'West Riding people', about Anglicans and Nonconformists and indeed about the whole community, academic or otherwise, of Leeds. I cannot but surmise that Sir David Evans, the very Welsh Vice- Chancellor in Michael Innes' Leeds detective story *The Weight of the Evidence*, nevertheless impersonates the very Scottish Sir James uncannily well. Thus the lines 'the Vice-Chancellor crinkled the corners of his eyes into the kindliest smile – much as a dog-lover might do when subjected to the gambollings of an over-obstreperous puppy' seem to catch the note of the comments in his private journal again and again. He stood a little aloof and above them all, wondering in his Journal whether Anglicans were Christians or Nonconformists gentlemen.[10] He appeared resolved to press ahead with the establishment of Theology. He was thinking in terms of a Faculty and had already been in correspondence on the subject, obtaining relevant information from elsewhere, a year or more before the news of Mrs Fawcett's legacy was received. In the following years there can be little doubt that it was he, more than anyone else, who provided the driving force in this matter.

I have referred already to Rawdon and the other Theological Colleges. It is to them that we should next turn. There were in the thirties three Free Church theological colleges in the vicinity of Leeds – all three old, served by good scholars and with a reputation for being on the more liberal side of the theological spectrum within

---

[10] 'A good deal of English Non-conformity is Christianity without manners: just as a certain amount of Anglican religion is manners without Christianity.' Journal II, 1 June 1933.

their respective denominations. They both symbolized the powerful Free Church tradition of the West Riding and had become that tradition's principal institutional focal points. Here were dignified buildings, training grounds for a considerable number of ministers, producers of literature and of leadership, but needy recipients too of continual benefaction to keep going with rising standards and increasing costs.

The Yorkshire United Independent College at Bradford traced its Congregationalist origins to the establishment of a dissenting academy at Heckmondwike in 1756.[11] It owed its modern theological character to a strong-minded Scottish scholar, Andrew Fairbairn, who headed it for eight years from 1877 until being invited to become first Principal of Mansfield College, Oxford. The Baptist theological college at Rawdon equally traced its beginnings to the age of dissenting academies.[12] First founded at Horton, it was moved to Rawdon in 1859. Wesley College, Headingley, the third of the trio, was the first purpose-built Wesleyan theological college, being opened in 1868. By the early twentieth-century all three were well developed academically and several of their staff could easily have been university lecturers – in fact Underwood and Howells of Rawdon were already in the 1920s included in the Leeds university staff, as lecturers respectively for ecclesiastical history and Hebrew. A few – particularly in the biblical field – were scholars of international reputation. Of no one was this more true than of Vincent Taylor, a leading figure in our story.[13] Taylor chose to spend most of his working life on the staff of a small college in Headingley. He might as well have been Regius Professor of New Testament studies in any university. Perhaps he slightly lacked the flair of an absolutely first class mind but the reliability and depth of his scholarship was outstanding. His *Gospel According to St Mark* has been described by Dennis Nineham as 'the great modern English

[11]It moved to its final site in Emm Lane, Bradford, in 1877. See Kenneth W. Wadsworth, *Yorkshire United Independent College*, Independent Press, London 1954.
[12]See A. C. Underwood, *A History of the English Baptists*, The Baptist Union Publication, The Kingsgate Press, London 1947. Underwood was for many years, and still at the time of writing, Principal of Rawdon.
[13]Leeds recognized this with an honorary DD. For Taylor see the notice in *The University of Leeds Review*, December 1953, pp.393–5, also pp.206–10 of *A History of the Medhodist Church in Great Britain*, vol. 3, ed. Rupert Davies, A. Raymond George and Gordon Rupp, Epworth Press 1983.

commentary on the Greek text',[14] while his whole range of New Testament publications from the twenties to the fifties can hardly be rivalled by any other British scholar of his generation other than C. H. Dodd.

It would be impossible to understand the development of our department aright without appreciating the traditional strength of Nonconformity in the West Riding, the benefits these colleges looked for from co-operation with the local university but also the existing high standards of scholarship existing within the colleges: standards which an under-funded and even slightly amateur department within the university might not so easily be able to match. This explains the early preoccupation, lasting into the fifties,[15] with a Faculty rather than a Department. The argument for a Faculty was that the only practical way of co-opting the large amount of expertise available in the vicinity, and thereby obtaining a large and varied staff without the university having to pay more than one or two salaries, was to adopt after all the Manchester model, a sort of federation in which the various Colleges would form an integral part, with a faculty board representative of all the institutions involved. It seems clear that this is what the Colleges wanted and even, at least for a time, the Vice-Chancellor. They could point to the example of Manchester, London, or any of the ancient Scottish universities. The failure to bring it about – largely, I think, because of wider feeling in the university linked with Article X – has much to do with the undoubted frustration that subsequently ensued in the Colleges in regard to a department for long inadequately staffed to bear the burden by itself, but unable effectively to share it. But that is to anticipate.

To the three Nonconformist Colleges we must, of course, add the Anglican College of the Resurrection at Mirfield. It had been opened later than they, in 1902. As not only Anglican, but Anglo-Catholic (and in its early days under much attack for 'Romanizing'), it kept its distance from them. It was no less interested in the business of degrees and quickly opened a hostel in Leeds, in Springfield Mount, close to the university, in which its students could live while studying for a BA. In October 1928, that hostel was completed and blessed, the extremely imposing brick Tudor

[14]D. E. Nineham, *Saint Mark*, Penguin Books 1963, p.12.
[15]Professor Reid was still proposing the establishment of a Faculty in 1954–5.

building which we know today (since 1976) as the university's Adult Education Centre. It was opened in the presence of the Vice-Chancellor and the Bishop of Ripon and a wide range of ecclesiastics and academics.[16] The completion of the hostel in 1928 and the degree of collaboration between church and university it represented may be seen as a sort of prologue for the establishment of our department, but it must be stressed that the hostel was to enable impecunious ordinands study subjects other than theology. The latter they would do subsequently at Mirfield only. Unlike the Free Church Colleges, Mirfield was not much interested in a Leeds theology course – at least until the sixties.

When the Chair Committee first met in November 1932 it decided that the post should be advertised and appointed a subcommittee to consider applications including the Vice-Chancellor, Professor Hamilton Thompson and Bishop Burroughs of Ripon.[17] All three took a strong personal interest in the appointment. Baillie we have already considered. Hamilton Thompson was a mediaeval historian of great distinction, a scholar particularly interested in church history, a generous and humane Anglican layman.[18] He was the most distinguished figure in the Faculty of Arts at that time and extended a fatherly concern to the development of theology in Leeds, very similar to that which another great mediaevalist, T. F. Tout, had shown in Manchester a generation earlier. The Bishop of Ripon, the third of our trio, was a member of both Court and Council. He had been pressing the university to develop Theology for some time, but he had a very firm, decidedly Anglican, view of the form it should take.

When the applicants for the post were considered in March a short list of six was agreed upon, but it was already clear that in some ways easily the most attractive among them was a Roman Catholic, Christopher Dawson. Indeed in retrospect it would seem that he was

---

[16]*CR* (quarterly of the Community of the Resurrection) no. 104, 1928, Christmas, pp.12–19.

[17]Edward Arthur Burroughs, Bishop of Ripon 1926 until his death in 1934, author of *A Faith for the Firing Line, World Builders All*, etc. He was a Crown nominee to the Court, and an elected Court representative on the Council of the university.

[18]It is worth noting that both Hamilton Thompson and James had recently contributed to the symposium *Essays Catholic and Critical* by Members of the Anglican Communion, edited by E. G. Selwyn and published in 1926.

at this stage the only candidate with any real academic distinction and plausibility. The minutes of the Sub-Committee include the following: 'The Sub-Committee considered whether the appointment of a member of the Roman Catholic Church would be prejudicial to the prospects of maintaining and developing co-operation between the local theological institutions whose students were in attendance at the University. The question of whether a candidate's adherence to the Roman Catholic faith would preclude his co-operation with members of other denominations was also considered. At the same time it was noted that under the terms of the Charter no test whatever of religious belief or profession could be imposed upon any person for admission to a Professorship or any other office within the University.'

Dawson was a layman, already a scholar of recognized distinction, a naturally irenic person and a lecturer in Exeter university. In the previous years he had published prolifically: it was in fact his most creative period. The *Age of the Gods* appeared in 1928, *Progress and Religion* – a very widely admired work – in 1929, a remarkable essay on St Augustine in 1930, *The Making of Europe* in 1932, *The Spirit of the Oxford Movement* in 1933. His references – from Walter Moberly, H. A. L. Fisher, Ernest Barker, Dean Inge and others – were excellent. Ernest Barker, his ex-tutor at Oxford, declared 'I always knew that in intellectual power he stood alone among all the men I had ever taught'.[19] He was not a theologian nor a philosopher – though he was rather nearer to being both than was James. He was a wide-ranging historian of religion and culture and a thinker of considerable power, not least in regard to politics. He was also a Yorkshireman, possessing a family home at Harlington in Wharfedale.

As a recent biography of Christopher Dawson by his daughter, Christina Scott, has raised the issue of his non-appointment at Leeds, it seems appropriate to throw as much light on the matter as is now possible. Candidates were interviewed on two days in May. Dawson and another, seemingly the bishop's choice, in the second group on the 29th. The Committee minutes are extremely guarded. The conclusion reached was to refer the matter to the Sub-Committee which met three days later and was also unable to decide anything beyond agreeing to interview two further candidates (nine

[19]Christina Scott, *A Historian and His World*, A Life of Christopher Dawson, 1889–1970, Sheed & Ward 1984, p.110

were interviewed in all). Fortunately Baillie's Journal tells us a great deal more of what actually happened: 'Dawson made a good impression but the majority of the Committee seemed clearly unsympathetic, especially the Bishop of Ripon who plainly indicated that Dawson could not expect to cooperate with the colleges owing to his "spiritual allegiance" to Rome. This Dawson dissented from and gave his reasons, which were good. Dawson's mind is subtle . . . I helped Dawson as much as I could. He is obviously not robust and rather a recluse pale scholar. Much discussion about the possibility of taking a Roman Catholic . . .' The second candidate, all in all, failed to make an acceptable impression on most of the Committee. Finally, while the Bishop wished to report back to the Council that they could not find a man, the Vice-Chancellor objected to this course.

At the Sub-Committee on 1 June it transpired – again following the Journal – that the Bishop had seen the second candidate after the last meeting and got others 'to see him behind the scenes. He then said he had been unfairly treated and should be reconsidered. The Bishop's advocacy will not do him good service . . . H. Thompson resented the actions and views of the Bishop'.

The position was, clearly enough, extremely embarrassing. It is true that Dawson was intensely reserved, 'recluse' is not too unfair a description. He was a rather impractical person, far from strong in health, and it is unlikely that he could ever have made a good head of department. One wonders, however, whether such points stood heavily against him. He was clearly a distinguished scholar and a singularly ecumenical Christian. He, at least, was not unwilling to co-operate with anyone. The other candidates, at this stage, were essentially nonentities. When Baillie admits 'Much discussion about the possibility of taking a Roman Catholic', one might ask whether in spirit the Charter was not already broken. Yet, if the Vice-Chancellor and Professor Hamilton Thompson too tried hard to be fair and were most unwilling to be pushed by the bishop into accepting a candidate they did not really consider up to it, they felt no less unable to make an appointment starkly opposed to the bishop's advice. The argument continually used was that no Catholic could co-operate with the colleges. The question (in the case of Dawson) rather was: could the colleges co-operate with a Catholic? In fact they were, it seems, never asked and when an appointment was finally made, and they did not care for it, they complained that they had not been represented on the selection board. If they did not care for James, could they conceivably have preferred Dawson?[20]

It should be remembered that the first Free Churchman was only appointed to a chair of Theology at Cambridge or Oxford two years later (C. H. Dodd in 1935), so it would be more than surprising if the idea of appointing a Roman Catholic had not greatly raised the hackles of many. While it could have been, in theory at least, a gloriously imaginative appointment, Leeds was noted for caution rather than imagination.

If he was not to be appointed – and in theory Baillie refused to rule it out – an academically satisfactory alternative had simply got to be found. The new names brought forward on the 1 June proved no better than the rest, but on 20 June at a Sub-Committee meeting the Vice-Chancellor announced yet another name, Dr E. O. James. This was the very first time his name had appeared. A letter of application and supporting references were read out. He was interviewed two days later and immediately appointed. Clearly James seemed a thoroughly acceptable candidate: 'By far the best man we have seen', Baillie confided to his diary. He too was already an author of several books and a scholar of stature; he was also ecclesiastically acceptable as an Anglican priest; but acceptable too to the secularist opposition just because he was an anthropologist rather than a theologian. We will probably never know how in those three weeks James was persuaded to apply and thus rescue the university from the awkward predicament in which it found itself: that of either appointing Dawson and, arguably, wrecking the whole scheme for a Faculty of Theology because the colleges would not co-operate with him, or appointing some manifestly inferior candidate and appearing to have discriminated on grounds of religion and infringed its charter.

Dawson was deeply disappointed. 'It was a great disappointment about Leeds' he wrote to George Every that August, 'and I don't think it would have happened if it had not been for that wretched Bishop of Ripon and his sister. They had much the same attitude to Catholics as the Nazis have to the Jews!'[21]

---

[20]Mirfield, at least, might well have preferred him, especially as Fr Symonds of Mirfield was a friend of his father and had visited the latter at Hartlington just before he died in February 1933.

[21]Scott, *A Historian and His World*, pp.110–11.

Two subsequent events may throw just a little more light to round off this discussion of the predicament of 1933. In 1940 the Registrar wrote to the colleges about the possibility in future of one or another member of their staff being appointed to the selection board in future appointments to the Department of Theology. While the university declared itself willing to do this, the Registrar thought it necessary to quote clause X in full and add, fiercely enough, 'this means that in making any appointment, even in the Theological Department, a candidate's religious persuasion (if any) cannot be taken into account in any way by the members of the appointing committee; it is the candidate's academic and personal qualifications alone that can be considered. Should a Mahomedan, Turk or infidel happen to be the man academically best suited for the position, say, of Professor of Biblical Exegesis, then he would be recommended without any qualms'.[22] Did he protest too much?

Secondly, when the chair was again vacant in 1945 and the selection board, chaired by the Vice-Chancellor and including a new Bishop of Ripon and – this time – several college staff (Vincent Taylor, Underwood and Fr Symonds of Mirfield), met to consider procedures, it was decided 'for various reasons' (unstated) not to advertise but to proceed by private inquiries in Oxford, Cambridge and Manchester. It seems strange not to advertise a chair. Was it, just conceivably, so as to make absolutely sure that no highly qualified 'Turk or infidel' could possibly get on to the short list and so renew for the university the dilemmas of 1933?

Finally one might add that if, in 1933, Leeds was unable to claim a national first in leaping the residual barrier of anti-Catholic prejudice, twenty-five years later it actually did so in a closely related area. When J. M. Cameron was appointed Professor of Philosophy here in 1959, it was still the first appointment of a Catholic to a Philosophy chair in any English university, and of someone almost as much theologian as philosopher.[23]

James was a man of great erudition and numerous publications. Two books of his were published in 1933, the year of his Leeds appointment, *Origins of Sacrifice* and *Christian Myth and Ritual*. He

[22]Letter of Registrar to heads of all four colleges, 15 March 1940.
[23]See, for instance, the collection of essays he published a little later (including his Leeds Inaugural), *The Night Battle*, 1962, or his edition of Newman's *Essay on the Development of Christian Doctrine*, 1970.

was, as he always saw himself, an anthropologist in the school of James Frazer and Robert Marett. He was also a priest, of exceptionally High Church sympathies and had for years been Vicar of the Church of St Thomas Becket in Oxford, a church famed for the extremity of its Anglo-Catholic worship. His studies and his ministry were united, it seems clear, by a passion for ritual, ritual in all its strange and baffling complexity, which he saw as the heart of religion. After his appointment to Leeds Underwood, the Principal of Rawdon, expressed to the Vice-Chancellor considerable bitterness about it[24] and 'doubts as to the future of the faculty of Theology'. While admitting that James was an authority on early religions, Underwood claimed that he 'had no background as a scholar, and was no philosopher'. It was a jaundiced judgment. James was not a philosopher any more than he was a theologian, but he was a scholar of the history of religions of immense breadth and ceaseless curiosity – qualities noticeable already in such early pieces as his articles on 'Rain' and 'Smoking' in the tenth and eleventh volumes of Hastings's *Encyclopedia of Religion and Ethics*. He was, indeed, in his own field a systematizer of both originality and balance. He was not, of course, a field anthropologist. While increasingly he would appeal to the authority of Malinowski and such as were, he saw himself as weaving together and interpreting the findings of others – rather in the style of Frazer whom he greatly admired (though not uncritically) and whose central concept of divine kingship he had very much adopted. Indeed, to appreciate the perceptive sanity of James's scholarship at its mature best, it would be almost sufficient to read his superb article on Frazer in the 1950 *Dictionary of National Biography* (272–8). While Frazer's hidden agenda was the undermining of all religion as just one ghastly folly after another, James's was, nevertheless, rather its tolerant vindication in evolutionary terms. For him, one feels, ancient Egypt was almost more important for understanding Christianity than ancient Israel: Egypt had become the principal paradigm for primitive religion and primitive religion was to be understood in continuity, rather than contrast, with modern and world religions. He was in due course founder of the British section of the *International Association of the History of Religions*, whose Bulletin is in fact now published from our Department. We may see him as the first major exponent within the

---

[24]Sir James Baillie's Journal, II, 6 July 1933, The Brotherton, Special Collections.

British theological world of what is today called 'the Phenomenology of Religion' and some of his writing – in the field of ritual, in particular – is still quite usable. He was also, by all accounts, an unusually tolerant academic, very far removed not only from *odium theologicum* but also from its younger, almost equally virulent, cousin *odium anthropologicum.*[25]

Having said all this it remains true that James's training and interests lay in anthropology not theology. He was hardly the man to build up a department of theology, let alone a faculty, and he could occasionally put his foot into it pretty badly when allowing his anthropological and evolutionary enthusiasms to run away with him. Take a strange little section of his *History of Christianity in England* entitled 'The Ethnology of the Reformation'[26] in which he declares it 'significant that at the Reformation the round-headed (or brachycephalic) extrovert Alpines and Mediterraneans, among whom the herd instinct is strong, remained Catholic while the long-headed (or dolichocephalic) northern introverts, with their intense individualism, readily adopted Protestantism'. If in the sixteenth century and afterwards England remained more Catholic than the rest of northern Europe and even experienced a further Catholic revival in the nineteenth century, this is to be explained by 'numerous invasions and large-scale infiltrations' by round-headed southerners with their built-in herd instinct which have 'from Neolithic times onwards' introduced 'a basic southern strain' into the English population. However, he adds, England has also enjoyed 'a very definite Nordic strain in the population going back to the influx of the Beaker folk'. This left its mark on the English temperament 'affording a predilection for the qualities which emerged in Protestantism'. And what about Ireland? Here, James claims, 'Mediterranean influences predominated. The Beaker folk never reached its coasts, and the later Norse invasions were only sporadic. Therefore, except in the north where Scottish and Nordic elements prevailed, Protestantism has made little headway'. It might be hard

---

[25]As Professor S. H. Hooke remarked in the appreciation of him at the beginning of the Festschrift edited by S. G. F. Brandon, *The Saviour God, Comparative Studies in the Concept of Salvation* presented to Edwin Oliver James, to commemorate his seventy-fifth birthday, Manchester 1963.
[26]E. O. James, *A History of Christianity in England*, 1948, 80–1.

to find a more absurd example of the attempt to explain culture and religious history in terms of a crude physical anthropology: the sort of social Darwinianism one does not expect to encounter as late as the 1940s. This is not a fair example of James' published work, but it does demonstrate, all too painfully, the dangers of an arm-chair anthropologist and folk-lorist wandering far into the roads of theological history. Occasionally even Homer nods.

Professor James delivered his Inaugural on the 12 October 1933[27] – barely a fortnight after taking up his Professorship: I am glad I did not have to do the same. One year later, October 1934, witnessed a major new move. 'An Appeal' or Memorial was presented to the Council of the university calling for the creation of 'A Faculty of Theology together with the Degrees corresponding thereto' – precisely what, in fact, the Vice-Chancellor had declared in 1931 would be made possible by Mrs Fawcett's legacy but which was still showing no real sign of materialization. The Theology lobby was not going to give up. There were no less than forty-seven signatories to the Appeal beginning with the Archbishop of York, William Temple, and three other bishops and including the Secretary of the Leeds Free Church Council, the General Secretary of the Yorkshire Congregational Union, three local MPs, Lord Mayors and ex-Lord Mayors of both Leeds and Bradford, the President of the Bradford Chamber of Commerce, the Chairman of the Bradford National Council of Women and the staff of the three Free Church Theological Colleges. Clearly this was no easy appeal to reject and it was not intended to be. Its production had been organized at Wesley College by Vincent Taylor, shortly to become its Principal, but behind Taylor one can, I suspect, detect the hand of Baillie himself. He had in fact been occupied that summer obtaining further information from Manchester. For him the establishment and filling of the chair remained but a first step in a larger operation. Maybe, he – correctly – foresaw further resistances ahead and the organization of this rather massive memorial seems designed to strengthen his hand. It was certainly needed. Indeed the Senate was by no means keen to endorse the programme of the Memorialists. It was willing in principle to institute a degree in Theological Studies but not, at least at the present stage, a Faculty. It insisted that the major portion of the teaching for such a degree should

[27]It is summarized in the *Gryphon*, November 1933, 47–8.

be 'supplied by full-time members of the University Staff lecturing within the University' but it also stressed that provision for additional members of staff of Theology could not at present be met from university funds.[28] From that first, almost intransigent, response it had to retreat a little. By April 1936 a compromise had been worked out and the Council could now express its 'grateful appreciation' to the memorialists for their 'cordial interest' and declare that their Appeal 'could not fail to meet with a sympathetic response'. It went on, tactfully enough, to agree to rather less than half a loaf: no Faculty of Theology, no BD as a first degree, only a BA Honours in Theology which had to be taught entirely within the university in the first year, but up to two-thirds in the Colleges for second and third year students; one new full-time lecturer to be appointed by the university.

There was dislike of this upon both sides. Thus Professor Milne of Mathematics declared that the 'intrinsic character' of the University of Leeds 'as a fundamentally "internal university" is directly threatened by these proposals'.[29] The Theology students would never feel the widening benefits of sharing a common life with students of other disciplines, while the Head of the Department would lose his proper authority because he would be unable to control the staff of the Colleges. The Colleges, for their part, could hardly find it satisfactory. They received little effective recognition, none of the real sense of sharing in a common enterprise which Manchester provided; moreover, too much of the time of their students would have to be given up to studying the history of religions *à la James*, a subject they thought rather unimportant. James wanted the new lectureship to be in Philosophical Theology – a subject which he might have been expected to teach himself. In fact it was in Hebrew – a subject the Colleges were well enough equipped to cope with anyway.

As a result of all this, as we have seen, from the autumn of 1936, just fifty years ago, the Department of the Philosophy and History of Religion became the Department of Theological Studies and – from the following year – a list of nine 'Recognized Teachers' from the Theological Colleges appears in the Calendar under the Professor's name. Moreover J. N. Schofield, hitherto on the staff of Rawdon, became a full university lecturer in Old Testament Studies and

[28]Senate, 6 February 1935.
[29]Memorandum, 26 February 1936.

Hebrew. There was a syllabus. There were students. Something at least had been accomplished. Shortly after this, however, the coming of world war put a stop to further progress. Years later, looking back on that time, James declared that by the end of the war 'only a skeleton remained of that organization I had tried to create prior to the catastrophe that befell a stricken world in the Long Vacation of 1939'.[30] That comment does, perhaps, conceal the rather ineffectual nature of James's contribution to Leeds. While employed by this university he had continued to live in Oxford. Without resources or, one feels, the sympathy of the Colleges, an anthropologist rather than a theologian, he had remained somewhat marginal to the whole enterprise. Perhaps because there was so little of a core to the department, Hebrew itself pulled away in 1941 to become a department of its own: far from becoming a skeleton it at least seemed to flourish in those years. Indeed by the time of James's resignation in 1945 to take up a chair in London, there was hardly even a skeleton left.[31] Probably the only significant development of the war years in regard to the Department was the loan of the Holden Library to the university in 1940 by the diocese of Ripon. This generous initiative of Bishop Lunt provided the department with a sound core for the splendid library facilities which have now been built up. In 1945 the chair was marked 'vacant' in the Calendar and the only person actually in the Department was Schofield, by now Senior Lecturer and Head of a quite different department, *Hebrew Language and Literature* (soon to become Semitics). It is not surprising that when in due course Laurence Browne was appointed to the chair he declared, pitifully enough, 'It is impossible to run a Department with one Professor and no staff'.[32]

By 1949 the department had a staff of four. There were now lecturers for Old Testament, New Testament and Church History. The course of the History of Religions had been reduced and James' Primitive Religion dropped entirely as 'a difficult subject for beginners, bristling with uncertainties'. It was replaced by a more

[30]*University of Leeds Review*, 2 December 1952, p.146.
[31]It may be noted that a special series of theological lectures, the Scott Holland lectures, were delivered in the university by Fr Lionel Thornton of Mirfield in 1943–4. These provided the substance for volumes 2 and 3 of his large work *The Form of the Servant*, Dacre Press, 1952 and 1956 (see Preface to part 1, p.x and to part 2, p.vii).
[32]Memorandum for consideration at meeting of 7 June 1946.

conventional introduction to world religions, followed by either Islam or Hinduism and taught by Browne.

When James left, some wanted the chair to become one of Comparative Religion, but as the original legacy had been for a chair in Theology, that title was at last admitted and has prevailed ever since. Nevertheless Laurence Browne came from the chair of Comparative Religion in Manchester (which he held part-time, combined with a living in Northamptonshire!) so in a way both sides were satisfied. He had worked in India, taught at the School of Islamics in Lahore, and had a wide competence also in biblical studies and church history. He was older than James, only a few years off retirement, a very quiet man, and in his pleasant, sensitive writings[33] he represents a liberal, but still essentially missionary, approach to the study of other world religions. Probably his most personal scholarly work, and still the most useful, is *The Eclipse of Christianity in Asia*, published by Cambridge in 1933, a historical study ending with the fourteenth century.

Our department by the 1950s, it seems fair to say, as built up by Browne and continued by Professor Reid, was somewhat small, sound as a bell in its scholarship and a fairly traditional theological orientation, but unadventurous. If one compares it – unfairly, of course – with the Faculty of Theology at Manchester, celebrating fifty years of existence in 1954, one must be struck by the rather limited significance and output of our Leeds department when set against a Manchester Faculty of very considerable prestige presided over at that time by H. H. Rowley. Our first twenty-five years witnessed, it seems fair to say, more problems than achievements. They hardly prepare one to expect the altogether larger, more sustained work of the next twenty-five years in which – while neither the highest standards of individual academic precision nor creative personal idiosyncracies have been missing – there has been a consistency in harnessing a wide variety of skill and concern within the work of a unified team such as to bring Leeds to an increasingly well recognized position within the national and indeed international world of Theology and Religious Studies. It would not be possible, nor

[33]For instance, the following: 'Much as I would like one day to see my cat and dog growing in intelligence and grace, and discussing with me some of the deep things of life, I do not feel that the time has come for any profitable speculation on the future of individual animals.' *Theological Essays*, L. M. Grensted and others, p.44.

appropriate, to attempt to evaluate in detail this more recent work, but I would like now, first to outline some of the altered circumstances of latter years, and then to say something about the future which must, in the end, be still more important for us than a review of the past.

Hardly had the Department attained internally a reasonably adequate size of staff, than its social, ecclesiastical and cultural context shifted almost out of recognition. The Department had, after all, been brought into existence principally at the request of neighbouring Theological Colleges – particularly Free Church theological colleges – and so as to serve them in the role of nucleus for what was originally intended to be an independent Faculty of Theology. Almost all its early students in point of fact did belong to the colleges and – presumably as a corollary – they included no women. The first woman to graduate in the department did so in 1947, the second in 1954. By the start of the sixties, however, all this had changed: the ordinands were in a minority, the women almost a majority; most of the students, both men and women, were now intending to teach as lay people in the schools, but there were also some who approached the subject out of interest only, without any vocational or professional interest.[34] Today, committed future teachers are fewer, the variety of reasons for choosing the subject greater, than ever. In the mid fifties, when this change was starting to get under way, the colleges still appeared to be flourishing. There were still nine 'Associate Lecturers' – college members of staff – on the departmental prospectus for the years 1957–8, although in practice it seems that – with the exception of Vincent Taylor – they did little or nothing outside their respective colleges.[35]

Then, in 1958, the Yorkshire United Independent College was closed. Rawdon followed in 1964. Wesley College, Headingley, in 1967. An Annual Report of the first, back in 1830, had expressed the hope that the institution would exist 'as long as the sun and moon endure'.[36] It celebrated its bicentenary in 1956, and had its memorial history written including forward looking references to 'the abiding

---

[34]See memorandum on the Department of Theology, signed by Professor Tinsley, October 1962 (University Archives).

[35]'The associate lecturers do not make any significant contribution to the departmental teaching.' Memorandum of 1955.

[36]Wadsworth, *Yorkshire United Independent College*, p.108.

task'. It then disappeared. Another ten years and its sister colleges were gone as well. David Thompson, Britain's leading contemporary historian of the free churches, remarked laconically in a recent survey article of twentieth-century history 'Yorkshire has lost its Colleges from all nonconformist denominations'.[37]

What had happened? The heavy steady decline of the principal Free Churches in England throughout this century has been well documented. It does not require analysis here. The fifties had been an age of slight recovery for most churches and it was only at their close, and in the far more abrasive sixties, that it finally became necessary to face institutionally the consequences of a long erosion. Yorkshire, the West Riding particularly, was a traditional stronghold of Nonconformity: a natural nineteenth-century environment for the establishment of their colleges. When our three were founded, there were none at Oxford or Cambridge. But from the later nineteenth century the pull of the latter proved more and more irresistible. Still today, the existence of Mansfield, Regent's Park and Manchester at Oxford, Westminster and Wesley at Cambridge speak for what happened. The Free Churches determined to break so far as they could into the old Anglican strongholds at the ancient universities, and put more of their heart and their resources there. When, with decline, something had to go, Oxbridge was spared, Yorkshire condemned. It may also be true that it was felt that the University of Leeds, which had, as we have seen, always held the colleges somewhat at arms length, had less to offer than Manchester or even Bristol. Whatever explanations we proffer, the fact remains that by the end of the 1960s, while Mirfield had been drawn for the first time into an active relationship with the department, with which we are very happy (both our firsts last year were Mirfield men),[38] the latter had now – for better or worse – been abandoned by its principal erstwhile wives and had to serve a clientele profoundly different from that for which it had been instituted and without most of the external support it had hitherto counted upon.

It has responded to this predicament creatively enough. West

[37]David Thompson, p.98 of *The Testing of the Churches*, ed. R. Davies, Epworth Press 1982.
[38]'Formerly the policy was markedly to discourage new students from reading Theology at Leeds, because of the way it was taught there', *CR*, no.294, 1976, Michaelmas, p.12.

Yorkshire has itself been changing profoundly in ethos and the composition of its population. Leeds, long an unusually multi-coloured city, the receiving point of a wave of Irish immigration in the 1840s and a Jewish wave fifty years later, was now facing a third wave – this time from the Caribbean and South Asia. It was becoming a city of Sikhs and an almost ideal centre for the contemporary study of 'Comparative Religion' – to use a slightly old-fashioned term, one favoured by Professor James. It is one of the curiosities of our story that, at its start, when the Colleges wanted Theology, the University gave them a Professor who could lecture about little except the history of religions. Religious Studies stood high on its syllabus for the ten years of the James era; they then diminished more and more until – by the mid-fifties, in the age of J. K. S. Reid – with a staff of five, they occupied no more than perhaps a third of the attention of one of them. By then the pendulum had swung from one extreme to the other and the department had become, very emphatically, one of biblical studies and Christian theology – indeed, a sort of outpost of the most professional but hard-edged tradition of theology in Britain, the modern Scottish School. The *Scottish Journal of Theology* was, for those years, actually edited from Leeds. The biblicist, Calvinist and Barthian publications of J. K. S. Reid[39] were distinguished enough, but they are about as remote as it would be possible to imagine from the ethos of E. O. James. The genially detached tone of the one had given way to the intensely committed note of the other.

It was the achievement of Professor Tinsley, appointed in 1962 – just half way through our period – to draw together enduringly these rather contrary legacies. Very much of a Christian theologian himself, a skilled interpreter of all the major Protestant theologians of this century,[40] he was far less a man of one school than Reid, and very much more sympathetic to the lessons of anthropology,

---

[39]See, in particular, Calvin, *Theological Treatises*, translated with Introductions and Notes by J. K. S. Reid, 1954; J. K. S. Reid, *The Authority of Scripture*, A Study of the Reformation and Post-Reformation Understanding of the Bible, 1957; John Calvin, *Concerning the Eternal Predestination of God*, translated with an introduction by J. K. S. Reid, 1961.

[40]See the five volumes of selections from modern theologians (Barth, Bultmann, Tillich, Niebuhr and Bonhoeffer) published by Epworth Press with introductions and notes by E. J. Tinsley, 1973.

philosophy and secular literature.[41] He was thus drawn to reinvigorate the Department's pristine concerns with the history and philosophy of religion, particularly through the appointment in 1963 of two outstanding scholars, Trevor Ling for Comparative Religion and Hugo Meynell for the Philosophy of Religion.[42] He was helped in this by his close collaboration and friendship with Professor Cameron in Philosophy. From 1970 to 1973, for the only time in its history, the Department actually had two professors, Tinsley in Theology and Ling in Comparative Religion. That represents the ideal model, balancing the two concerns which have been here from the start instead of neglecting one for the sake of the other, and it is a pity it could not be continued. In 1974 the department was renamed 'Theology and Religious Studies' (its fourth title). The revival of the Religious Studies side has, furthermore, led more recently to a major development of research, initially within the contemporary context of West Yorkshire: the *Community Religions Project* specializes in the study of the developing character of the religions of Britain's ethnic minorities. From it has come, this very year, a new monograph series published by the Department, of which the first volume was Dr Knott's study of *Hinduism in Leeds*. Our 'Comparative Religion' in the James era was very much a concern with the past and the primitive; today it is far more one with the close and the contemporary.[43]

I have said surprisingly little about biblical studies. The department has been fortunate in including among its staff, both past and present, a number of distinguished scripture scholars. To mention

---

[41]Cf. his inaugural lecture, E. J. M. Tinsley, *Christian Theology and the Frontiers of Tragedy*, delivered 4 February 1963, University of Leeds. Curiously, both his predecessor and successor delivered papers the same year on the character of theology in a modern university, and the three are well worth reading together: see J. K. S. Reid, 'Scotland – the Biblical Tradition', pp.133–45, and David E. Jenkins, 'Oxford – the Anglican tradition', pp.146–62, both in the Downside symposium volume *Theology and University*, ed. John Coulson, Darton, Longman & Todd 1964.

[42]Dr Meynell was shared with the Department of Philosophy, his appointment being half in each Department.

[43]It is worth noting that the published volume of the 1985 Congress at Sydney of the International Association for the History of Religions (IAHR), *Identity Issues and World Religions*, contains 27 papers finally selected out of more than 200. Of these two are by present members of the department of Leeds, one is by a former staff member and one by a former student, both now working abroad. This represents a good 50% of the total British contribution.

just two: in the Browne years Matthew Black was lecturer in the New Testament and Peter Ackroyd in the Old: both were outstanding scholars and teachers who went on to chairs in St Andrew's and London and reached without question the very top of their fields internationally.[44] Yet it remains a fact that of the seven people appointed to chairs in this department not one has been primarily a biblical scholar. The contrast with Manchester, Bristol or, probably, any other department of Theology in Britain is striking. For whatever reason our department, while it has never questioned the necessity of a lively biblical section, has noticeably diverged from standard British practice in placing its primary concern elsewhere, and this divergence is, I believe, an element in its wider significance.

It is to be noted too that if the old college connections disappeared in the 1960s new partners were emerging. The College of Trinity and All Saints opened in Leeds in 1966. Ripon and York St John as also North Riding – older Colleges of Education – were at the same time developing degree work in Religious Studies validated by Leeds. The department's current importance cannot be gauged regardless of these now very considerable external responsibilities in a field designated by the DES a national priority area in the school curriculum. All this represents, clearly enough, a history of both loss and gain.

In the immediate future I would see three principal cutting edges to the department's research and claim that all three have a clear public importance. For all, furthermore, we could argue for Leeds something of an at least potential primacy in national terms. The first I have referred to already: the study of the on-going religious character of Britain's new ethnic minorities, for which we have recently been awarded a four year Leverhulme Research Fellowship; the second is African religion and in particular the interaction

[44]See the Festscrifts in their honour: *Neotestamentica et Semitica*, Studies in honour of Matthew Black, ed. E. Earle Ellis and Max Wilcox, Edinburgh 1969; *Text and Interpretation*, Studies in the New Testament presented to Matthew Black, ed. Ernest Best and R. McL. Wilson, Cambridge 1979; *Israel's Prophetic Tradition*, Essays in Honour of Peter Ackroyd, ed. Richard Coggins, Anthony Phillips and Michael Knibb, Cambridge 1982. It is worth recalling that at the same time as Black and Ackroyd were the department's New and Old Testament lecturers, Vincent Taylor of Wesley and W. D. Davies of the United Independent College (later professor at Princeton and a world authority on Rabbinic Judaism) were amongst its Associate Lecturers: the biblical strengths of Leeds in 1950 were surely remarkable!

208 The Theology of a Protestant Catholic

of the two world religions, Christianity and Islam, with its traditional religions. The premier international review in this field, *The Journal of Religion in Africa*, published by Brill in Holland, is now edited from the department and we would hope to build up a steadily stronger African connection – something admittedly new for the department, but not for me. The third is the interaction of politics and religion, once again in its contemporary dimension. Over the last few years, the period of David Jenkins's professorship and since, this has been developing as a major departmental concern and I hope we can further enlarge it. My own recently published *History of English Christianity 1920–1985*[45] is in fact in large measure a politico-religious history. Though completed before arriving in Leeds, it fits very neatly with the department's current interests.

Behind these specific research and teaching specializations, which by no means exhaust the department's current research interests, lie the requirements of its basic shape: both Theology and Religious Studies. We have seen how, across our story, there has been a recurring duality of concern, a sort of oscillation back and forth, between Christian theology and comparative religion, the one more committed, the other more detached. The point is that we are both and have been so from the start. The recognized strength of Leeds in national terms is widely seen to be just this, that here these two different, if closely related, subjects are integrated into a unity in which each continually challenges and questions the other – and no one was better at maintaining the intensity of that self-questioning atmosphere than my immediate predecessor, Professor David Jenkins, who went on from here to provoke both church and nation with tools of theological dialectic sharpened in Leeds.[46] If we let either slip, we would quite sacrifice our specific *raison d'être* for some relatively trivial saving in cost. Sheffield has an excellent department of Biblical Studies, Lancaster of Religious Studies, but the specific point of Leeds is different and it would be lost if, through cuts, we were forced effectively to abandon the shape really adopted from the beginning and emphatically developed from the 1960s. Back in 1954

[45]Adrian Hastings, *History of English Christianity* 1920–1985, Collins 1986.
[46]See both his inaugural lecture, David E. Jenkins, 'Universe and University – Reflections on Having the Nerve to do Theology', *The University of Leeds Review* 1982, pp.119–36, and David E. Jenkins, 'Professors, Bishops and the Search for Truth', *University of Leeds Review*, 1984, pp.97–100.

Professor Reid declared in a Memorandum for the *Senate Committee on Priorities*: 'This Department teaches a number of very diverse subjects – so diverse as to make it, so far as I can see, quite unique' (26 January 1954). That is still more true now than then. Biblical studies, involving apart from much else, the teaching of two languages (Hebrew and Koine Greek), cannot possibly be sustained with less than a staff of three. Comparative Religion – that is to say, the study of non-Christian and non-biblical religious traditions, including at least two major world religions such as Islam and Buddhism, together with the sociology and phenomenology of religion – again requires a minimum of three. There is thirdly, and equally centrally to the department, the area of Christian studies – the theological development of doctrine, the history of the church, the contemporary interaction of Christianity with politics and culture. Add to all that the Philosophy of Religion. Again, we cannot cope here with less than three. That suggests a round minimum of nine full-time staff – not so as to mount a wide range of marginal courses, but to ensure that the department covers with integrity and in reasonable depth the central areas of its discipline. Between 1975 and 1981 we had an establishment of 10½. This was then reduced to 8, and the University's Development Committee (to use our current language of double speak) has proposed to cut it further to 7 by 1990 – a lower figure than for any year since 1966. With a staff limited to seven it would be next to impossible to remain genuinely, as we still are at present, a rounded department of both Theology and Religious Studies. Something would have to give and the developments of the last twenty years would be gravely undermined. At present, fortunately, we are in fact more than eight: the presence of a research fellow and two or more part-time lecturers – one of which we owe to Mirfield – means that we still have a teaching staff equivalently of nine. With that we can just cope. With seven we could not.

Here, as elsewhere, the University must decide: a simple model of nearly all round reductions must, fairly soon, destroy the effective competence of almost every smaller department. Choices have to be made, and one can only plead for one's own cabbage patch. But there is a matter of regional policy at stake. Neither York nor Bradford has any department in our field. That of Hull, formerly as large as ours, has just been amalgamated into a School of Humanities and in terms of staff seems set to be cut down to two or three. It is hard to believe that Hull will continue as a major centre of theological study. The department at Sheffield, while vigorous enough, is rigidly limited to biblical studies. Leeds is now alone among the five universities of Yorkshire in possessing a full department of either Theology or Religious Studies: it has, I believe, in these circumstances a quite special responsibility to maintain it unmutilated – all the more so as its current vigour is indisputable.

Public religion in Leeds has always been, it seems to me, a somewhat muted thing – the very opposite to that of a cathedral city. Perhaps a city so familiar with cloth is not likely to be over-respectful of 'the cloth'. No church dominates its centre. The Town Hall, its great architectural pride, is a masterpiece of Victorian civic religion of the most assured and this-worldly sort. Yet Leeds has been and remains a city of many faiths: a city of the Free Churches, of Roman Catholics, of Jews, of Sikhs, of Hindus as much as of its Parish Church – they can all claim it with some reason as their own. Maybe, as the march of our history goes on, it leaves their buildings in ruins, like Kirkstall Abbey, or almost closed, like St John's, or changed into office or furniture shop. Yet *Faith in Leeds* is still there, as a lively recent report of that name showed well enough. Leeds religion, then, is somewhat changeable yet open and friendly, pluralist, ecumenical: and that is just how our department – like our university – has long been and is today, I trust, more than ever. We do not seek to impose anything but we do say that the understanding of religion, in all its power, vision, blindness, eccentricity, is an important and vital part of our culture. The very diversity of Leeds makes it a better place, I would claim, than Cambridge or Oxford for carrying on this task, realistically and untriumphalistically. Britain cannot afford to restrict the study of theology to the ancient universities. We have depended on local religious leaders in the past for support and in the world of the eighties, in which Mr Tebbit no less has urged us all to get out on our bicycles and find the wherewithal, we may need to appeal to them again today. You need a department of theology. It continues to serve you in all sorts of ways, not least through our very considerable number of part-time postgraduate students. Every area of academic life is having today to turn for additional financial support to its wider constituency. We may have to do the same. Please, do not let us down.

When Manchester celebrated its theological Golden Jubilee in

1954, it invited, among others, Professor Grensted to give a lecture. He had known the Faculty almost from the beginning, and looking back to that beginning he remarked 'It certainly never occurred to me then that Faculties could have a history and a growth, or that theology, with its roots so firmly in the unalterable past, could itself be alive and changing'.[47] Now that here at Leeds we, if less grandly, are recalling fifty years of theological existence, I thought it appropriate to offer this brief survey to show that we too have 'a history and a growth'. Our theology too is 'alive and changing'. May it stay that way, I will not say 'as long as sun and moon endure', but just as long as Leeds has a university.

[47]*Theological Essays* in Commemoration of the Jubilee by L. W. Grensted and others, 1954, 20.

★ 20 ★

Three Oranges

Some years ago, in 1975 to be exact, I was travelling in west Africa from Bobbio Dioulasso, the capital of what is today Burkino Faso, towards Accra. I had spent the night in Bolgatanga in northern Ghana and had gone in the morning to the open sandy area where a bus was in due course to leave for Tamale, some hundreds of miles of dusty roads to the south. I entered the bus, took a seat and began to wait. It would not leave until it was quite full and that might be a long time. It would certainly be many hours before we reached our destination. I was a complete stranger in northern Ghana and had no provisions for the journey.

Some distance away across the square a woman was selling fruit placed on the ground and a man was buying a few oranges. I think I looked at the fruit a little enviously, but I suppose I felt too unsure of myself to leave the bus, walk over and buy something too. Then suddenly I saw the man approaching the bus. He came up to my window and to my immense surprise offered me three oranges in great simplicity. He smiled and departed. Nothing more was said. Perhaps we had in fact no common language and, of course, I never saw him again. He did not know my name, nor I his. It still seems to me a truly amazing action.

How grateful I was in the hot hours that followed as we journeyed south, to suck those oranges, one by one. I had been an outsider, the sole white person in the bus or the market place. My anonymous black benefactor had been able to foresee the need of this traveller passing through his town and to go out of his way to spend a little money – and I doubt if he had so much of it – to guard against my wants.

Christmas is a time of present giving. That is very much part of the pleasure of the season and always has been. Half the point of carols and wassail songs always was to provide the occasion for hospitality and gift giving between strangers. The danger with Christmas presents is that they remain wholly within a closed circle of privileged family and friends, a too carefully arranged, conventional exchange.

The best present comes straight from the heart, a clear expression of affection, concern, gratitude. The first present you ever receive from one you greatly love will remain for ever in a class of its own. It is the freedom, the sincerity, the unexpectedness, the underlying meaning, in a present which makes it truly memorable. Of course, old loves too need new symbols and it is utterly right for the old wife to give a present to her husband as she has done at Christmas fifty times before. But why not think too of someone you have never given anything to before, and probably won't again? Somehow that remains the quintessential Christmas gift. The gift to the youngest child, like the gifts of the wise men to the infant Jesus in Matthew's Gospel. Gold, frankincense and myrrh. They had never seen the child before, they never did again. Travellers in a far land, they remain world famous as gift givers, but we do not even know their names.

All so like that gift I received at Bolgatanga. A black man to a white stranger, far, far away. Just three oranges. No more. Yet they still seem like gold to me. I have never received a gift I cherish more and I hope maybe sometime before I die that I too will give a present as nice as that.